Financialization, Austerity, and Inclusion in Latin America and the Caribbean

Financialization, Austerity, and Inclusion in Latin America and the Caribbean

Rana S. Gautam, Diogo L. Pinheiro and Dwight Wilson

LEXINGTON BOOKS/FORTRESS ACADEMIC
Lanham • Boulder • New York • London

Published by Lexington Books/Fortress Academic
Lexington Books is an imprint of The Rowman & Littlefield Publishing Group, Inc.
4501 Forbes Boulevard, Suite 200, Lanham, Maryland 20706
www.rowman.com

86-90 Paul Street, London EC2A 4NE

British Library Cataloguing in Publication Information Available

Library of Congress Cataloging-in-Publication Data

Names: Gautam, Rana S., editor. | Pinheiro, Diogo L., 1979- editor. | Wilson, Dwight, 1974- editor.
Title: Financialization, austerity, and inclusion in Latin America and the Caribbean / Rana S. Gautam, Diogo L. Pinheiro, Dwight Wilson.
Description: Lanham : Lexington, [2024] | Includes bibliographical references and index. | Summary: "Gautam, Pinheiro, and Wilson analyze the spread of financialization in Latin America and the Caribbean, highlighting the ideational origins of financialization outside the region, its effects on government budgeting and social inclusion, and options for increased inclusivity"— Provided by publisher.
Identifiers: LCCN 2023046224 (print) | LCCN 2023046225 (ebook) | ISBN 9781793647955 (cloth) | ISBN 9781793647962 (ebook)
Subjects: LCSH: Financialization--Latin America. | Financialization—Caribbean Area. | Latin America--Economic conditions—1982- | Caribbean Area—Economic conditions—1945-
Classification: LCC HG185.L29 F563 2024 (print) | LCC HG185.L29 (ebook) | DDC 330.98—dc23/eng/20231030
LC record available at https://lccn.loc.gov/2023046224
LC ebook record available at https://lccn.loc.gov/2023046225

In memory of Stan Swamy
RG

In memory of Celso V. Pinheiro
DP

To Gabriela and Ana Sofia
DW

Contents

Figures

Tables

Preface

This project emerged from the meeting of cross-cutting perspectives. Two are from the Global South and one from the north. Two originate from outside Latin America and the Caribbean, while the third supplies an insider view from Brazil. Two of the coauthors had disciplinary training in sociology, while the other had a political science background. Even though we come from different perspectives, we are equal coauthors in this project; our names appear alphabetically. Finally, we combine quantitative and qualitative methodological methods to our investigation.

This multidisciplinary and multi-perspectival intersection is only appropriate for a topic like financialization. The concept has confounded definitions and expectations. Judgments of the causes, parameters, and effects of financialization depend heavily on the interpretive lens one brings to its study, which can be found in everything from finance to anthropology. Overlapping with, but distinct from, neoliberalism, and globalization, this relatively recent phenomenon (or old, depending on one's perspective!) has generated a prolific new research paradigm and yet maps so wide a territory that the resulting pictures often fail to connect.

Our motivation in taking up this subject, therefore, is to combine the views from our different approaches to draw a fuller picture, even as we recognize that it will not be complete. Despite these differences in approaches to studying the social world, we are unified in our belief that the purpose of empirical investigation is to understand how societies confront large-scale processes like financialization, structure choices about policies, arrange advantages and disadvantages, and ultimately, shape life opportunities for people.

The book began a follow-up to, and widening of, questions addressed in a paper by one of the authors that was presented at the 23rd Conference of the Americas in 2020. We would like to thank the sponsors of that conference for providing a forum to explore these issues and the participants for their insights and feedback.

We would also like to thank Ana Muñoz Jaramillo for her research and editorial assistance. Our gratitude also extends to our colleagues at UNG, who have supported us along the way, in particular: Drs. Bibek Chand, Alex Wisnoski III, George Danns, Donna Danns, Diane Cook, John O'Sullivan, and the faculty at the Departments of Sociology and Human Services and Political Science and International Affairs. We are also grateful to Drs. John Finn and Matthew Flynn. We must also acknowledge the immense support provided by the administration of the University of North Georgia through its Presidential Incentive Award, which allowed us to dedicate ourselves to this project.

We couldn't have done this without the endless patience and support of our families and friends: Paula, Camila, Rafael, Ligia, Dale, Sujata, Sushma, Appu, Raja, Gabriela, Ana Sofia, and many others. Finally, we must thank Nicolette Amstutz, Alexandra Rallo, and Ryan Dradzynski at Lexington Books for their patience and guidance.

Rana S. Gautam
Diogo L. Pinheiro
Dwight Wilson
Gainesville, GA, March 3, 2023

Chapter 1

The Puzzle of Financialization

Few ideas come to embody the world we inhabit. Financialization is arguably one such concept; it points to profound economic, political, and cultural transformations witnessed around the world since the turn of the twenty-first century. The changes are ubiquitous. A tell-tale sign of financialization is the debt that governments, firms, and households have accumulated. By one estimate, for each dollar of new investment between 2000 and 2020, the global economy created nearly two dollars in debt.[1] Or, take Rishi Sunak's elevation as the prime minister of the United Kingdom, the latest example of the rise of an investment banker or hedge fund honcho to the pinnacle of political power. Then, there are everyday online investors who whipped the frenzy of a meme stock, such as what happened with Game Stop stocks. Financialization is a target of social movements; and an instrument for social empowerment and change. Some hail financialization, others loathe financialization, but few can ignore financialization.

The rising tide of financialization is also unmistakable in Latin America and the Caribbean (LAC). Consider the much-publicized Global Financial Center Index or GFCI (Wardle and Mainelli 2022), which ranks the world's leading financial centers. LAC is home to 13 of the 119 major global financial centers on the GFCI list.[2] Cayman Islands, a prominent tax-free international offshore center, leads the region in the GFCI ranking. Nearly 60 percent of global hedge funds are domiciled in the idyllic archipelago in the Caribbean sea (Fichtner 2016). A majority of the top 50 global banks also hold licenses in the Cayman Islands (CIMA 2021). Chile's capital city Santiago is another global financial powerhouse in the region. Chile has been a trailblazer of sorts, embracing privatization, liberalization, and deregulation under the military dictatorship of Augusto Pinochet in the 1970s, even before Reaganomics or Thatchernomics gained toeholds in the West. To its credit, Chile pioneered for the world the privatized pension system with a defined contribution that channeled investments into the capital market under the aegis of private fund managers.

Indeed LAC has come a long way from the days when the church (in the nineteenth century) doubled as money lender and American economist E. W. Kemmerer (in the early twentieth century) preached the virtues of central banks in the region.[3] Then, to some, the region had an "atrophied financial system" (Ceballos, Didier, and Schmukler 2014, p. 4), owing to state dirigisme over the financial sector, especially during the 1960s and 1970s. And not too long ago, Latin America was the quintessential hotbed of financial instability and crises.

Since the late twentieth century, LAC has been at the forefront of financial liberalization. The region has led emerging economies' quest to open financial markets to cross-border capital flows and foreign institutions. Latin America has been the fastest-growing banking market in the world, outpacing even China, one of the fastest-growing economies in the world (Baquerizo et al. 2019). Overall, the capital market structure resembles that of advanced economies (Didier and Schmukler 2013). Bond and equity markets have gained ground relative to institutions such as banks, which traditionally dominated the capital market in emerging economies. The derivative markets, especially currency derivatives, have also grown. The institutional investors weigh heavily on capital markets, the capital flow has shifted in favor of the private sector, and financial services have become internationalized.

But not everyone seems ready to celebrate the metamorphosis of LAC's financial market from a so-called atrophied system to one that mirrors the financial sector of advanced economies. For that matter, many are glum, some even angry. Before the COVID-19 pandemic took a firm grip on the region, in 2019, Latin America was roiled by a wave of social unrest. From Chile to Colombia and Bolivia to Haiti, masses of angry people poured onto the streets, protesting against economic hardship, government apathy, and a plethora of other issues. In Chile the much-touted privatized pension system, called the pillar of the country's capital market, was the target of people's ire (Laing 2019). The signature economic reforms of the Augusto Pinochet era, the pension system has failed to deliver financial security promised to beneficiaries. As a result, many, such as Maria Luz Navarete, a septuagenarian civil servant of 30 years who works as a janitor after retirement, have to rely on a side job to make ends meet. To its credit, the pension system has provided a large stock of savings, with about half of the assets under management invested domestically (Evans and Pienknagura 2021). However, economic growth has benefited only a handful.

When it comes to the Cayman Islands, the plot only thickens. On paper, financialization has brought a deluge of primarily foreign companies to the island. So much so that there are more companies than people living there; to be precise, there were about 1.6 registered companies per person in Cayman Islands in 2021.[4] A single five-storied building, the Ugland House in the capital city of George Town, is home to 18,000 companies and other entities.[5] Nonetheless, the torrent of business firms of all stripes has failed to lift all boats. "There is a disconnect between the quality of our economy and the quality of life for our people," the deputy premier Christopher Saunders lamented at a press conference (Cayman News 2022). In Bermuda, the region's third major financial center, poverty has been a lingering problem. "There is no official poverty and inequality data. My estimate is that 40 percent of the population lives below the median household income. The pandemic has exacerbated the island's economic woes," said Robert Stubbs, the research head of SEED Bermuda, who is also a member of Bermuda's Wage Commission (Robert Stubbs, virtual interview, October 25, 2022). "The tax base is woefully inadequate to support a meaningful safety net. The economic system that taxes labor and not income produces systemic poverty and widens inequality."

Financialization has become a lightning rod of controversy. On one hand, financial development is viewed as yet another false prophet of growth and progress. Nobel laureate Joseph Stiglitz (2012) blames the financial sector's meteoric rise for spiraling inequality. His fellow laureate, Michael Spence (2008), the chair of the World Commission on Growth and Development, cautions against the "mistake of equating financial-sector development or anything else, with a sufficient condition for growth" (p. 33). Still, others suggest financialization dampens investment in productive assets, spurs speculation, and corrodes democracy (Godechot 2021; Nölke 2021; Palley 2014; Sen 2021). Global capital mobility has been blamed for financial meltdowns and economic recessions that turned into human rights crises (Balakrishnan, Heintz, and Elson 2016, Balk, Gautam 2019; Nolan 2014).

On the other hand, the financial sector's growth is presented as the sine qua non for growth, prosperity, and development. Microfinance was the basis for the 2006 Nobel Peace Prize to Bangladeshi economist Muhammad Yunus and the organization he founded, Grameen Bank, for bottom-up economic and social development. It is argued that financial development promotes efficiency, fuels economic growth, lowers transaction costs, spreads risk, smoothens consumption, relocates economic value through time, and distributes capital more broadly (Demirguc-Kunt, Klapper, and Singer 2017; Goetzmann 2016). Financial development can be an ally in achieving global development objectives of poverty reduction, gender equality, and access to education and healthcare (Claessens and Feijen 2007).

This book attempts to untangle the puzzle of financialization. We examine financialization's rise, its consequences for social policy, and its effect on social inclusion in LAC since 1980. The popular ideas about economic reforms are, to borrow Moises Naim's (1999) words, "as faddish as skirt lengths and tie widths." So, how did financialization emerge as the flavor of the season? Was it the lost decade of the 1980s that left social planners and the elite with no other model of development? Or did the multilateral financial institutions force their hands? How has the embrace of financialization transformed social policy? And, what do these changes entail for social inclusion in LAC? We attempt to answer these questions in this book.

A greater understanding of financialization and its public policy effects could not be more urgent. The COVID-19 pandemic, Ukraine war, slowing growth, and galloping inflation have pushed the world into, what the IMF managing director Kristalina Georgieva (2022) calls, "a new danger zone," where high rates, high inflation, and greater uncertainty become normal. Nearly 54 low and middle-income countries are highly vulnerable to debt crisis (Jensen 2022). Ten such countries are from Latin America.

LAC offers a unique opportunity to examine financialization. After all, the region has been a laboratory for economic ideas. It was the purveyor of the Import Substitution Industrialization (ISI) approach to economic policy, which became the principal economic development model for most newly independent states after 1945 (Frieden 2006). Chile embraced the neoliberal mantra of privatization, trade openness, liberalization, and limited government in the 1970s before these ideas took hold in the advanced economies of the West. The Brady Plan to restructure distressed commercial bank loans in Latin America into liquid, tradable securities effectively created a sovereign emerging bond market (Agnoli and Vilán 2008). Latin America also was the cradle of the Washington Consensus, which fundamentally altered the policy landscape worldwide and became the catalyst for financial liberalization and international capital flow far greater than initially anticipated (Rodrik 2006).

The region's complex financial history weighs heavily on its people even today. Take the case of Haiti, one of the first countries to break free from the yoke of slavery and colonialism but remains the poorest country in the western hemisphere. A *New York Times* investigation faulted the exploits of French and American banks for the "crippling legacy of financial extraction and dashed hopes—even by the standards of a nation with a long history of both" (Apuzzo et al. 2022).

We would be remiss not to acknowledge the region's pioneering role in social policy. For example, under Jose Batlle y Ordonez's presidency between 1903 and 1915 in the early 1900s, Uruguay adopted free universal education, public pension, public health system, and other progressive measures, which became features of wealthy societies only in the late twentieth century. We mentioned Chile's pension reforms earlier. And, in more recent years, Brazil and Mexico are credited with breaking new ground by introducing conditional cash transfers as both safety net programs and an instrument for improving child health and education, replicated around the world, including advanced economies such as the United States.

Finally, as we come from different academic disciplines, our effort here necessarily takes a multidisciplinary approach—primarily drawing from sociology, international relations, economics, and the capability approach—to examine the phenomenon of financialization. We believe that this represents an advantage in understanding financialization, which has stoutly disobeyed academic boundaries.

1.1 FINANCIALIZATION AND ITS MANY FACES

Financialization has been a hot-button issue. An amazingly diverse body of literature—heterodox economics, economic sociology, anthropology, political science, and many others—has examined financialization's causes, facets, and consequences.[6] The discussion has centered mainly around the mature capitalist societies of the West, but there has been a growing interest in financialization in the Global South. In this body of work, that we term as the "critical approach" to the financial sector's rise, there is near agreement that financialization has been a negative force for advanced and emerging economies (Sawyer 2022).

The term financialization is rarely, if at all, invoked in mainstream economics or finance literature, where the discussion on the financial sector, especially as it relates to emerging economies, is typically couched in terms of financial development, financial deepening, and financial inclusion. The mainstream literature has examined some aspects of financialization, including its implications for social policy, poverty, inequality, and financial stability. It has mainly been sanguine about the financial sector's rise. Without global finance's engagement, challenges of international development and climate change would be hard to surmount (Cerra 2022; Claessens and Perotti 2007).

But the larger sociopolitical questions associated with financialization have received little or no attention in the mainstream literature (Sawyer 2013).

Despite its proliferation across the cognate areas of social sciences, financialization remains a vague term in the academic literature without a universally accepted definition. A commonly cited definition of financialization is as "the increasing role of financial motives, financial markets, financial actors and financial institutions in the operation of domestic and international economies" (Epstein 2005b, p 3). Another explanation of financialization is as a regime of accumulation in which profit is generated through financial activities or channels rather than trade and commodity production (Krippner

2005). Financialization is also presented as a form of neoliberalism that imposes the financial sector's interest on the macroeconomy and economic policy (Palley 2014). It is sometimes narrowly defined as the increased activity of non-financial businesses on the financial market (Stockhammer 2004). Financialization has been a catch-all phrase for a range of "discrete structural changes" (Dore 2008, p. 1097), with profound implications for the nature of economic growth and development as well as for the distribution of power, income, and wealth. We will revisit the idea of financialization in chapter 2; here we focus on some of the characteristics of the structural transformation brought about by financialization.

Financialization marks an important epoch in the development of capitalism witnessed in the advanced economies of the West since the 1980s (Epstein 2005a; Krippner 2005; Lapavitsas 2011). A new form of capitalism dominated by the financial markets has replaced the post-war Fordist accumulation regime reliant on mass production and mass consumption. Financialization has become a powerful organizing force woven into the structure of governance of the state, large corporations, and households alike. Nonetheless, as Sawyer (2013) notes, the era of financialization should not be mistaken as the beginning of financialization. The process of financialization—the development of money, credit, bonds, etcetera—has been unfolding for centuries.[7] The current phase of financialization reflects quantitative and qualitative shifts in the financial system. Sawyer aptly points out that there are some ongoing aspects of the previous processes (e.g. growth in financial transactions), some acceleration of past activities (e.g. deregulation), and a few novel features (e.g. securitization).

Financialization, however, is hardly a Western phenomenon limited to mature economies.[8] The emerging economies also have been witnessing financialization, albeit, as some critics (e.g. Caldentey and Vernengo 2021) assert, prematurely and before the process of industrialization has run its full course. Chile's retail sector is illustrative of financialization in LAC in particular and the developing world in general. Like many non-financial firms in the West, the large department stores in Chile also offer financial services via credit cards used for in-store purchases, cash advances, and payments at other stores. Retail outlets have become non-trivial providers of household credits in recent years (Didier and Schmukler 2013). Retail stores in Argentina, Brazil, Colombia, and Peru have replicated the Chilean model.

But, financialization is not a one-size-fits-all process. It varies across countries, regions, and income groups. There are both broad similarities and differences in the forms of financialization seen in advanced and emerging economies. We saw earlier how the overall structure of LAC's financial sector parallels those in the developed economies. At the same time, Latin America's banking industry has been on a high growth trajectory, unlike the lackluster performance of the banking sector in many of the high-income countries. No change has been as transformative as the region's increasing footprint of foreign banks (Cull and Peria 2010). Further, microfinance and remittances are a few important empirical manifestations of financialization unique to the Global South (Bonizzi 2013b).

Importantly, financialization in emerging economies takes the form of what Alami and colleagues (2022) call "international financial subordination."[9] It is shaped by the subordinate position of the emerging economies in the world system. Financialization in the Global South rests on international capital flow, which, as the experience of both 1970s and 1990s has shown, depends on the liquidity surplus and business cycle in the core countries (Becker et al. 2010; Lapavitsas and Soydan 2022). The hierarchical international monetary system, where some currencies occupy a lower rank in the international monetary position, relegates developing countries to this lower position, which limits their ability to pursue independent monetary and financial policies. The emerging economies are also subjugated to the strict discipline of multilateral agencies such as the IMF and global credit rating agencies. Further, financialization in the Global South centers around the mechanism of interest-bearing capital and thus on banks and on interest rates as well. The social base of financialization is large with a significant proportion of the population, voluntarily or involuntarily, bound to the process of financialization via pension scheme, home loans, consumer credit, health insurance, social programs, and much more. Finally, financialization is a politically and socially contested process since it requires major regulatory changes.

Financialization has been a potent force for transforming social institutions, including the state. Foreign trade, investments, and multilateral lending have encouraged the growth of autonomous central banks (Polillo and Guillén 2005). It has resulted in the executive branch ceding control of monetary policy to central banks. With the rise of the shareholding state, governments are themselves players in the capital market (Wang 2021). The 100 largest sovereign funds collectively manage assets of over $ 10 trillion and, in the process, shape megatrends of the world (PwC n.d.; SWFI n.d.). At the same time, governments rely on capital markets to raise bonds and leverage financial services for development and service delivery. The state now has the added responsibility to protect foreign institutional investors from political, climate, and demand risks underpinning development asset classes (Gabor 2021). Finally, within the state hierarchy, finance ministries occupy a position of preeminence that allows them to influence the functioning of all government departments effectively.

With the state, social policy too has been reconfigured by the rising tide of financialization in the LAC. The region's financial development since the late twentieth century has been predicated on concern for macroeconomic stability and the rising tide of neoliberalism (Ceballos, Didier, and Schmukler 2014; Correa and Vidal 2012). Also, insulated from political and social tugs, central banks preferred a technocratic approach to monetary policy that privileged inflation targeting, overlooking other goals like employment and investment (Epstein 2002). Inflation targeting and fiscal austerity constrict the space for social spending. Moreover, the global sovereign credit rating agencies further impose market discipline on governments that limit the fiscal space for social policy. The possibility of rating downgrades that enhance borrowing costs prevented many governments from pursuing sufficient fiscal expenditure during the COVID-19 pandemic (Ghosh 2021).

Financialization, in fact, has undermined the very logic of social policy (Lavinas 2018), prompting a sea change in the approach to social welfare in the Global South. We will examine later how social inclusion, often narrowly understood as access to economic opportunity, credit, or financial products and services, has become the cornerstone of social policy. In brief, microfinance, conditional cash transfers, basic pensions, and social floors dominate the social protection agenda in the developing world. Credit has become a policy instrument not only for boosting debt-based consumption of durable goods by the working and middle classes but also for fulfilling basic human needs such as housing, education, and health (Reis and de Oliveira 2021).

Social policy has also become a vehicle for expanding financial services and products. Social welfare programs underpin and even create financial markets, specifically mass markets for consumer finance, mortgages, and pensions (Schelkle 2012). For example, consider the case of conditional cash transfer (CCT) programs in Brazil, where the beneficiaries of the programs receive payment via banking services like debit cards, ATM, conventional teller, or telebanking. Most of the CCT programs in LAC work through the banking system.

We aim to contribute to the existing body of literature by examining how financialization has fostered what we call the politics of austerity in LAC. We analyze how these changes impacted social spending. And finally, does financialization live up to the promise of social inclusion?

1.2 MEASURING FINANCIALIZATION

Financialization is a multifaceted concept notoriously hard to measure. It takes many different forms—financial reforms, capital flow, stock market capitalization, private debt, domestic credit, microcredit, financial crises, and much more—each with its own distinctive logic. These different empirical manifestations of financialization can lead to divergent outcomes. For example, international remittances are credited for a modest reduction in poverty and inequality in LAC (Acosta et al. 2008). Similarly, microcredit aimed at small entrepreneurs has had a modestly positive effect. In contrast, financial crises such as the 2007–2008 Wall Street Meltdown have a devastating economic and social effect, with the burden of the crisis disproportionately borne by politically weaker and marginalized groups (Alesina and Drazen 1991; Reinhart and Rogoff 2009b). The mounting public and private debt could well turn out to be another recipe for economic disaster (Roubini 2022).

What one makes of financialization could well depend on how one operationalizes it. So, at the very outset, we would like to clarify how we measure financialization in this book; our intention is not to offer a comprehensive measure of financialization or financial development.[10]

We use outstanding international private debt securities as a percentage of GDP from the World Development Indicators (n.d.) as a proxy for financialization. As discussed in chapter 4, outstanding international private debt securities are a common measure of financialization in the literature. It indicates long-term bonds and notes and money market instruments placed on the international market. It is an indicator of the market-side depth of the financial system. We saw earlier that the evolution of bond and money markets has been an important feature of financialization and financial development in LAC. Global finance has become a critical linchpin of the international development agenda (Gabor 2021). The structural transformation of the local finance system toward market-based finance to better accommodate global portfolio investments has important implications for public policy that we aim to untangle in the book.

Our second indicator of financialization is total domestic credit to the private sector by financial corporations such as monetary authorities, deposit money banks, insurance corporations, and pension funds. We include central banks in our calculation of the credit-to-GDP ratio because they control monetary policy that has been consequential for social welfare policies. Credit has become an alternative policy tool to enable income-strapped household finance consumption, with central banks often pursuing ultra-loose credit policy (Roubini 2022). We take up the issue of credit in the next chapter. The point we want to emphasize here is that the domestic credit-to-GDP ratio also indicates the financial sector's size relative to economic output. It is a crude indicator of the pervasiveness of financialization in terms of the scope and reach of the financial sector (Sawyer 2022). The indicators capture the institutional side of the financial sector.

Both our measures of financialization are admittedly narrow and capture only a few facets of the market and institutional sides of the financial system. We also acknowledge that standard financial sector matrices, such as bond market debt and financial deepening or credit-to-GDP, may not capture the economic and social transformation associated with the evolving capitalist accumulation (Lapavitsas and Soydan 2022). But the two indicators help us understand the public policy dynamics for the reasons discussed earlier.

1.3 THE THEORETICAL ARGUMENT

From the export-led growth phase until the Great Depression to the inward-looking ISI approach in the post-war period and the subsequent embrace of globalization, Latin America's economic destiny has been intricately linked to distant forces far away from its shore. The oil crises, the global liquidity glut, the end of the Bretton Woods system, the Volker shock, and the Washington Consensus are only a few examples of external drivers of the region's economic journey. LAC has had little control over trade cycles, investment and consumption patterns, debt accumulation, and technology transfer (Bulmer-Thomas 2003). By and large, Latin America has "operated in a world in which rules were made by others" (p. 392).

Financialization continues the long trend in Latin America's history of economic development. We assert here that financialization has been an external import. There was no Latin American equivalent of the forces that shaped financialization in the United States and Europe: institutional investors were either wholly controlled by the government or too small to make a difference; credit markets were almost entirely directed by government policy, and state banks were the primary actors in local credit markets. The growth of international financial markets in the 19070s, and their political force in the 1980s led to the adoption of a set of policies that entrenched finance as the commanding force in Latin America. First, through financial deregulation in the 1990s, and then through the expansion of credit markets in the 2000s, Latin America went from being one of the regions of the world where finance was the most regulated to one of the least, and one where policymakers from a variety of backgrounds have been replaced by technocrats seen as credible by financial markets.

1.3.1 The Two Tales of Financialization

We alluded earlier to the fact that the literature on financialization is largely polarized and lopsided. The mainstream economic view represents financialization as an unstoppable force of global reach that will unlock powerful solutions to poverty and other social ills if only wisely embraced according to the universal prescriptions of liberal economics. The critical view taken by many scholars studying the question from the perspective of financial subordination, more widely accepted in financialization studies of the social sciences, views in financialization studies, tells us that financialization is an unstoppable force that will enrich an elite few while harming the life prospects of the large majority.

Each side, we argue, is half-right. The mainstream view underscores that increasing financial integration is an entrenched and unavoidable fact of the world, that carries the potential for benefits. The critical view appropriately highlights the historically subordinate position of LAC in the global economy and its imposition of rules of the game from the outside, as we note above, and the highly skewed distribution of the advantages of financialization.

While both are partially correct, the sides converge, we believe, on a mistake. Characterizing financialization only as a global force external to national borders with singular sources and effects reifies a complex social process and directs attention away from the active role agents play in the mediation and implementation of financialization. The mistake is defining financialization in a mechanistic fashion that overlooks the complex, social characteristic of financialization.

The only significant disagreement concerns whether benefits spread widely or narrowly. Correcting this mistake, furthermore, points the way toward a means to bridging the gap between them, and moving toward a more fruitful approach to financialization than the current situation of two literatures largely speaking past one another.

The critical literature examining the issue from the perspective of subordinate financialization positions less developed economies as actors without significant influence, pushed by global financial structures with only the choice of acceptance or rejection of the terms imposed by financial markets and institutions, a choice with no substantive freedom as global finance cannot plausibly be refused without significant economic dislocation given the subordinate status of these economies and their need for international capital. Conventional liberal economics similarly tells the story of markets as operating beyond human intervention, emphasizing macroeconomic indicators of financial growth and stability as the measure of success, independent of the social costs of uneven benefits of financialization.

As the critical view highlights, it is the case that the benefits of financialization have been uneven and have aggravated inequalities in LAC. However, we argue that this is not a necessary outcome of financialization, as there are a multitude of mechanisms and policies that may be classified under the rubric of financialization.

If this debate sounds familiar, the contours are much the same as those surrounding the discussion concerning globalization that emerged in the last decades of the twentieth century. Polemics over globalization similarly tended to emphasize either the many potential benefits or the many potential drawbacks of global integration.[11] In either case, there usually emerged a picture of globalization as an impersonal, global tidal wave, the question was simply whether to ride it or resist it. Rather than the debate being decided in favor of either view, a broad consensus has emerged that globalization is not a singular force of nature beyond the influence of individual nations. Instead, a panoply of domestic variables shape the opportunities and outcomes of global interconnectedness. There is no single story of globalization. Financialization is not the same as globalization, it presents its own challenges. Nevertheless, we find a similar dynamic at work in financialization studies that colored discourse in previous decades. While financialization may have been an external force that profoundly shaped LAC, its results were neither uniform nor consistent.

1.3.2 A Bridge Not Too Far

We propose to bridge the two literatures, underscoring what each view gets right and wrong, by emphasizing the social nature of financialization and refocusing attention on the agents that compose such a complex social system. Agents as diverse as the "Chicago Boys" (so named because of their University of Chicago training), local economists who were once upon a time staunch development state supporters, technocrats trying to bridge the gaps between local and global financial markets, and policymakers trying to operate under newfound restrictions on what policies were accepted by the market. In this way, we propose to reveal that domestic actors in LAC, while subjected to externally originating financial pressures, the implementation of financialization may take different forms, its demands negotiated in ways that are not uniformly negative at the national level, but different actors may distribute benefits and losses according to their varying interests. The rules, as we see it are externally imposed. The rules of any complex game are endlessly interpretable and may be implemented with impressive creativity without fundamentally altering the nature of the game.

Missing from both is the acknowledgment that national-level actors in LAC are significant players in financialization. Even as they play by rules created in the Global North for economic contexts very different than their own, governments and national-level financial elites are invested in and constructing financialization in their own fashion and for their own purposes. We wish, therefore, to return to an agentic perspective that can incorporate the motive power of actors in LAC, incorporating the insights of the mainstream and critical perspectives while avoiding the shared mistake of rigid structuralism.

Theory and evidence should always remain in conversation. Observations are unavoidably directed by theory, and empirical findings necessarily inform theory, leading us to revise, reject, or provisionally maintain our views in light of observations. In financialization studies, a rupture has opened between the two, and both sides in the debate have suffered from the loss of the other's contributions. Both the conventional economic and critical views have been guided by theory mismatched to the complexity and sometimes contradictory evidence presented by the real world.

Rather than persist with competing but incommunicative theories that lead us to differing streams of evidence, we will argue that conjecturing new theoretical models and attending closely to the empirical evidence is the best method to adopt if we hope to ameliorate the corrosive social consequences highlighted by the critical perspective while taking advantage of the opportunities accented by the conventional economic perspective.

The views are marked by different varieties of myopia that converge in the structuralism that displaces agency. Theoretical myopia suffered by investors and policymakers alike drives them in adopting policies based on a flawed understanding of markets as complicated mechanisms that have an optimal operational state that can only be achieved by eliminating interference from influences from outside the mechanism itself. This draws a picture of economies as extremely intricate, but intelligible and self-sustaining processes which are manageable through proper restraint. This quite explicitly removes agents from any position of influence. In the extreme case, such myopia produces the current condition of the Cayman Islands as described above. Policy is distorted by a misconceived theoretical lens.

Despite accurately capturing the many perils associated with ever-deepening financial ties and the social exclusion that often accompanies them, the critical view similarly suffers from a blind spot that is also an artifact of a failure to appreciate the role of actors at the national level and their positions as participants in a socially constituted process who possess the power to choose among paths offered within the financialized international context. The tendency here is to similarly regard structures as external, material forces rather than inherently social ones created through mutual interactions.

In this case, the blind spot obscures empirical evidence that financialization's effects are significantly diverse. In contrast to the conventional economic view's production of distorted policy and it is, consequently, empirical observation that is distorted by theoretical misconception.

While a major motivation of our research concerns material effects, we recognize that economic and other material aspects of the world do not carry independent meaning. Instead, social outcomes are laden with the interpretations we bring to them, pointing to the importance of the constructed dimension of ideas. Therefore, the correction to the theoretical blindspot, we suggest, is to attend more closely to the overlooked complexity of financialization and the place of agents as constituents in it. This entails an ideational approach that highlights the motive importance of ideas.

Cognitive approaches to economic processes, while traditionally neglected, have in recent decades become more mainstream. Treatments in political science, sociology, and anthropology of economics in general and financialization, in particular, have employed ideational variables to enrich our understanding of these complex processes far beyond the axiomatic and mathematical approaches of traditional economics. By neglecting the fact that economic decisions are made by agents interacting with and anticipating the decisions and actions of other agents themselves behaving in the same way, traditional economic approaches "de-socialize" what are essentially social activities. By emphasizing the importance of ideas, constructivist or ideational theories acknowledge the reality that bare material facts lend themselves to rearrangement in a panoply of explanations. Constructivist International Political Economy, for example, has examined the important role of shared ideas in shaping divergent national economic postures in a globalizing economy (e.g. Abdelal, Blyth, and Parsons 2010), while sociological institutionalist studies have documented how ideas at the level of managers and firms have important consequences for entire economies (e.g. Fligstein 1993).

We agree that ideational factors are essential for making sense of the process of financialization. We are left with other questions, however, that we do not believe are sufficiently answered by most ideational perspectives. Among the unknowns surrounding financialization are its sources and reasons for its persistence. How did financial liberalization embed itself so fully in LAC, when its origins lie in the distinctive conditions of highly developed capitalist economies? We trace this process to the adoption and spread of the ideas animating financialization abroad, independent of the conditions of the Global South.

Additionally, we wish to uncover the manner in which ideas shape financialization, and whether financialization carries with it effects that reach beyond the financial dimension. Put another way, does financialization affect changes in policy and social outcomes outside the immediate sphere of the financial industry? If so, what are the sources of these ideas and why do they influence changes beyond the typical understanding of the realm of financialization?

An appreciation of economic phenomena as complex systems, constituted by agents reacting and adapting to other agents in recursive fashion, points toward a fuller, more realistic reading of financialization than provided by either the conventional economic or critical views, and is better equipped to answer these questions. By overlooking the central role of agents in the ideational construction of a process like financialization, each side draws overly broad conclusions about its failings and its potential.

Rather than executives and policymakers responding rationally to structural, material conditions of an exterior economic reality, as claimed by neoliberal economics, the policy prescriptions associated with financialization are derived from the ideological convergence of many social actors. This convergence emerges from the competition of ideological frameworks providing divergent interpretations of the economy and functioning of markets. We term the set of prescriptive ideas derived from neoliberal economic theory "market ideology" to underscore its interpretive and normative functions. In much of Latin America and the Caribbean market ideology was imported by foreign-educated economists, who gradually displaced the state-centric development approaches that had dominated the region for several decades.

If financialization is driven by such ideational factors, its full social effects cannot be grasped without accounting for these nonmaterial variables and will lead to confusion about the potential for financialization to yield the benefits it has promised and misplaced confidence in orthodox neoliberal policies as a universal panacea for developing economies.

Thus far, we agree with the critical perspective that comes to similar conclusions. Nonetheless, as suggested earlier, we believe that a similar oversight has affected the appraisal of financialization from a critical perspective. In this case, the minimization of agents' participation in financialization understates the influence held by decision-makers in LAC. These act within confines established by a financialized global system, but nevertheless have the power to integrate their economies into a globalized financial system so as to benefit some social sectors at the expense of others. By choosing how to implement the austerity policies favored by financial markets, maintaining some budget items while sacrificing other areas of spending, and by national level elites actively shape the domestic effects of financialization. Again, these actors do not simply react to an exterior economic structure as posited by economic theory, but also as sometimes claimed by government officials in LAC.

In making this contribution to the theory and empirical testing of financialization, we hope to contribute to a less polarized conversation over financialization that will move our understanding toward more productive policymaking, which will promote more inclusive distribution of the benefits of this inescapable aspect of modern capitalism.

1.4 THE PLAN FOR THE BOOK

Chapter 2 provides a historical sociology of financialization in LAC. It situates LAC's current phase of financialization in the larger context of its economic history. During the export-led growth period, the national governments of the region primarily created national banks to finance the production and export of raw materials and fund the state's operations. Larger Latin American economies, like Brazil, Mexico, and Argentina, also set up their first stock exchanges, primarily aimed at raw materials exports. As a result of these processes, most Latin American economies emerged in the early 1970s with relatively significant financial institutions, which were wholly subordinate to the coordination and development goals of the state (Bonizzi 2013a; Levy and Bustamante 2018; Whitener 2019). After the export-led growth model gave way to the inward-looking Import Substitution Model (ISI), governments vigorously pursued policies to create state apparatuses such as national development banks to finance and promote the risky investments needed to create local industries of vital interest to state. These financial institutions existed in a world of significant state regulation of financial flows, with capital accounts heavily regulated (Pinheiro, Chwieroth, and Hicks 2015), multiple exchange rate regimes dedicated to promoting (or discouraging) different forms of economic activity (Collins 1996; Frieden, Ghezzi, and Stein 2000), and personal credit, to the extent that it existed, guided by development considerations.

The emergence of financialization marks a shift in the role of the financial sector in the region. We argue that the current era of financialization can be understood as the inversion of the relative relevance of finance on one hand, and government finance and productive activities on the other. Rather than supporting the sectors related to the export of primary commodities, like in the period after independence, or supporting state investment and industrialization efforts, like in the immediate post-war period of the twentieth century, finance and financial concerns mold public policy to its logic. Government policy, social spending, and even social inclusion mechanisms became subjected to the logic and technology of finance. The speed of this conversion in Latin America can be demonstrated by comparing existing measures of financial openness across the world.

In chapter 3, we establish our expectations for the empirical tests in chapters 4 and 5. In order to understand the effects of financialization we must determine where it comes from and why it persists. We consider alternative views of policy change in the production of financialization, determining that prevailing models privilege understandings of financial and economic systems as external mechanical structures that operate independently of agentic input. Instead of such a "de-socialized" and structural view, we take the position that in order to properly understand financialization we must grapple with its status as a complex system of interacting agents. As such, we must acknowledge the participation of actors at the national level in LAC who, though constrained by large-scale international forces, can implement financialization policies according to their own lights and to benefit some domestic sectors over others.

In order to integrate this view we take an ideational perspective, centering the role of actors' ideas. Financialization in LAC is the product of ideas generated in a different context responding to different conditions. We do not quibble against ideas born afar, nor do we valorize home-grown champions. But, unlike structural and psychological explanations, we bring into the calculus ideas and agency that shape the process. Financialization, as imported into the region, took on the form of a set of policy ideas that floats free of the material context of the world in which it operates. Without discounting the importance of economic conditions, we draw attention to the ideational dimension to uncover beliefs underpinning the process of financialization. These beliefs incorporate the assumptions that rational actors pursuing similar, predictable goals will reliably produce the most efficient allocation of resources, contributing to healthier economic growth.

This stylized, policy-oriented version of neoliberal economic theory produces a commitment to austerity in social spending that travels with financialization is not rooted in simple market incentives but in shared notions about the proper role of the state or, perhaps more accurately, the impropriety of an active role for the state in promotion of social welfare. The theoretical underpinning of this orientation posits easily grasped propositions about economies, propositions that we argue, do not account for the fundamental unpredictability of complex social systems like economies and financial markets. Therefore, our argument leads us to expect that higher levels of financialization will be associated with lower levels of health and education spending, independent of the real-world economic effects of financialization. Rather than straightforward economic criteria, the assumptions that undergird market ideology propel the budget-cutting austerity policies that have marked the last several decades while blinding policymakers to the—at best—mixed evidence regarding financialization's advertised benefits.

To this point we converge with critical views of financialization of the subordinate or dependent financialization schools. However, chapter 3 further argues that these approaches, which dominate the studies of financialization as such, share the broad theoretical assessment of financialization as an exterior and structural constraint on national-level actors. A comparison is drawn between the debates of earlier decades surrounding globalization and free trade. This discussion was similarly polarized with critical scholars predicting dire results on both social spending and social inclusion. Ultimately, empirical observation has revealed the diversity of outcomes that have accompanied integration into the global economy. Experience has shown that many social and institutional factors intervene at the national level to mediate the effects of global competition. With this empirical history in mind, we expect that action at the national level similarly mediates outcomes in the complex interactions of financialization in ways that predominant structural theories tend to overlook.

The subsequent chapters test the various policy implications related to social spending and social inclusion. We rely on a cross-national sample of

LAC countries for which data are available between 1980 and 2020. Chapter 4 focuses on the effect international private debt securities outstanding have on health, education, and overall welfare spending. We turn the spotlight on international debt securities since it is likely to have the greatest impact on public expenditure. We find empirical support for our postulate that financialization measured as outstanding international debt securities leads to a long-term decline in health and education spending but an increase in total welfare spending.

We next answer why reliance on international bonds for state funding dampens social spending. We do so by examining how levels and spending changes influence Sovereign Risk Ratings issued by credit rating agencies. The dominant view in the mainstream economic discourse is that social spending increases the risk of default or macroeconomic instability, adversely impacting their sovereign rating and ability to raise funds in the international capital market. However, our empirical analysis shows that social spending is not directly related to either defaults or banking crises. This suggests that financialization instead serves as a way through which external policy paradigms take hold of Latin American politics.

In chapter 5, we turn our attention to the social consequences of the two dimensions of financialization under consideration. Before we embark on our investigation, we provide our rationale for evaluating financialization's social impact. For one, there is no one set of gold standards for assessing social arrangements and programs. Efficiency, equity, or some other criterion could serve as the benchmark. And, as Amartya Sen (2000) cautions, our choice of measurement has a bearing on the information we include or exclude from the evaluation process. We use extreme poverty and inequality levels to analyze the social consequences of financialization. The idea that less poverty is better for society has been around since the Enlightenment era in the eighteenth century. Ending extreme and other forms of poverty by 2030 is the top goal of the United Nations Sustainable Development Goals, an objective severely undermined worldwide by the COVID-19 pandemic. Income inequality poses a severe social and moral challenge. Moreover, reducing extreme poverty and inequality are necessary for social inclusion, which has become an important guiding principle for social policy. Social inclusion entails benefit sharing that requires a reduction in both poverty and inequality.

Our empirical analyses here present a more nuanced understanding of how the different channels of financialization, namely private credit and international debt securities, impact inclusive growth in the LAC. First, we find that private credit enhances the growth of post-tax and transfer income inequality, therefore worsening relative inclusion in the region. Private debt securities have a statistically weak opposite effect on relative inclusion. When it comes to absolute inclusion or extreme poverty, we find that international private securities negatively affect the growth of extreme poverty, thus bolstering absolute inclusion. The effect of private credit on extreme poverty growth too is negative but statistically weak.

Chapter 6 concludes by highlighting our contribution to the understanding of financialization in LAC. Financialization has been a defining feature of the transformation witnessed since the late twentieth century. Our primary motivation has been to uncover the downstream effects of financialization on social spending and human welfare indicators, bringing some greater clarity to the question of whether financialization "works" as neoliberal economic theory predicts. The process of financialization is not only an external, foreign influence, however, and the principles of neoliberalism were subsequently embraced at the domestic level, transforming national economies.

We demonstrate that financialization has an independent causal effect on social spending. The type of debt owed by governments exercises a direct form of pressure on the budgeting decisions of national policymakers. While welfare and social security spending are significantly impacted by the strength of labor movements, budget cuts to education and healthcare are directly related to levels of international bond debt and private credit. Importantly, there is no direct connection between these budget items and the propensity for governments to default on debt.

Our findings thus present a complex reality, perhaps not surprising for a multifaceted process without a universal definition. We conclude with a call to integrate the mainstream economic and critical literatures which largely fail to speak to one another. Both the potential benefits and dangers to social inclusion are part of this reality. An understanding of financialization as a social process amenable to agentic intervention and national choices allows us to integrate the insights of the contrasting views and to move beyond their theoretical weakness.

NOTES

1. See Woetzel (2021); also Roubini (2022) on this point.

2. Cayman Islands, Santiago, Bermuda, Mexico City, São Paulo, Rio de Janeiro, British Virgin Islands, Bogota, Bahamas, Panama, Trinidad and Tobago, Buenos Aires and Barbados made it to the Global Financial Index 32. The rankings are based on five broad areas of business environment, human capital, infrastructure, financial sector development and reputation.

3. See Bulmer-Thomas (2003) and Thorp (1998) for historical perspective on economic development including capital markets in Latin America. See also Burns (1999) for discussion on what she calls spiritual economy.

4. According to the Cayman Island General Registry (n.d.) there were 116,996 active registered companies in 2021. Economic and Statistics Office (2022) put the total the total population at 71,105 in 2021.

5. The former president Barack Obama singled out the building in a speech in 2009, calling it as "either the biggest building or the biggest tax scam on record" (Keating 2012). But activities at the Ugland House are neither unusual nor illegal. See also GAO (2008) report to the U.S Senate's committee on finance.

6. Our review here is admittedly selective. See Epstein (2005a), Zwan (2014), Davis and Kim (2015), Mader, Mertens and Zwan(2020), Lapavitas (2011), and Sawyer (2013) for systematic review of the literature on the topic.

7. Economic historian Nial Ferguson (2008) reminds us that the financial sector crucially shaped the course of history. Banks financed the Renaissances, bonds tipped the scale of war, stock markets built empires, and monetary meltdown ignited revolutions. William Dalrymple (2019) provides illuminating discussion on common stock, East India Company, and colonization of India. See also Goetzmann (2016) for the role of finance throughout history.

8. See Bonizzi (2013b), Becker et al. (2010), Lapavistsas and Soydan (2022), Alami et al. (2022), and Sawyer (2022) for in-depth review of financialization in Global South.

9. See also Bonizzi, Kaltenbrunner and Powell (2021) for an overview on subordinate financialization in emerging economies; and Reis and de Oliveira (2021) on Latin America's peripheral financialization.

10. See Karwowski and Stockhammer (2017), Lapavitsas & Soydan (2022) and Swayer (2022) for discussion on measuring financialization in emerging and developing. Also see Sahay et al. (2015) for discussion on measuring financial development.

11. See, for example, Stiglit's (2002) discontent with and Bhagwati's (2004) defense of globalization.

BIBLIOGRAPHY

Acosta, Pablo, Cesar Calderón, Pablo Fajnzylber, and Humberto Lopez. 2008. "What Is the Impact of International Remittances on Poverty and Inequality in Latin America?" *World Development* 36 (1): 89–114. https://doi.org/10.1016/j.worlddev.2007.02.016.

Agnoli, Myriam Quispe, and Diego Vilán. 2008. "Financing Trends in Latin America." In *New Financing Trends in Latin America: A Bumpy Road towards Stability*, edited by Bank for International Settlement, 36: 15–27.

Aguilera, Ruth V., and Gregory Jackson. 2003. "The Cross-National Diversity of Corporate Governance: Dimensions and Determinants." *Academy of Management Review* 28 (3): 447–65. https://doi.org/10.2307/30040732.

Alami, Ilias, Carolina Alves, Bruno Bonizzi, Annina Kaltenbrunner, Kai Koddenbrock, Ingrid Kvangraven, and Jeff Powell. 2022. "International Financial Subordination: A Critical Research Agenda." *Review of International Political Economy.* https://doi.org/10.1080/09692290.2022.2098359.

Alesina, Alberto, and Allan Drazen. 1991. "Why Are Stabilizations Delayed?" *The American Economic Review* 81 (5): 1170–88.

Alves, Carolina. 2022. "Fictitious Capital, the Credit System, and the Particular Case of Government Bonds in Marx." *New Political Economy* 18. https://doi.org/10.1080/13563467.2022.2130221.

Apuzzo, Matt, Constant Méheut, Selam Gebrekidan, and Catherine Porter. 2022. "How a French Bank Captured Haiti." *The New York Times*, May 20, 2022, sec. World. https://www.nytimes.com/2022/05/20/world/french-banks-haiti-cic.html.

Balakrishnan, Radhika, James Heintz, and Dianne Elson. 2016. *Rethinking Economic Policy for Social Justice: The Radical Potential of Human Rights*. New York: Routledge.

Banerjee, Abhijit, Dean Karlan, and Jonathan Zinman. 2015. "Six Randomized Evaluations of Microcredit: Introduction and Further Steps." *American Economic Journal: Applied Economics* 7 (1): 1–21. https://doi.org/10.1257/app.20140287.

Baquerizo, Hugo, Alvaro Cubria, Roberto Marchi, and Alexandre Sawaya. 2019. "Lessons from Leaders in Latin America's Retail Banking Market." McKinsey & Company. https://www.mckinsey.com/industries/financial-services/our-insights/lessons-from-leaders-in-latin-americas-retail-banking-market.

Beck, Thorsten, Asli Demirgüç-Kunt, and Ross Levine. 2007. "Finance, Inequality and the Poor." *Journal of Economic Growth* 12 (1): 27–49. https://doi.org/10.1007/s10887-007-9010-6.

Becker, Joachim, Johannes Jäger, Bernhard Leubolt, and Rudy Weissenbacher. 2010. "Peripheral Financialization and Vulnerability to Crisis: A Regulationist Perspective." *Competition and Change* 14 (3–4): 225–47. https://doi.org/10.1179/102452910X12837703615337.

Bhagwati, Jagdish N. 2004. *In Defense of Globalization*. New York: Oxford University Press. http://site.ebrary.com/id/10103674.

Bonizzi, Bruno. 2013. "Financialization in Developing and Emerging Countries: A Survey." *International Journal of Political Economy* 42 (4): 83–107. https://doi.org/10.2753/IJP0891-1916420405.

Bonizzi, Bruno, Annina Kaltenbrunner, and Jeff Powell. 2021. "Subordinate Financialization in Emerging Capitalist Economies." In *The Routledge International Handbook of Financialization*, edited by Philip Mader, Daniel Mertens, and Natascha van der Zwan, 177–87. New York: Routledge.

Bulmer-Thomas, Victor. 2003. *The Economic History of Latin America Since Independence*. 2nd ed. New York, NY: Cambridge University Press.

Burns, Kathryn. 1999. *Colonial Habits: Convents and the Spiritual Economy of Cuzco, Peru*. Duke University Press.

Cayman Island General Registry. n.d. "Company Statistics." Cayman Islands General Registry | An Official Website of the Cayman Islands Government. Accessed November 1, 2022. https://www.ciregistry.ky/companies-register/company-statistics/.

Cayman News. 2022. "CIG Rakes in Near $447 Million in Just the First Quarter." *Cayman News Service*, May 12, 2022.

Ceballos, Francisco, Tatiana Didier, and Sergio L. Schmukler. 2014. "Overview." In *-Emerging Issues in Financial Development: Lessons from Latin America*, edited by Tatiana Didier and Sergio L. Schmukler, 1–24. Washington, D.C: The World Bank.

Cecchetti, Stephen G., and Enisse Kharroubi. 2018. "Why Does Credit Growth Crowd Out Real Economic Growth?" Working Paper W25079. Cambridge, MA: National Bureau of Economic Research. https://doi.org/10.3386/w25079.

Cecchini, Simone, and Bernardo Atuesta. 2017. "Conditional Cash Transfer Programmes in Latin America and the Caribbean: Coverage and Investment Trends." *Social Policy* 224. Santiago: United Nations. https://repositorio.cepal.org/handle/11362/42109.

Cerra, Valerie. 2022. "An Inclusive Growth Framework." In *How to Achieve Inclusive Growth*, edited by Valerie Cerra, Barry Eichengreen, Asmaa El-Ganainy, and Martin Schindler, 1–31. Oxford, UK: Oxford University Press.

Chandrasekhar, C.P., and Jayati Ghosh. 2018. "The Financialization of Finance? Demonetization and the Dubious Push to Cashlessness in India." *Development and Change* 49 (2): 420–36. https://doi.org/10.1111/dech.12369.

Chinn, Menzie D., and Hiro Ito. 2008. "A New Measure of Financial Openness." *Journal of Comparative Policy Analysis: Research and Practice* 10 (3): 309–22. https://doi.org/10.1080/13876980802231123.

Chwieroth, Jeffrey M, and Andrew Walter. 2020. "Financialization, Wealth and the Changing Political Aftermaths of Banking Crises." *Socio-Economic Review* 20 (1): 55–84. https://doi.org/10.1093/ser/mwaa017.

Čihák, Martin, Aslı Demirgüç-Kunt, Erik Feyen, and Ross Levine. 2012. "Benchmarking Financial Systems Around the World." Policy Research Working Paper WPS 6175. Washington, DC: World Bank Group. https://doi.org/10.1596/1813-9450-6175.

CIMA. 2021. "Fact Sheet of the Cayman Islands Monetary Authority." 2021. https://www.cima.ky/fact-sheet.

Claessens, Stijn, and Erik Feijen. 2007. "Financial Sector Development and the Millennium Development Goals." Working Paper 89. Washington, DC: The World Bank. https://doi.org/10.1596/978-0-8213-6865-7.

Correa, Eugenia, and Gregorio Vidal. 2012. "Financialization and Global Financial Crisis in Latin American Countries." *Journal of Economic Issues* 46 (2): 541–48. https://doi.org/10.2753/JEI0021-3624460229.

Cull, Robert, and Martinez Maria Soledad Peria. 2010. "Foreign Bank Participation in Developing Countries: What Do We Know About the Drivers and Consequences of This Phenomenon?" Policy Research Working Paper 5398. The World Bank. https://doi.org/10.1596/1813-9450-5398.

Dalrymple, William. 2019. *The Anarchy: The East India Company, Corporate Violence, and the Pillage of an Empire*. New York: Bloomsbury Publishing.

Davis, Gerald F., and Suntae Kim. 2015. "Financialization of the Economy." *Annual Review of Sociology* 41 (April): 203–21. https://doi.org/10.1146/annurey-soc-073014-112402.

Demirguc-Kunt, Asli, Leora Klapper, and Dorothe Singer. 2017. "Financial Inclusion and Inclusive Growth: A Review of Recent Empirical Evidence." Policy Research Working paper WPS 8040. Washington, DC: World Bank Group. World

Bank Group. https://documents.worldbank.org/en/publication/documents-reports/documentdetail/403611493134249446/Financial-inclusion-and-inclusive-growth-a-review-of-recent-empirical-evidence.

Didier, Tatiana, and Sergio L. Schmukler. 2013. "Financial Globalization: Some Basic Indicators for Latin America and the Caribbean." In *Emerging Issues in Financial Development: Lessons from Latin America*, edited by Tatiana Didier and Sergio L. Schmukler, 175–204. Washington, DC: The World Bank. https://doi.org/10.1596/978-0-8213-9828-9.

Dietz, Miklos, Attila Kincses, Archana Seshadrinathan, and Dee Yang. 2022. "Banking on a Sustainable Path: Global Banking Annual Review 2022." McKinsey & Company. https://www.mckinsey.com/industries/financial-services/our-insights/global-banking-annual-review.

Dore, Ronald. 2008. "Financialization of the Global Economy." *Industrial and Corporate Change* 17 (6): 1097–1112. https://doi.org/10.1093/icc/dtn041.

Economic Commission for Latin America and the Caribbean (ECLAC). 2022. "Capital Flows to Latin America and the Caribbean: 2021 Year-in-Review and First Four Months of 2022." LC/WAS/TS.2022/1. Santiago: United Nations. https://repositorio.cepal.org/handle/11362/47917.

Economics and Statistics Office. 2022a. "The Cayman Islands' 2021 Census of Population and Housing Report." 1-362: Government of the Cayman Islands.

———. 2022b. "The Cayman Islands' 2021 Census of Population and Housing Report." Government of the Cayman Islands. https://www.eso.ky/2021-population-and-housing-census-report.html.

Engelen, Ewald. 2008. "The Case for Financialization." *Competition & Change* 12 (2): 111–19. https://doi.org/10.1179/102452908X289776.

Epstein, Gerald A. 2002. "Financialization, Rentier Interests, and Central Bank Policy." In *Financialization of the World Economy*. University of Massachusetts, Amherst: Department of Economics and Political Economy Research Institute. https://peri.umass.edu/publication/item/77-financialization-rentier-interests-and-central-bank-policy.

———. ed. 2005a. *Financialization and the World Economy*. Northampton, MA: Edward Elgar.

———. 2005b. "Introduction: Financialization and the World Economy." In *Financialization and the World Economy*, edited by Gerald A. Epstein, 3–16. Northampton, MA: Edward Elgar.

Evans, Christopher, and Samuel Pienknagura. 2021. "Assessing Chile's Pension System: Challenges and Reform Options." Working Paper WP/21/232. International Monetary Fund. https://www.imf.org/en/Publications/WP/Issues/2021/09/09/Assessing-Chile-s-Pension-System-Challenges-and-Reform-Options-465415.

Ferguson, Niall. 2008. *The Ascent of Money: A Financial History of the World*. New York, NY: The Penguin Press.

Fernández-Arias, Eduardo, and Peter J. Montiel. 1996. "The Surge in Capital Inflows to Developing Countries: An Analytical Overview." *The World Bank Economic Review* 10 (1): 51–77.

Fichtner, Jan. 2016. "The Anatomy of the Cayman Islands Offshore Financial Center: Anglo-America, Japan, and the Role of Hedge Funds." *Review of International Political Economy* 23 (6): 1034–63. https://doi.org/10.1080/09692290.2016.1243143.

Fine, Ben. 2009. "Financialisation and Social Policy." In *Social and Political Dimensions of the Global Crisis: Implications for Developing Countries*. Geneva: UNRISD (United Nations Research Institute for Social Development).

———. 2013. "Financialization from a Marxist Perspective." *International Journal of Political Economy* 42 (4): 47–66. https://doi.org/10.2753/IJP0891-1916420403.

Fiszbein, Ariel, Norbert Rüdiger Schady, Francisco H. G. Ferreira, Margaret Grosh, Niall Keleher, Pedro Olinto, and Emmanuel Skoufias. 2009. *Conditional Cash Transfers: Reducing Present and Future Poverty*. Washington, DC: The World Bank.

Frieden, Jeffry A. 2006. *Global Capitalism: Its Fall and Rise in the Twentieth Century*. 1st ed. New York: W.W. Norton.

Gabor, Daniela. 2021. "The Wall Street Consensus." *Development and Change* 52 (3): 429–59. https://doi.org/10.1111/dech.12645.

GAO. 2008. "Cayman Islands: Business and Tax Advantages Attract U.S. Persons and Enforcement Challenges Exist." GAO-08-778. Washington, DC: Government Accountability Office.

Gautam, Rana S. 2019. *Human Rights Practices during Financial Crises*. Cham: Palgrave Pivot.

Georgieva, Kristalina. 2022. "The IMF's Role in a More Shock-Prone World." IMF. 2022. https://www.imf.org/en/News/Articles/2022/10/14/sp101422-imf-managing-director-speech-to-the-plenary-meeting.

Ghosh, Jayati. 2021. "Credit-Rating Agencies Could Derail Economic Recovery | by Jayati Ghosh." Project Syndicate. March 16, 2021. https://www.project-syndicate.org/commentary/credit-rating-agencies-could-derail-economic-recovery-by-jayati-ghosh-2021-03.

Godechot, Olivier. 2021. "Financialization and the Increase in Inequality." In *The Routledge International Handbook of Financialization*, edited by Philip Mader, Daniel Mertens, and Natascha van der Zwan, 413–24. New York: Routledge.

Goetzmann, William N. 2016. *Money Changes Everything: How Finance Made Civilization Possible*. Princeton, NJ: Princeton University Press.

Heng, Dyna, Anna Ivanova, Rodrigo Mariscal, Uma Ramakrishnan, and Joyce Cheng Wong. 2016. "Advancing Financial Development in Latin America and the Caribbean." Working Paper WP/16/81. IMF (International Monetary Fund). https://www.imf.org/en/Publications/WP/Issues/2016/12/31/Advancing-Financial-Development-in-Latin-America-and-the-Caribbean-43854.

Jensen, Lars. 2022. "Avoiding 'Too Little Too Late' on International Debt Relief." Development Futures Series Working Papers. New York, NY: UNDP (United Nations Development Programme). https://www.undp.org/publications/dfs-avoiding-too-little-too-late-international-debt-relief.

Kaltenbrunner, Annina, and Juan Pablo Painceira. 2018. "Subordinated Financial Integration and Financialisation in Emerging Capitalist Economies: The Brazilian

Experience." *New Political Economy* 23 (3): 290–313. https://doi.org/10.1080/13563467.2017.1349089.

Kaminsky, Graciela Laura, and Sergio L. Schmukler. 2003. "Short-Run Pain, Long-Run Gain: The Effects of Financial Liberalization." *IMF Working Papers* 03 (34): 1. https://doi.org/10.5089/9781451845280.001.

Kaplan, Stephen B. 2013. *Globalization and Austerity Politics in Latin America*. Cambridge Studies in Comparative Politics. New York: Cambridge University Press.

Karwowski, Ewa, and Engelbert Stockhammer. 2017. "Financialisation in Emerging Economies: A Systematic Overview and Comparison with Anglo-Saxon Economies." *Economic and Political Studies* 5 (1): 60–86. https://doi.org/10.1080/20954816.2016.1274520.

Keating, Joshua E. 2012. "House of 19,000 Corporations." *Foreign Policy*, 2012. https://foreignpolicy.com/2012/01/24/house-of-19000-corporations/.

Klapper, Leora, Mayada El-Zoghbi, and Jake Hess. 2016. "Achieving the Sustainable Development Goals: The Role of Financial Inclusion." Washington, DC: CGAP. https://www.cgap.org/research/publication/achieving-sustainable-development-goals.

Knafo, Samuel, and Sahil Jai Dutta. 2020. "The Myth of the Shareholder Revolution and the Financialization of the Firm." *Review of International Political Economy* 27 (3): 476–99. https://doi.org/10.1080/09692290.2019.1649293.

Krippner, Greta R. 2005. "The Financialization of the American Economy." *Socio-Economic Review* 3 (2): 173–208. https://doi.org/10.1093/SER/mwi008.

Kwon, Roy. 2019. "Turn the Bull Loose: A Test of the Moderating Effect of Economic Liberalization on the Link Between Financialization and Income Inequality in Developed Economies." *Social Science Quarterly* 100 (3): 808–24. https://doi.org/10.1111/ssqu.12578.

Laing, Aislinn. 2019. "Chile's Fiery Anger Fueled by Fears of Poverty in Old Age." *Reuters*, November 1, 2019, sec. americas-test-2. https://www.reuters.com/article/us-chile-protests-pensions-idUSKBN1XB3U8.

Lapavitsas, Costas. 2011. "Theorizing Financialization." *Work, Employment and Society* 25 (4): 611–26. https://doi.org/10.1177/0950017011419708.

Lapavitsas, Costas, and Aylin Soydan. 2022. "Financialisation in Developing Countries: Approaches, Concepts, and Metrics." *International Review of Applied Economics* 36 (3): 424–47. https://doi.org/10.1080/02692171.2022.2052714.

Lavinas, Lena. 2018. "The Collateralization of Social Policy Under Financialized Capitalism." *Development and Change* 49 (2): 502–17. https://doi.org/10.1111/dech.12370.

Mader, Philip, Daniel Mertens, and Natascha van der Zwan, eds. 2020. *The Routledge International Handbook of Financialization*. New York, NY: Routledge.

Martin, Randy, Michael Rafferty, and Dick Bryan. 2008. "Financialization, Risk and Labour." *Competition & Change* 12 (2): 120–32. https://doi.org/10.1179/102452908X314849.

Mawdsley, Emma. 2018. "Development Geography II: Financialization." *Progress in Human Geography* 42 (2): 264–74. https://doi.org/10.1177/0309132516678747.

Menaldo, Victor, and Daniel Yoo. 2015. "Democracy, Elite Bias, and Financial Development in Latin America." *World Politics* 67 (4): 726–59. https://doi.org/10.1017/S0043887115000192.

Naim, Moises. 1999. "Fads and Fashion in Economic Reforms: Washington Consensus or Washington Confusion? - Moises Naim - Paper Prepared for the IMF Conference on Second Generation Reforms, Washington, DC" 1999. https://www.imf.org/external/pubs/ft/seminar/1999/reforms/naim.htm.

Nolan, Aoife, ed. 2014. *Economic and Social Rights after the Global Financial Crisis.* Cambridge: Cambridge University Press.

Nölke, Andreas. 2021. "Financialization and the Crisis of Democracy." In *The Routledge International Handbook of Financialization*, edited by Philip Mader, Daniel Mertens, and Natascha van der Zwan, 425–36. New York: Routledge.

OECD. 2019. "Equity Market Development in Latin America: Enhancing Access to Corporate Finance." OECD. https://www.oecd.org/corporate/ca/equity-markets-latin-america.htm.

Palley, Thomas I. 2014. *Financialization: The Economics of Finance Capital Domination*. Houndmills: Palgrave Macmillan.

Pérez Caldentey, Esteban, and Matías Vernengo. 2021a. "Financialization, Deindustrialization and Instability in Latin America." Working Paper 547. University of Massachusetts, Amherst: Political Economy Research Institute. https://doi.org/10.7275/27121089.

———. 2021b. "Financialization, Premature Deindustrialization, and Instability in Latin America." *Review of Keynesian Economics* 9 (4): 493–511. https://doi.org/10.4337/roke.2021.04.03.

Polillo, Simone, and Mauro F. Guillén. 2005. "Globalization Pressures and the State: The Worldwide Spread of Central Bank Independence." *American Journal of Sociology* 110 (6): 1764–1802. https://doi.org/10.1086/428685.

PwC. n.d. "Sovereign Investors 2020: A Growing Force." United States: PwC (PricewaterhouseCoopers). https://www.pwc.com/gx/en/industries/sovereign-wealth-investment-funds/publications/sovereign-investors-2020.html.

Quispe-Agnoli, Myriam, and Diego Vilán. n.d. "Financing Trends in Latin America." In *Recent Financing Trends in Latin America: A Bumpy Ride Towards Stability*, 15–27. BIS Papers No 36. Atlanta, GA.

Rajan, Raghuram G. 2010. *Fault Lines.* Princeton: Princeton University Press.

Reinhart, Carmen M., and Kenneth S. Rogoff. 2009. *This Time Is Different.* Princeton: Princeton University Press. https://press.princeton.edu/books/paperback/9780691152646/this-time-is-different.

Reis, Nadine, and Felipe Antunes de Oliveira. 2021. "Peripheral Financialization and the Transformation of Dependency: A View from Latin America." *Review of International Political Economy*, 1–24. https://doi.org/10.1080/09692290.2021.2013290.

Rodrik, Dani. 2006. "Goodbye Washington Consensus, Hello Washington Confusion? A Review of the World Bank's." *Journal of Economic Literature.*

Rodrik, Dani, and Arvind Subramanian. 2009. "Why Did Financial Globalization Disappoint?" *IMF Staff Papers* 56 (1): 112–38.

Roubini, Nouriel. 2022. "The Unavoidable Crash | by Nouriel Roubini." Project Syndicate. December 2, 2022. https://www.project-syndicate.org/commentary/stagflationary-economic-financial-and-debt-crisis-by-nouriel-roubini-2022-12.

Sahay, Ratna, Martin Čihák, Papa N'Diaye, Adolfo Barajas, Ran Bi, Diana Ayala, Yuan Gao, et al. 2015. "Rethinking Financial Deepening: Stability and Growth in Emerging Markets." IMF Staff Discussion Notes SDN/15/08. International Monetary Fund. https://www.imf.org/en/Publications/Staff-Discussion-Notes/Issues/2016/12/31/Rethinking-Financial-Deepening-Stability-and-Growth-in-Emerging-Markets-42868.

Santos, Paulo L. dos. 2013. "A Cause for Policy Concern: The Expansion of Household Credit in Middle-Income Economies." *International Review of Applied Economics* 27 (3): 316–38. https://doi.org/10.1080/02692171.2012.721755.

Sawyer, Malcolm. 2013. "What Is Financialization?" *International Journal of Political Economy* 42 (4): 5–18. https://doi.org/10.2753/IJP0891-1916420401.

———. 2022. *Financialization: Economic and Social Impacts*. Newcastle: Agenda Publishing.

Schelkle, Waltraud. 2012. "In the Spotlight of Crisis: How Social Policies Create, Correct, and Compensate Financial Markets." *Politics & Society* 40 (1): 3–8. https://doi.org/10.1177/0032329211434687.

Sen, Amartya. 2000. *Development as Freedom*. New York, NY: Anchor Books.

Sen, Sunanda, Philip Mader, Daniel Mertens, and Natascha van der Zwan. 2021. "Financialization, Speculation and Instability." In *The Routledge International Handbook of Financialization*, 448–57. New York: Routledge.

Sorelle, Mallory E. 2022. "Privatizing Financial Protection: Regulatory Feedback and the Politics of Financial Reform." *American Political Science Review*, October, 1–19. https://doi.org/10.1017/S0003055422001071.

Stein, Jeff. 2019. "As Bank Profits Soar, Wall Street's Political Spending Hits New High." *Washington Post*, April 30, 2019. https://www.washingtonpost.com/business/2019/04/30/bank-profits-soar-wall-streets-political-spending-hits-new-high/.

Stiglitz, Joseph E. 2002. *Globalization and Its Discontents*. New York: W.W. Norton. https://wwnorton.com/books/globalization-and-its-discontents/.

———. 2012. *The Price of Inequality*. New York, NY: W. W. Norton & Company.

Stockhammer, Engelbert. 2004. "Financialisation and the Slowdown of Accumulation." *Cambridge Journal of Economics* 28 (5): 719–41. https://doi.org/10.1093/cje/beh032.

SWFI. n.d. "Top 100 Largest Sovereign Wealth Fund Rankings by Total Assets." Accessed February 9, 2023. https://www.swfinstitute.org/fund-rankings/sovereign-wealth-fund.

The Commission on Growth and Development. 2008. "The Growth Report: Strategies for Sustained Growth and Inclusive Development."

Thorp, Rosemary. 1998. *Progress, Poverty and Exclusion: An Economic History of Latin America in the 20th Century*. Washington, DC: Inter-American Development Bank.

Torre, Augusto de la, Alain Ize, and Sergio L. Schmukler. 2011. *Financial Development in Latin America and the Caribbean: The Road Ahead*. Washington, DC: The World Bank. https://doi.org/10.1596/978-0-8213-8847-1.

"Ugland House Explained | Overview." n.d. Accessed October 27, 2022. https://www.uglandhouse.ky/overview.

UNEP-WCMC. 2016. *The State of Biodiversity in Latin America and the Caribbean: A Mid-Term Review of Progress Towards the Aichi Biodiversity Targets*. Cambridge: UNEP-WCMC.

Wang, Yingyao. 2021. "Financialization and State Transformations." In *The Routledge International Handbook of Financialization*, edited by Philip Mader, Daniel Mertens, and Natascha van der Zwan, 188–99. New York: Routledge.

Woetzel, Jonathan, Jan Mischke, Anu Madgavkar, Eckart Windhagen, Sven Smit, Michael Birshan, Szabolcs Kemeny, and Rebecca J. Anderson. 2021. "The Rise and Rise of the Global Balance Sheet: How Productively Are We Using Our Wealth?" McKinsey Global Institute.

World Bank. n.d. "World Development Indicators." n.d.

Zwan, Natascha van der. 2014. "Making Sense of Financialization." *Socio-Economic Review* 12 (1): 99–129. https://doi.org/10.1093/ser/mwt020.

Wardle, Mike, and Michael Mainelli. 2022. "The Global Financial Centers Index 32." Z/Yen Group."

Chapter 2

The Uneven Process of Financialization in Latin America

We saw in chapter 1 that financialization takes distinct forms in different regions of the world. In this chapter, we historicize the rise of financialization in LAC. We map the evolution of the financial sector during different phases of economic development, linking the import of a subordinate form of financialization to the ascent of the global financial sector.

As is the story of financialization in much of the world, the expansion of private credit in Latin America and the Caribbean (LAC) is nothing short of remarkable. We noted in the previous chapter the foray of the retail industry into the credit business. Credit has become a prominent means through which the masses in the region have become part of a society of mass consumption. At the same time, the way this credit works is sui generis. A history of inflation, high interest rates, and default rates made it so that very few people qualified for the sorts of personal credit available in developed countries. So, a Brazilian couple looking for a nice romantic dinner may be able to finance its check in ten monthly installments, where the restaurant charges the couple one-tenth of the bill, plus interest, every month, rather than the whole balance appearing on the credit card statement at once and using up much of the card's limit. Or a domestic servant may be able to afford the latest smartphone by financing it over five years through consigned credit, a modality of loans where your monthly installments are automatically deducted from your paycheck. This sort of expansion of access to credit markets was one of the key features of the emergence of the Pink Wave in Latin America, transforming the previously impoverished population into potential mass consumers. As one economist has noted, the end result has been one where more people have access to color TVs and refrigerators than to sanitation and clean water (Lavinas 2017).

Increased access to TVs while having restricted access to clean water are good illustrations of the two sides of the effects of financialization in Latin America: more people having access to mass markets even as the state has reduced capacity to provide certain critical services and infrastructure. The key question to ask, then, is how did this come to pass? A substantial literature has discussed financialization, which refers, broadly speaking, to the historical process through which financial markets became dominant organizing forces in society. This involves not only the growing importance of finance in the national economy of select countries but also the spread and legitimization of what Fligstein (2001) calls the "shareholder conception of control" wherein financial considerations become a larger part of structures of governance of larger corporations and governments. Financialization in LAC has followed its own course that a significant body of the existing literature tends to overlook.

This chapter asks the following questions: what did the financial sector of Latin American economies look like prior to the emergence of financialization? How did the emergence of Import Substitution Industrialization affect the financial sector in Latin America? And did these Latin American specificities lead to a different process of financialization? The story this history tells is markedly different from the processes described in the literature about the global north: rather than an internal response to numerous crises of legitimacy (Krippner 2011), we highlight here how elite decision-makers embraced financialization in Latin America as a response to the external pressures created by the rise of finance and institutional investors in the United States.

The remainder of the chapter is organized as follows: we first discuss the basic definition of financialization, and how it is a relevant concept to understand recent Latin American history; we then set the stage, by discussing the origins of Latin America's financial sectors; next, we briefly review the literature on the origins of financialization in the global north; we then finalize by discussing the process of financialization in Latin America, which generally happened in three waves in most countries.

2.1 WHAT IS FINANCIALIZATION?

"Financialization" is one of the most widely used terms within the social sciences to describe the changes to the global economic order over the past 50 years or so. It is also, alongside terms like "neoliberalism," "globalization," and "post-Fordism," a term for which a multitude of definitions have been offered (Bonizzi 2013; Fine 2012; Kaplan 2018; Krippner 2005; Levy and Bustamante 2018). Here, we use perhaps the most widely used definition as a starting point, from Krippner (2011, 4): "the tendency for profit making in the economy to occur increasingly through financial channels rather than productive activities." But while this definition captures the core of the matter at hand, it is clearly insufficient to clearly delineate the processes we seek to discuss here. The shift in emphasis from productive investment to financial investment brings along with it a shift in the logic of both private and public decision-makers and a reorganization of the technical and technocratic apparatus through which financial transactions take place. To put it into more concrete terms, previously finance played an auxiliary role in support of productive activities; now financialization has reversed the relationship such that productive activities are subjected to the restrictions imposed by the logic of finance. From the point of view of governments, rather than regulating financial flows in service of their preferred policies, policy options are restricted with an eye toward bond markets and how faceless investors might react to each alternative.

The intellectual underpinnings of these changes are related to the rise of the "portfolio theory of the firm" (Greenwald and Stiglitz 1993) and the rise of shareholder value conception of control. These ideas lay the foundation for the creation of markets and of new instruments that shape financialization. One such major development occurred in 1952 when Harry Markowitz (1952) fully elaborated the strategy of portfolio management. Mixing advanced statistics and linear programming (i.e. forecasting), Markowitz helped create the modern perspective on risks and information, thereby generating both the modern branch of mainstream economics called "economics of information" (Hirshleifer and Riley 1992) and the trading and investing strategies that have been adopted by most major corporations (Negus 1998; Fligstein 1996). While its impact on corporate diversification has been well documented, another effect of this new perspective involved a more fundamental conception of risk. Markowitz developed the notion of "Value at Risk" (VaR) that basically estimated how much a certain portfolio stood to lose in a single day. If the creation of credit ratings reduced complex information to a number or a letter, this innovation further simplified things by reducing risk to volatility. Before this development, risk assessment was based on probabilistic enumerations of possible events—that is, probabilities of profits (or some other measure) going up or down. With the advent of portfolio management, risk assessment became concerned almost exclusively with volatility—it's not whether profits are going up or down, but how much they are fluctuating (Izquierdo 2001; LiPuma and Lee 2004). This is based on an assumption that markets will create a trade off between potential pay-offs and stability, so that the correct strategy can minimize risks while maintaining approximately the same returns.

Another major change occurred in the 1970s, as the VaR idea was further advanced by the option pricing models—more specifically, the Black and

Scholes model (MacKenzie and Millo 2003). In a relatively short period, academic economists and financial analysts reduced problems associated with incomplete information and the unpredictability of future events to statistical measures of dispersion based on a given assumed distribution. This eliminated the once-common distinction between uncertainty and risk. Once again, this development was not based purely on concerns about efficiency, but also on attempts to legitimize new and forming markets and ways of doing business (MacKenzie and Millo 2003). Risky investing was seen as no different from gambling in a casino, with several gambling houses around Chicago taking bets on future prices of commodities, future bankruptcies, and other economic matters. By providing a sort of scientific basis to this type of investing, economists were also thinking about legitimizing such types of investing, eventually leading to the creation of derivatives and futures markets.

The key idea here, then, is that financialization refers not only to the primacy of financial markets, but to the primacy of the logics of finance: risk as quantifiable, manageable through diversification, and as the primary signal through which all other decisions follow. We will revisit how this discourse has shaped policy decisions in the next chapter.

2.1.1 Early Financial Institutions in Latin America

During the colonial era, Latin America had no local banks or financial institutions, as the metropoles held tight control over the colonial economies. The first bank in Latin America is generally considered to be Banco do Brasil, founded in 1808 (Marichal 2008). As the Napoleonic wars forced the Portuguese royal family to flee Europe, Brazil was elevated to the status of United Kingdom, losing its colonial status. It was not merely a commercial bank: many of its intended functions were those that in the current day are generally reserved to central banks, like the issuing of currency (Cardoso 2010). The elevation of Brazil to an equivalent position as that of Portugal in the empire had drastic consequences for the local economy. As a colony, Brazilian ports were closed to foreign trade and local economic activities were generally restricted to the extraction of goods by colonial authorities. With the head of the Portuguese empire moving to Brazil, the ports were opened to other nations and foreign trade boomed. As a result, demand for currency skyrocketed, and it is in this context that this first bank was created. It did also provide credit to local merchants, but only as a secondary activity. This version of Banco do Brasil would go out of business in 1838, be recreated in 1851, be closed as a result of the financial crisis of the early 1890s, and then be reformed in its current configuration as a commercial bank in 1905.

If Banco do Brasil was first because of the particular history of Brazil-Portugal relations, the rest of Latin America saw their first banks emerge a few years after the independence wars of Spanish America. The fragmented process of independence in Spanish America led to the end of the Spanish-backed silver currency regime in the region, and the emergence of different regional financial arrangements (Irigoin 2009). In Mexico, the first bank was the Banco de Avío, created in 1830 as an investment bank, to finance the nascent manufacturing firms in Mexico (Marichal 2008). Much like in Brazil, commercial banking played a lesser role in the Mexican economy, and it wasn't until 1864 that the first commercial bank was founded, with the creation of the Bank of London, Mexico, and South America.

But it is perhaps in Argentina that we see the genesis of what would become the standard relationship between finance and an agriculture-centered export economy. The first Argentinean bank was created in 1822 with the founding of Banco de Depósitos de Buenos Aires, which was a mixture of commercial bank and state investment bank, financing public works and projects (Marichal 2008). Banks like this one financed the state through inconvertible paper currency (Irigoin 2000). As Irigoin (2000) highlights, this was crucial in the growth of the export-oriented agriculture business in the country. Inflationary public financing heavily favored that economic sector: inflation led to currency devaluations, which kept these exports competitive in the international markets; at the same time, the inherent volatility of high inflation makes agricultural investments seem safer by comparison, especially if oriented toward external markets. This particular model, centered around facilitating the exports of primary goods at the cost of high inflation, came to dominate the region from the late nineteenth to the mid-twentieth century (Cardoso and Faletto 1979).

At their genesis, then, banks were primarily created by national governments as ways to finance the production and exports of raw materials and the operations of the state. Larger Latin American economies, like Brazil, Mexico, and Argentina, also created the first stock exchanges in the region, though once again this is primarily aimed at the exports of raw materials.

The period after the Great Depression is marked by the first consistent attempts to industrialize the region, and sees with it another wave of expansion of financial institutions, though once again subjugated to the logic of a particular economic development model, and in support of those activities rather than as an end onto itself (Baer 1972; Whitener 2019). This is especially the case after the Second World War and the Bretton Woods accords. In Latin America, the creation of the United Nation's Economic Commission for Latin America (CEPAL) marks a definitive shift toward Import Substitution Industrialization (ISI). ISI, as a developmental strategy, focused on heavy regulation of capital flows, high tariffs, and a state-dominated financial sector aimed at promoting nascent industries (Bielschowsky 1998; Rodríguez 1993). State banks heavily subsidized sectors seen as strategic and stock markets were dominated by companies where the majority shareholder is the government. Founded by influential economists in the region, like Raúl Prebisch and Celso Furtado (Mallorquin 1999; Dosman 2008) CEPAL provided the theoretical framework for a developmentalism that centered industrialization as the cornerstone of economic development. The key idea behind ISI is based on a critique of the then-ruling notion of Ricardian comparative advantages in trade and a repudiation of the existing economic model centered around the export of primary goods (Diniz 2009; Furtado 1970; 1976; Prebisch 1962; Sapsford, Sarkar, and Singer 1992). The argument had it that economies that revolve around the export of primary goods, even if to their comparative advantage, were doomed to stagnation. Limited markets for primary commodities meant significant price competition and long term declining terms of trade (Diakosavvas and Scandizzo 1991; Grilli and Yang 1988). Even if in the short-term currency devaluations keep a nation's exports competitive, in the long term the loss of relative value of these exports when compared to that of manufactures would mean a relative impoverishment of the country in international markets. And absent those devaluations, a high volume of exports in one sector of the economy would create exchange rate pressures that would make other sectors of the economy less competitive (Bresser-Pereira 2008).

The solution to the challenges of being an exporter of primary commodities, then, was to engage in ISI. As the name suggests, state intervention was supposed to foster economic development through interventions that fostered a nascent local manufacturing base. On one hand, tariffs and import restrictions were supposed to protect these new industries from competition from industrialized nations, while on the other, a state apparatus was created to finance and promote the risky investments needed to create local industries. One such example was the creation, in Brazil, of the Banco Nacional de Desenvolvimento Econômico (BNDE) in 1952 (later renamed Banco Nacional de Desenvolvimento Econômico e Social—BNDES). A national development bank, it primarily funded government construction projects and industries considered vital to the "national interest" (Barboza, Furtado, and Gabrielli 2019). This market is the beginning of the expansion of a state apparatus dedicated to the planning and development of local industries. More specialized banks, such as the Banco Nacional de Habitação (BNH, created in 1964) (Botega 2007) soon followed. The BNH, for example, was a bank dedicated exclusively to financing construction and real estate development, as construction was identified as a sector with strong industrial linkages in the input-output matrices that guided much of public investment in the period (Teixeira and de Carvalho 2005). Most other Latin American nations underwent a similar process: Argentina with the creation of the Banco Nacional de Desarrollo in 1944 (Martínez Sola

2017); and Chile created the Banco del Estado de Chile in 1953 (Arellano 1985), for example.

As a result of these processes, most Latin American economies emerge in the early 1970s with significant financial institutions, but institutions that are wholly subordinate to the coordination and development goals of the state (Bonizzi 2013; Levy and Bustamante 2018; Whitener 2019). These financial institutions existed in a world of heavy state regulation of financial flows, with capital accounts heavily regulated (Pinheiro, Chwieroth, and Hicks 2015), multiple exchange rate regimes dedicated to promoting (or discouraging) different forms of economic activity (Collins 1996; Frieden, Ghezzi, and Stein 2000), and personal credit, to the extent that it existed, guided by development considerations. A sort of public-private partnership where state institutions "guide" private investment as a development strategy (Offner 2019).

2.2 THE EMERGENCE OF FINANCIALIZATION IN THE CORE

The period from the end of the Second World War to the early 1970s is commonly described as one of "embedded liberalism" (Blyth 2002). The source of this embedded liberalism is the Bretton Woods accords. Bretton Woods refers to the New Hampshire town of the same name where 44 allied nations met in 1944 to discuss the international economic arrangements following the war. Key allied nations, especially the United States and Great Britain, thought that having a system that fostered economic liberalism, while at the same time preventing major crises and fluctuations, would help prevent major wars and depressions (Block 1977). The resulting accords were in large part influenced by the then-ruling Keynesian ideas (with the participation of Keynes himself, one of the main negotiators on behalf of the United Kingdom) The Bretton Woods System, as it was called, attempted to reconcile the liberalism that existed during the Gold Standard period with the expansionist policies that most countries adopted following the Great Depression. These accords led to the creation of the International Monetary Fund (IMF) and the International Bank for Reconstruction and Development (which later would become a part of the more encompassing World Bank), as well as a set of very specific economic policies to be followed by its members. The IBRD would help finance different construction projects, while the IMF would serve as an international lender of last resort, helping to maintain the basic policies of the Bretton Woods System. Among these policies the main ones were the following (Block 1977):

1. Countries could maintain trade and transaction restrictions for up to five years after the implementation of these accords. However, even after

these five years were up, the IMF could only demand that these restrictions be lifted under extraordinary circumstances.

2. While members should remove all restrictions on current transactions, members would be allowed to use capital controls to restrict the transfer of capital. As a matter of fact, it was stipulated that the IMF, under some circumstances, could actually require that countries adopt capital controls in order to have access to the resources of the IMF.
3. Member nations agreed to maintain a system of fixed exchange rates. The exchange rate of each country would be pegged to the dollar. The U.S. dollar became the international reserve currency, and, in turn, was pegged to gold ($35 = 1 ounce). Nations were supposed to maintain this fixed rate by buying and selling each other's currency, providing a compromise between government intervention and market forces. Countries could adjust the fixed exchange rate, but larger changes had to be approved by the IMF.
4. Countries with trade deficits were to finance these by using their reserves and buying the currencies needed from the IMF. However, once these deficits became chronic, a country could eventually lose its right to draw funds from the IMF. From this point on, the IMF could impose conditions for access to more funds.

The key aspect of these policies is that they allowed for stable international trading while at the same time allowing countries to use capital controls and expansionist monetary policy to pursue Keynesian goals of full employment and economic growth. The particular changes this system went through, and the main reasons for its collapse, are beyond the scope of this project. Yet this much should be stated: in February of 1973, the United States, under the Nixon presidency, decided to devalue the dollar—a decision that was followed in March of the same year by the decision by European countries to allow their currencies to float (Block 1977; Widmaier 2004). Thus started an era marked by what Mundell (1968) called the "impossible trinity" (Quinn and Inclan 1997). That is, countries could only pursue two of the following three policies at any given time: fixed exchange rates, free movement of capital, and expansionary monetary policy. Countries that decided to follow the old policies would have to control significantly the mobility of capital. The emphasis here is on the fact that under the previous system, currency fluctuations were minimal, virtually eliminating one source of risk for those investing in other countries: the risk of currency fluctuations affecting the rate of return of investments. On top of this, currency fluctuations can lead to a government default on its debt, since countries that had debt tied to foreign currencies were faced with the risk that such debt would balloon overnight because of shifts in the exchange rate. All of the sudden, then, countries that pursued expansionist monetary or fiscal policies could see either speculative attacks against their currencies (if they still adopted a system of fixed exchange rates) or sudden fluctuations in their exchange rates (if it was allowed to float) that could lead to more devastating consequences, such as an exploding debt and withdrawal of external investment. This is especially important given the fact that bonds and securities have replaced loans by major international banks as the main borrowing instruments for governments of different countries, both in the developed and developing world. By 1976, 60 percent of all foreign debt was owed to private financial sources (Frenkel and O'Donnell 1994).

With the end of the Bretton Woods accords in 1973, fluctuations that were once absorbed by central banks and diluted by capital controls were "privatized." Now, fluctuating exchange rates and mobile capital could wipe out or generate profits in an instant. Risk ratings were eventually adapted to describe the movements of currencies, bonds, or interest rates instead of stocks, stock options, and corporate bonds. Therefore, in order to understand the origins of financialization, we must understand the role that financial economists and analysts played in spreading and establishing these notions. As several sociologists have emphasized, professionals play an important role in the diffusion of certain frames of thinking and acting (DiMaggio 1997; DiMaggio and Powell 1983; Edelman, Uggen, and Erlanger 1999; Edelman, Fuller, and Mara-Drita 2001). They play a crucial role in institutional chance by facilitating what some call "frame transpositions." In other words, financial analysts and economists adapted ready-made models and ideas ("frames") and applied them to a new situation. In this particular case, the rise of Chicago school economics is already well documented (Blyth 2002; Carruthers, Babb, and Halliday 1998; Dezalay and Garth 2002; Fourcade-Gourinchas and Babb 2002). So instead of just looking at the rise of monetarism and its variations, the key development here is how certain economists used very specific notions legitimated by the rise of this particular way of doing economics to create this new way of talking about economic development.

It is against this backdrop that financialization takes hold over the core economies of the capitalist West. In perhaps the most comprehensive work on the rise of financialization, Krippner (2011) points to the way in which finance and financial markets offered a "solution" to a particular set of crises in motion during the 1970s and 1980s. As the embedded liberalism of the postwar economy started to reach its limits, governments were facing three different sets of crises: fiscal, social, and a crisis of legitimacy. The slowdown of economic growth, the internal distributional conflicts regarding expansionist welfare policy, and the increasing limitations on consumer aspirations create a moment of profound social crisis. This crisis coincided with a period where governments were reaching a fiscal crisis: the OPEC oil shock of the early 1970s, coupled with the previously mentioned economic slow down and accompanying stagflation meant that governments were unable (or at least unwilling to pay the political price) to pursue an expansion in spending to satisfy the increasing demands of an ever more frustrated population This led to a fundamental crisis in the legitimacy of the state, as leaders like President Ronald Reagan and Prime Minister Margaret Thatcher rose to power by promising to improve people's lives through government retrenchment rather than government action.

These crises happened against a backdrop of growing importance of finance. Derivatives markets, where investors can buy and sell futures contracts, stock options, and the like, were once seen as little more than minor markets, not dissimilar from gambling opportunities. But as the sort of portfolio management perspectives grew with economics and emerging notions of risk took over, derivatives went from a sort of gambling done from amateurs to a serious market that followed complex pricing strategies to disperse risk (MacKenzie and Millo 2003). The Chicago Board of Exchange, for example, was created in 1973 to become a market for derivatives, and within 5 years hundreds of thousands of contracts were traded in a single day (MacKenzie and Millo 2003), and currently over 300 million contracts are traded on a single month (Chicago Board of Exchange 2022). Similarly, the OPEC oil shock generated a windfall for oil-producing countries flooded markets with "petrodollars" (Whitener 2019). On the corporate front, uncertainty regarding long-term investment led to corporations shifting from long-term investments in facilities and production to immediate mergers and acquisitions. As such, just as governments reached these previously discussed moments of crises, financial markets were trading and controlling ever larger sums in terms of assets and contracts. As Krippner (2011) argues, the ultimate emergence of financialization is not the result of a long-term plan, but rather of it providing a set of easy short-term solutions that proved too attractive to resist. Government deficits could be financed through bond markets, short-term investment gains could be generated through the deregulation of trusts and markets, much like deregulation of consumer financial products provided an easy way to promote consumer spending in the face of stagnating wages. The takeover of finance was complete, and in the core countries of North America and Western Europe, it was the result of internal crises, internal dynamics, and internal developments: institutional investors, financial institutions, derivatives, and stock exchanges were an integral part of the economies of these societies and played an active role in shaping them. Regulations were either abolished or, through the careful creation of an international architecture of finance, rendered moot. The Cayman Islands, for example, a British overseas territory, became home, at least legally, to 60 percent of all global hedge fund assets (Fichtner 2016). As we will see in the next subsection, the development of financialization in Latin America is a story that starts and is primarily shaped outside its borders, as the force of finance becomes irresistible, and ultimately shapes domestic politics in an irreversible way.

2.3 FINANCIALIZATION COMES TO LATIN AMERICA

The emergence of financialization in Latin America can be understood as the inversion of the relative relevance of finance on one hand, and government finance and productive activities on the other. Rather than supporting the sectors related to the export of primary commodities, like in the period after independence, or supporting state investment and industrialization efforts, like in the immediate postwar period of the twentieth century, finance and financial concerns mold public policy to its logic. Governments restrict spending lest they face capital flight, being considered "investment grade" by institutional investors gets touted in political campaigns even by left-wing candidates, agribusinesses make their production decisions with an eye toward futures markets. This inversion happened particularly quickly in Latin America. The speed of this conversion in Latin America can be demonstrated by comparing existing measures of financial openness across the world. Chinn and Ito (2008) developed a widely used measure of capital account liberalization. Figure 2.1 looks at the average scores for the different regions of the world:

As figure 2.1 highlights, in a span of a little over a decade Latin America went from being one of the regions with the lowest scores of financial openness to being the region with the second highest openness scores. But while this transition was quick, it is the result of a historical process that can be divided into four different phases: a preamble, where the end of the Bretton Woods system, the OPEC oil shock, the emergence of the so-called petrodollars, and the rise of financialization in the nations of the core see Latin American nations become highly indebted due to the flood of money from financial investors; a first stage, where the external debt crises of the early 1980s sees the appointments of an ever greater number of U.S.-trained economists to key government positions to negotiate with external debtors; a second stage marked by the radical adoption of financial deregulation of the structural adjustment of the 1990s; and a third stage, during the height of the Pink Wave of the 2000s, where the previous left-wing goals of decommodification of certain sectors succumb to the logic of finance, and social policy shifts to policies aimed at social inclusion as mass consumerism.

The end of the Bretton Woods accords had deep implications for Latin America. It marked the beginning of the end for the system of pegged exchange rates, which in turn added a layer of uncertainty to international

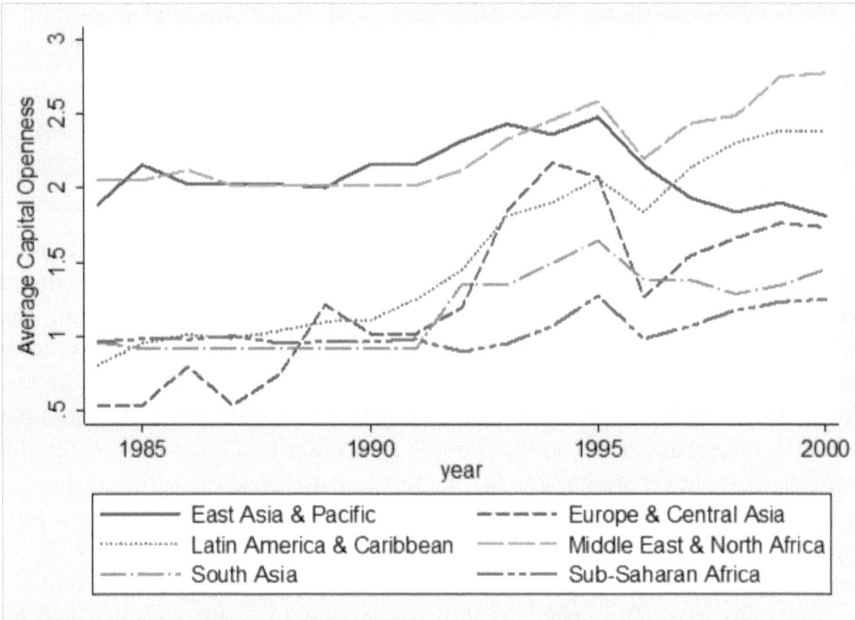

Figure 2.1 Average Latin American Capital Account Openness Across Time and Region. *Source*: Data Sourced from Chinn and Ito (2008).

transactions, as exchange rate fluctuations then become a risk unto themselves (Block 1977). But it was only the first major event to happen during this preamble of financialization in Latin America. The next big event was the OPEC oil shock of 1973–1974. That oil shock had two major consequences for Latin America: first, it created the conditions for the stagflation of the American economy of the 1970s; and second, it created a glut of so-called petrodollars, as oil-producing nations benefited from the rise in oil prices (Kaplan 2013; Whitener 2019). So as investors looked for alternatives to the limited profits of the American economy, and as financial markets were flooded with excess dollars from oil-producing nations, Latin America became an attractive alternative for investment. The relatively cheap credit available at the time and the global slowdown in economic growth led Latin American nations to borrow heavily during the 1970s. As figure 2.2 shows, between 1975 and 1980 external debt as a share of Gross National Income (GNI) had doubled (World Bank 2022b).

This sudden and significant increase in the external debt of Latin America sets the stage for the first stage in the financialization of the region. By the end of the 1970s, the policy paradigm (Hall 1993) used to combat the existing stagflation underwent a major shift. The rise of monetarism and the exhaustion of policies centered around the usual price control tools led to a

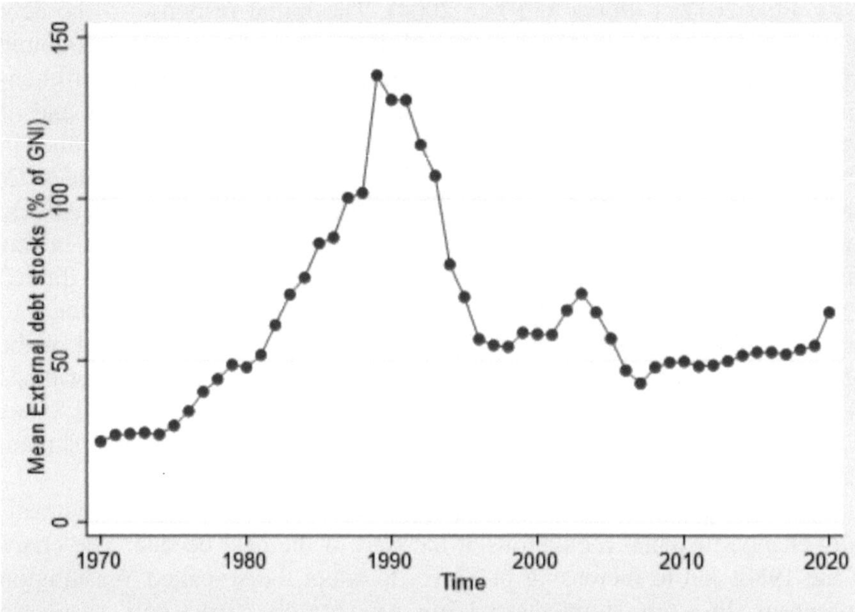

Figure 2.2 External Debt as Percentage of GNI. *Source*: Data Sourced from World Bank (2022b).

major break in how the American government faced that crisis (Blyth 2002). The "Volcker shock" saw the American Federal Reserve drastically raise interest rates in a very short amount of time. The Federal Funds Rate, which had fluctuated around 5 percent in 1977, reached nearly 20 percent by 1980, after the appointment of Paul Volcker in 1979. This spelled doom for Latin American economies. First, a large amount of the external debt acquired during the 1970s by Latin American governments was owed to American commercial banks, which now charged much higher interest rates as well. Second, these high-interest rates in the United States caused a wave of capital flight north, causing significant imbalances in capital accounts for the region (Pastor 1989).

The result was the start of the Latin American external debt crisis (Pastor 1989). In August of 1982, Mexico informed American authorities and the IMF that it would not be able to service its external debt. Other countries followed suit, and in the coming years another 16 Latin American nations would end up defaulting or rescheduling their debt (Ocampo 2014). Debt and financial crises were not new phenomena in Latin America. But what made this crisis different was the emergence of a new set of policies and priorities at institutions like the IMF (Przeworski and Vreeland 2000; Vreeland 2003; 2007) and the role of commercial banks as primary creditors (Bonizzi

2013; Fine 2012; LiPuma and Lee 2004). The initial response to the debt crisis was disjointed, and the region sunk into a "lost decade" for economic growth. But this period marks an important first step in the process of financialization of Latin America. As a result of the nature of the crisis and of the debtors, many nations turned to neoclassical, U.S.-trained economists in key government positions (Chwieroth 2007; 2008; Dezalay and Garth 2002; Kaplan and Thomsson 2017). As Dezalay and Garth (2002) have extensively documented, a crucial step in the rise of neoliberalism in Latin America was the decline in the role of lawyers and diplomats and the rise of U.S.-trained technocratic economists in the region, as LAC nations became indebted to banks and financial institutions rather than governments. By the end of the 1980s, the majority of ministers of the economy and central bank presidents were professionally trained economists, educated either in the United States or in Latin American institutions dedicated to the teaching of mainstream economics (Kaplan 2013; 2017).

These strategically placed economists, however, would only start to drastically change financial regulations at the start of the next decade. The crises of the 1980s led to increasing pressures to adopt the so-called Washington Consensus. In a few short years, Latin America goes from being a region where financial markets and capital accounts are strongly regulated to one where deregulation and privatization become the norm. Structural adjustment policies promoted by the IMF and other international organizations lead to a period of rapid privatization, removal of capital controls, and austerity. Stock markets are dominated by newly privatized large corporations; state banks, while still powerful, lose market share, and the logics of financialization take root: financial markets are no longer supposed to exist in support of exports or industrialization, but as their own entity, following their own logics. The key development that marks the start of this second stage is the development of the Brady Plan (Morin 2021). The Brady Plan, named after Nicholas Brady, U.S. Treasury secretary, was developed in 1989. Latin America had just experienced a decade of low economic growth, rampant inflation, and an inability to refinance its external debt, leading to its uncontrolled growth (see figure 2.2). The Brady Plan had three main pillars: the main debtor banks would grant some form of debt relief in exchange for some form of collateral; that debt relief would also be contingent on significant structural reforms; and, finally, a requirement that the resulting new debt be tradeable so that banks could more easily adapt their risk portfolios through markets. And it is the last item that sets Latin America on an irreversible path toward financialization. Figure 2.3 shows government debt held in long-term bonds and notes and money market instruments placed on international markets as a percentage of GDP(World Bank 2022b; 2022a). The Brady Plan had an almost immediate impact on external debt. This large-scale adoption of

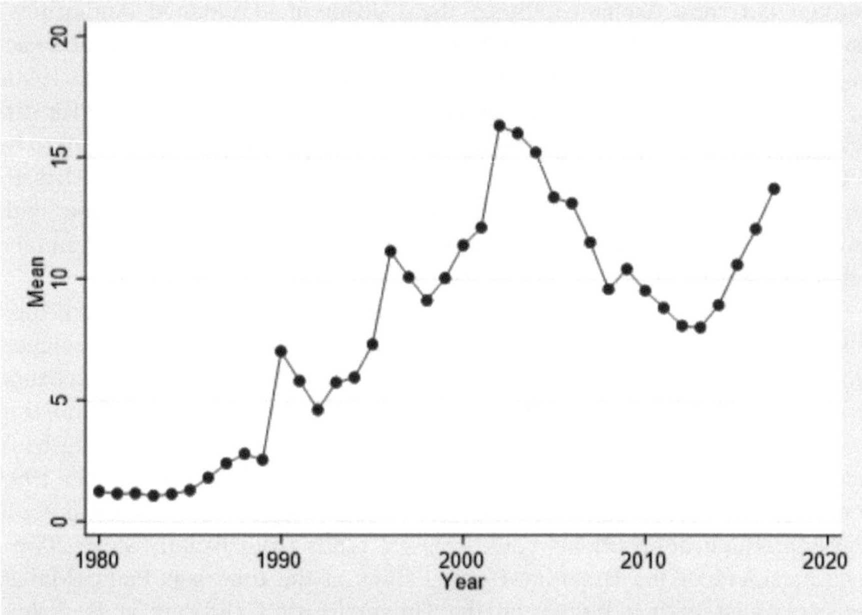

Figure 2.3 Outstanding International Public Debt Securities as Percentage of GDP. *Source*: Data Sourced from World Bank (2022a).

financing the government through bonds will have lasting consequences for government spending. As Kaplan shows, in general, and as we demonstrate in chapter 4, financialization of external debt is one of the key engines of austerity (Kaplan 2013).

As governments became more reliant on bond markets, a number of new concerns emerged for government finance. First, as government debt is subject to trade, volatility becomes a major concern: minor variations in economic outlook or exchange rates can generate a sort of vicious cycle that leads to increased risk of default. Second, exposure to risk in bond markets is more heavily regulated. The Securities and Exchange Commission (for the United States) and the Basel II accords (internationally) give a significant amount of power to credit rating agencies to determine just how risky a bond is, and institutional investors are restricted in terms of how much speculative grade investments they can carry (Pinheiro 2020; 2021). Third, one of the recommended ways to reduce risk to investors is to precisely deregulate the movement of capital across borders. The case of Brazil and its abolition of many forms of capital control is a good example of the latter.

Ever since the Great Depression, Brazil has had some of the strictest capital account regulations (Franco and Neto 2003). In 1931, Brazilian law granted the largest state-owned bank, Banco do Brasil, a monopoly on all foreign currency exchange. Since then, different "Exchange Authorities" have been created by the government, all with discretionary power to enact capital account controls. These powers were nearly absolute until the 1990s and included measures like the creation of different exchange rates for different types of transactions, and requirements for all foreign investment to be registered with a central authority (Franco and Neto 2003). As such, Brazilian capital account regulations were some of the strictest in the region, until two major waves of liberalization took place, one in circa 1993–1994 and the other in circa 1999.

The first significant wave of capital account liberalization in Brazil took place during the months that preceded and continued during the implementation of the "Plano Real," a set of monetary, capital account, and exchange policies that had the goal of fighting inflation and implementing liberalizing policies. Among these, there was a new set of instructions regulating bank accounts of foreign residents and institutions, clarified in a November 1993 letter by the Brazilian Central Bank, that significantly deregulated the process through which nonresidents could remove funds from Brazil (Sicsú 2006). The president of the Brazilian Central Bank at the time was Pedro Malan, an economist with a PhD from the University of California at Berkeley. These were the initial movements in what would become an internal struggle within the Cardoso presidency (1995-2002). While the Cardoso presidency as a whole marked a clear liberalizing impulse in Brazilian economic policy, internally there were significant disagreements between the so-called "developmentalist" group and those pushing for further liberalization (Abu-El-Haj 2007). Not surprisingly, there is almost a perfect correlation between these groups and the place where their members were trained. The "developmentalist" group included health minister Jose Serra (an economist with a PhD at Cornell, but a masters from the Economic Commission for Latin America), education minister Paulo Renato de Souza (an economist with a PhD from Universidade de Campinas in Brazil), minister of general administration Luis Carlos Bresser Pereira (PhD in economics from Universidade de Sao Paulo in Brazil) and the president of the state-owned Brazilian National Development Bank (BNDES) Luiz Carlos Mendonça de Barros (an economist with a PhD from Universidade de Campinas). The liberalizing group was generally thought of as including the president of the Brazilian Central Bank, Gustavo Franco (Harvard PhD), his replacement Arminio Fraga (Princeton PhD), and the minister of finance Pedro Malan (UC-Berkeley PhD).

If the first wave of liberalization during the "Plano Real" years was marked by a strong push by U.S.-trained economists in further deregulating the capital account, the second wave, in early 1999, was marked by a period of crisis and pressure from the IMF to further deregulate the exchange rate (Vreeland 2007). Foreign speculation in the wake of the Russian and East Asian crises in the late 1990s forced the Brazilian government to allow the exchange rate to be set by the market, removing the currency peg that was in place until then. More importantly, due to a severe balance of payments crisis, Brazil entered into a conditional agreement with the IMF. As part of this agreement, the Brazilian government accepted an obligation to become, "in the near future," fully compliant with Article 8 of the Articles of Agreement of the IMF (Franco and Neto 2003). These articles include provisions that explicitly require "avoidance of discriminatory currency practices" and "convertibility of foreign held balances."

The 1990s, then, saw the height of financial deregulation in Latin America. And while the processes that started that deregulation were tied to the response to the 1980s debt crises, their end result would the currency crises of the late 1990s. The "Tequila" crisis that hit Mexico in 1994-1995, the Brazilian crises of 1998-1999 (itself a sort of ripple effect of the Asian crisis on 1997) and the Argentinean crisis of 2001 all demonstrate the perils of reliance on influx of international capital as the basis of macro-economic policies, and how a loss of "confidence" by financial markets can have devastating effects on a country's economy (Mishkin 1999; Stallings and Studart 2003). All three crises had elements in common: an initial response to volatility that led central banks to raise interest rates to attract foreign capital; growing uncertainty about the government's ability to repay its debt given the high interest rates; and ultimately, economic collapse, currency devaluation, and high unemployment.

It is in this historical context that the last stage of financialization takes over. The crises of the late 1990s and early 2000s led to protests, social unrest, and a public backlash against the policies of the "Washington Consensus" (Kaplan and Thomsson 2017). From nongovernmental organizations to indigenous movements, a substantial transnational set of movements sought to rebuke the policies implemented during the 1990s height of neoliberalism (Almeida 2007; Pinheiro, Chwieroth, and Hicks 2015; Seoane and Taddei 2002). In many countries, an ascendant left won elections and took over federal governments for the first time in decades. The Pink Wave, as it is often called, saw various left-wing governments win elections in Argentina, Brazil, Chile, Uruguay, Venezuela, Bolivia and many other countries (Huber and Stephens 2012). Even nations ruled by parties not traditionally associated with the left sought a strengthening of ties with these new left-wing governments.

But this ascendant left, no matter what their intentions, still had to reconcile with the realities that they were assuming power at a moment where their government finances were dependent precisely on financial markets. Drastic breaks risked capital flight, a worsening of the economic conditions they were elected to ameliorate, and the potential return of inflation and shortages of imported goods. As a result, many of these new governments sought a more conciliatory approach to financial markets: they appointed economists aligned with the mainstream views of American economics to key government positions (Kaplan and Thomsson 2017); they sought to improve inequality through more focused spending on areas such as education and health, rather than through significant changes to the tax code (Huber, Mustillo, and Stephens 2008); and, perhaps more importantly, sought to improve the lives of the poorest segments of society not through the decommodification of certain goods and services, but through the expansion of credit and cash transfer programs (Lavinas 2017).

This marks the last stage in the financialization of Latin America. As a response to the crises of the late 1990s and early 2000s, one of the key policies implemented was the creation of a number of conditional cash transfer programs. Brazil created Bolsa Família, Mexico created the Programa de Educación, Salud y Alimentación and most of the region had similar programs in place (Colombia's Familias en Acción, Chile's Subsidio Unitario Familiar, etc). These programs included relatively small cash transfers to the poorest members of society but had a deep impact on consumption and poverty. In addition to these programs, there was also a great effort to democratize finance, an idea since championed by many of the key figures in mainstream economics (Shiller 2013). As Lavinas (2017) points out, it was a shift from inclusion through decommodification to inclusion through mass consumption. New forms of credit to low-income consumers were created, as well as new ways for consumers to establish creditworthiness and offer new forms of collateral, such as borrowing against future earnings and future cash transfers. Thus began a massive expansion of the domestic private credit sector. As figure 2.4 indicates, starting in the mid-2000s domestic credit as percentage of GDP went up every year:

2.4 CONCLUSION

Thus, the emergence of financialization in Latin America was complete. Government policy, social spending, and even social inclusion mechanisms became subjected to the logic and technology of finance. What sets Latin America apart from other stories of financialization are its external origins and its pace. There was no Latin American equivalent of the forces that shaped financialization in the United States and Europe: institutional investors were either wholly controlled by the government or too small to make a difference; credit markets were almost entirely directed by government policy, and state banks were the primary actors in local credit markets. The growth of international financial markets in the 1970s, and their political force in the 1980s, led to the adoption of a set of policies that entrenched finance as

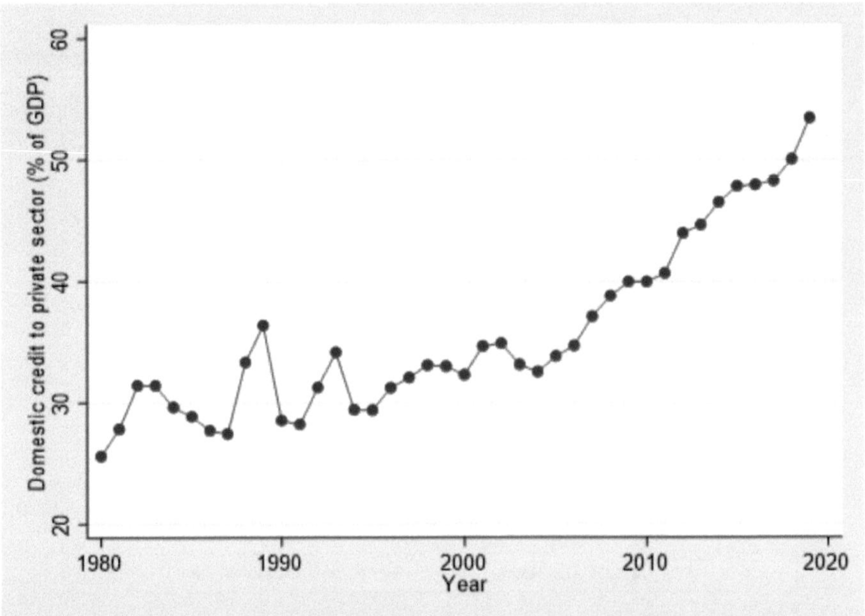

Figure 2.4 Domestic Credit to Private Sector as Percentage of GDP. *Source*: Data Sourced from World Bank (2022b).

the commanding force in Latin America. First through financial deregulation in the 1990s, and then through the expansion of credit markets in the 2000s, Latin America went from being one of the regions of the world where finance was the most regulated, to one of the least. The same institutions that were, once upon a time, set up to guide the economic development of the region through government intervention became the institutions responsible for financing the privatization of government companies (Offner 2019). At the low end of the income distribution, a population traditionally bereft of the protections of the state embraced the possibility of inclusion through mass consumption, leading some social scientists to refer to a "neoliberalism from below" (Gago 2017).

This process creates a very particular dilemma for governments in the region. The fiscal discipline demanded by financial markets when dealing with developing countries means that the pressure for austerity is stronger just as populations demand more protection from the volatility of a neoliberal world. Figure 2.5 below highlights the competing pressures these Latin American governments face.

Figure 2.5 shows the evolution of two different trends. One is the standardized average sovereign rating that key financial institutions have assigned to Latin American and Caribbean nations. Lower ratings mean that financial markets see these nations with distrust and expect greater austerity and interest

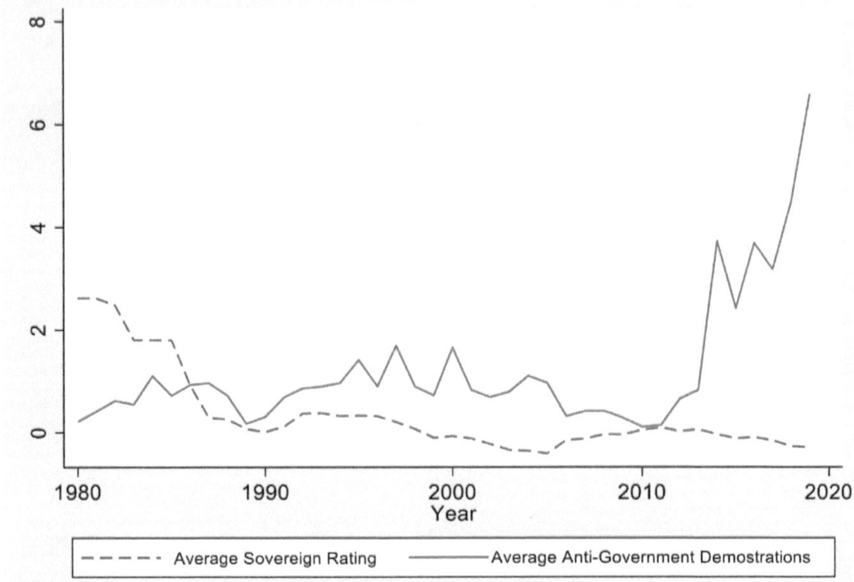

Figure 2.5 Sovereign Risk Ratings and Anti-Government Demonstrations. *Source*: Data Sourced from Banks and Wilson (2022) and Pinheiro (2020).

rates in exchange. As the graph shows, these ratings have tended to decline, sometimes quite substantially, with brief moments of improvement. In the opposite direction, we have graphed the average number of anti-government demonstrations we obtained from Banks and Wilson (2022). Dissatisfaction with government from institutional investors and from the population at large tend to coincide, then. Their demands, however, could not be further apart. As the research on welfare states has long shown, populations demand protection from the volatility of the market (Rodrik 2006) in the form of a greater safety net. But as research on financial globalization has shown, credit ratings and institutional investors demand greater austerity. This basic tension will shape much of social policy in Latin America during the twenty-first century.

BIBLIOGRAPHY

Abu-El-Haj, J. 2007. "From Interdependence to Neo-Mercantilism." *Latin American Perspectives* 34 (5): 92–114.

Almeida, Paul D. 2007. "Defensive Mobilization: Popular Movements against Economic Adjustment Policies in Latin America." *Latin American Perspectives* 34 (3): 123–39.

Arellano, José Pablo. 1985. "De La Liberalización a La Intervención: El Mercado de Capitales En Chile 1974–1983." *El Trimestre Económico* 52 (207 (3): 721–72.
Baer, W. 1972. "Import Substitution and Industrialization in Latin America: Experiences and Interpretations." *Latin American Research Review* 7 (1): 95–122.
Banks, Arthur S., and Kenneth A. Wilson. 2022. *Cross-National Time-Series Data Archive (Databanks International).* Jerusalem: Databanks International.
Barboza, Ricardo de Menezes, Mauricio Furtado, and Humberto Gabrielli. 2019. "A Atuação Histórica Do BNDES: O Que Os Dados Têm a Nos Dizer?" *Brazilian Journal of Political Economy* 39: 544–60.
Bielschowsky, Ricardo. 1998. "Evolución de Las Ideas de La CEPAL." *Revista de La CEPAL.*
Block, Fred L. 1977. *The Origins of International Economic Disorder : A Study of United States International Monetary Policy from World War II to the Present.* Berkeley: University of California Press.
Blyth, Mark. 2002. *Great Transformations: Economic Ideas and Institutional Change in the Twentieth Century.* Cambridge University Press. http://books.google.com/books?hl=en&lr=&id=sNXT0rpJuDkC&oi=fnd&pg=PR7&dq=info:XYVYaY67HkEJ:scholar.google.com&ots=pxxAKs8j4H&sig=HVUt7Yj8E4rJT6UTW4kXieqHC38.
Bonizzi, Bruno. 2013. "Financialization in Developing and Emerging Countries: A Survey." *International Journal of Political Economy* 42 (4): 83–107.
Botega, Leonardo da Rocha. 2007. "De Vargas a Collor: Urbanização e Política Habitacional No Brasil." *Espaço Plural* 8 (17): 65–72.
Bresser-Pereira, Luiz Carlos. 2008. "The Dutch Disease and Its Neutralization: A Ricardian Approach." *Brazilian Journal of Political Economy* 28: 47–71.
Cardoso, Fernando Henrique, and Enzo Faletto. 1979. *Dependency and Development in Latin America.* Berkeley: University of California Press.
Cardoso, José Luís. 2010. "Novos Elementos Para a História Do Banco Do Brasil (1808–1829): Crónica de Um Fracasso Anunciado." *Revista Brasileira de História* 30: 167–92.
Carruthers, Bruce G., Sarah L. Babb, and Terence C. Halliday. 1998. "Institutionalizing Markets, or the Market for Institutions? Central Banks, Bankrupcy Law, and the Globalization of Financial Markets." In *The Rise of Neoliberalism and Institutional Analysis*, edited by John L. Campbell and Ove K. Pedersen, 94–126. Princeton, NJ: Princeton University Press.
Chicago Board of Exchange. 2022. "Cboe Global Markets Reports Trading Volume for September 2022." CBOE. October 5, 2022. https://ir.cboe.com/news-and-events/2022/10-05-2022/cboe-global-markets-reports-trading-volume-september-2022.
Chinn, M. D., and H. Ito. 2008. "A New Measure of Financial Openness." *Journal of Comparative Policy Analysis: Research and Practice* 10 (3): 309–22.
Chwieroth, J. M. 2007. "Neoliberal Economists and Capital Account Liberalization in Emerging Markets." *International Organization* 61 (02): 443–63.
———. 2008. "Normative Change from within: The International Monetary Fund's Approach to Capital Account Liberalization." *International Studies Quarterly* 52 (1): 129–58.

Collins, Susan M. 1996. "On Becoming More Flexible: Exchange Rate Regimes in Latin America and the Caribbean." *Journal of Development Economics* 51 (1): 117–38.

Dezalay, Yves, and Bryant G. Garth. 2002. *The Internationalization of Palace Wars: Lawyers, Economists, and the Contest to Transform Latin American States*. University of Chicago Press. https://books.google.com/books?hl=en&lr=&id=TV6_IGm2f2UC&oi=fnd&pg=PR7&dq=Dezalay+and+Garth+2002&ots=cX1is8-1cW&sig=XT6R5Ead8W3HkJzpTXrxKNVC9Zw.

Diakosavvas, Dimitris, and Pasquale L. Scandizzo. 1991. "Trends in the Terms of Trade of Primary Commodities, 1900–1982: The Controversy and Its Origins." *Economic Development and Cultural Change* 39 (2): 231–64.

DiMaggio, Paul. 1997. "Culture and Cognition." *Annual Review of Sociology* 23: 263–287.

DiMaggio, Paul, and Walter W. Powell. 1983. "The Iron Cage Revisited: Institutional Isomorphism and Collective Rationality in Organizational Fields." *American Sociological Review* 48 (2): 147–60.

Diniz, Clélio Campolina. 2009. "Celso Furtado e o Desenvolvimento Regional." *Nova Economia* 19: 227–49.

Dosman, Edgar J. 2008. *The Life and Times of Raúl Prebisch, 1901–1986*. McGill-Queen's Press-MQUP.

Edelman, Lauren B., Christopher Uggen, and Howard S. Erlanger. 1999. "The Endogeneity of Legal Regulation: Grievance Procedures as Rational Myth." *American Journal of Sociology* 105 (2): 406–54.

Edelman, Lauren B., Sally Riggs Fuller, and Iona Mara-Drita. 2001. "Diversity Rhetoric and the Managerialization of Law." *American Journal of Sociology* 106 (6): 1589–1641.

Fichtner, Jan. 2016. "The Anatomy of the Cayman Islands Offshore Financial Center: Anglo-America, Japan, and the Role of Hedge Funds." *Review of International Political Economy* 23 (6): 1034–63.

Fine, Ben. 2012. "Financialization and Social Policy." In *The Global Crisis and Transformative Social Change*, edited by Peter Utting, Shahra Razavi, and Rebecca Varghese Buchholz, 103–22. International Political Economy Series. London: Palgrave Macmillan. https://doi.org/10.1057/9781137002501_6.

Fligstein, Neil. 1996. "Markets as Politics: A Political-Cultural Approach to Market Institutions." *American Review of Sociology* 61 (August): 656–73.

———. 2001. *The Architecture of Markets : An Economic Sociology of Twenty-First-Century Capitalist Societies*. Princeton: Princeton University Press.

Fourcade-Gourinchas, Marion, and Sarah L. Babb. 2002. "The Rebirth of the Liberal Creed: Paths to Neoliberalism in Four Countries1." *American Journal of Sociology* 108 (3): 533–79.

Franco, G., and D. M. P. Neto. 2003. "A Desregulamentação Da Conta de Capitais: Limitações Macroeconômicas e Regulatórias." Presented at the Aprimorando o mercado de câmbio brasileiro, Sao Paulo, December 4.

Frenkel, Roberto, and Guillermo O'Donnell. 1994. "The 'Stabilization Programs' of the International Monetary Fund and Their Internal Impacts." In *Money Doctors,*

Foreign Debts, and Economics Reforms in Latin America from the 1890s to the Present, edited by Paul W. Drake, 159–74. Wilmington, DE: Scholarly Resources Inc.

Frieden, Jeffry, Piero Ghezzi, and Ernesto Stein. 2000. "Politics and Exchange Rates: A Cross-Country Approach to Latin America." IDB Working Paper No. 137, Available at SSRN: https://ssrn.com/abstract=181468

Furtado, Celso. 1970. *Formacão Economica Do Brasil*. Sao Paulo: Companhia Editora Nacional.

Furtado, Celso. 1976. *Economic Development of Latin America: A Survey from Colonial Times to 1973*. 2nd ed. Cambridge Latin American Studies; Cambridge; New York: Cambridge University Press.

Gago, Verónica. 2017. *Neoliberalism from Below: Popular Pragmatics and Baroque Economies*. Duke University Press.

Greenwald, Bruce, and Joseph E. Stiglitz. 1993. "New and Old Keynesians." *Journal of Economic Perspectives* 7 (1): 23–44.

Grilli, Enzo R., and Maw Cheng Yang. 1988. "Primary Commodity Prices, Manufactured Goods Prices, and the Terms of Trade of Developing Countries: What the Long Run Shows." *The World Bank Economic Review* 2 (1): 1–47.

Hall, Peter A. 1993. "Policy Paradigms, Social Learning, and the State: The Case of Economic Policy Making in Britain." *Comparative Politics* 25 (3): 275–96.

Hirshleifer, Jack, and John G. Riley. 1992. *The Analytics of Uncertainty and Information*. Cambridge Surveys of Economic Literature. Cambridge ; New York: Cambridge University Press.

Huber, Evelyne, Thomas Mustillo, and John D. Stephens. 2008. "Politics and Social Spending in Latin America." *The Journal of Politics* 70 (02): 420–36.

Huber, Evelyne, and John D. Stephens. 2012. *Democracy and the Left: Social Policy and Inequality in Latin America*. University of Chicago Press.

Irigoin, María Alejandra. 2000. "Inconvertible Paper Money, Inflation and Economic Performance in Early Nineteenth Century Argentina." *Journal of Latin American Studies* 32 (2): 333–59.

———. 2009. "The End of a Silver Era: The Consequences of the Breakdown of the Spanish Peso Standard in China and the United States, 1780s–1850s." *Journal of World History* 20 (2): 207–44.

Izquierdo, A. Javier. 2001. "Reliability at Risk: The Supervision of Financial Models as a Case Study for Reflexive Economic Sociology." *European Societies* 3 (1): 69–90.

Kaplan, Stephen B. 2013. *Globalization and Austerity Politics in Latin America*. Cambridge University Press.

———. 2017. "Partisan Technocratic Cycles in Latin America." *Electoral Studies* 45 (February): 219–29. https://doi.org/10.1016/j.electstud.2016.10.004.

———. 2018. "Fighting Past Economic Wars: Crisis and Austerity in Latin America." *Latin American Research Review* 53 (1): 19–37. https://doi.org/10.25222/larr.292.

Kaplan, Stephen B., and Kaj Thomsson. 2017. "The Political Economy of Sovereign Debt: Global Finance and Electoral Cycles." *The Journal of Politics* 79 (2): 605–23. https://doi.org/10.1086/688441.

Krippner, Greta R. 2005. "The Financialization of the American Economy." *Socio-Economic Review* 3: 173–208.

———. 2011. *Capitalizing on Crisis: The Political Origins of the Rise of Finance.* Harvard University Press.

Lavinas, Lena. 2017. *The Takeover of Social Policy by Financialization: The Brazilian Paradox.* 1st ed. 2017 edition. New York, NY: Palgrave Macmillan.

Levy, Noemi, and Jorge Bustamante. 2018. *Financialisation in Latin America: Challenges of the Export-Led Growth Model.* Routledge.

LiPuma, Edward, and Benjamin Lee. 2004. *Financial Derivatives and the Globalization of Risk.* Public Planet Books. Durham: Duke University Press.

MacKenzie, Donald, and Yuval Millo. 2003. "Constructing a Market, Performing Theory: The Historical Sociology of a Financial Derivatives Exchange." *AJS - American Journal of Sociology* 109 (1): 107–45.

Mallorquin, Carlos. 1999. "Las Vicisitudes Teoricas En La Sociologia Economica de Celso Furtado." *Revista Mexicana de Sociologia* 61 (2): 213–41.

Marichal, Carlos. 2008. "Banking History and Archives in Latin America." *The Business History Review* 82 (3): 585–602.

Markowitz, Harry. 1952. "Portfolio Selection." *Journal of Finance* 7 (1): 77–91.

Martínez Sola, María Luz. 2017. "Ocasos y Resurgimientos de Los Bancos Nacionales de Desarrollo En Latinoamérica: Entendiendo Factores Que Pudieron Haber Afectado Las Diversas Trayectorias En Argentina y Brasil." *Revista Latinoamericana de Desarrollo Economico* 27: 101–39.

Mishkin, Frederic S. 1999. "Lessons from the Tequila Crisis." *Journal of Banking & Finance* 23 (10): 1521–33.

Morin, Johanna Gautier. 2021. "Global Production and Circulation of Dominant Ideologies: Mexico from the Default Debt Crisis to the Brady Plan (1982–1989)." In *Power and Influence of Economists*, edited by Jens Maesse, Stephan Pühringer, Thierry Rossier and Pierre Benz, 170–87. Routledge.

Negus, Keith. 1998. "Cultural Production and the Corporation: Musical Genres and the Strategic Management of Creativity in the US Recording Industry." *Media, Culture and Society* 20 (3): 359–79.

Ocampo, José Antonio. 2014. "The Latin American Debt Crisis in Historical Perspective." In *Life After Debt,* edited by Joseph Stiglitz and Daniel Heymann, 87–115. Springer.

Offner, Amy C. 2019. *Sorting out the Mixed Economy: The Rise and Fall of Welfare and Developmental States in the Americas.* Princeton University Press.

Pastor, Manuel. 1989. "Latin America, the Debt Crisis, and the International Monetary Fund." *Latin American Perspectives* 16 (1): 79–110.

Pinheiro, Diogo L. 2020. "The Origins of Sovereign Risk Ratings: Explaining the When and Why." *Comparative Sociology* 19 (3): 388–414.

———. 2021. "Sovereign Risk Ratings in Latin America: Measures of Economic Conditions or Policy Paradigm Compliance?" *Journal of Global South Studies* 38 (2): 343–73.

Pinheiro, Diogo L., Jeffrey M. Chwieroth, and Alexander Hicks. 2015. "Do International Non-Governmental Organizations Inhibit Globalization? The Case of

Capital Account Liberalization in Developing Countries." *European Journal of International Relations* 21 (1): 146–70.
Prebisch, Raul. 1962. "The Economic Development of Latin America and Its Principal Problems." *Economic Bulletin for Latin America*, 1–22.
Przeworski, Adam, and James Raymond Vreeland. 2000. "The Effect of IMF Programs on Economic Growth." *Journal of Development Economics* 62 (2): 385–421. https://doi.org/10.1016/S0304-3878(00)00090-0.
Quinn, Dennis P., and Carla Inclan. 1997. "The Origins of Financial Openness: A Study of Current and Capital Account Liberalization." *American Journal of Political Science* 41 (3): 771–883.
Rodríguez, Octavio. 1993. *La Teoría Del Subdesarrollo de La CEPAL*. Siglo xxi.
Rodrik, Dani. 2006. "Goodbye Washington Consensus, Hello Washington Confusion? A Review of the World Bank's *Economic Growth in the 1990s: Learning from a Decade of Reform*." *Journal of Economic Literature* 44 (4): 973–87. https://doi.org/10.1257/jel.44.4.973.
Sapsford, D., P. Sarkar, and H. W. Singer. 1992. "The Prebisch-Singer Terms of Trade Controversy Revisited." *Journal of International Development* 4 (3): 315–32.
Seoane, José, and Emilio Taddei. 2002. "From Seattle to Porto Alegre: The Anti-Neoliberal Globalization Movement." *Current Sociology* 50 (1): 99–122.
Shiller, Robert J. 2013. *Finance and the Good Society*. Princeton University Press, Princeton, NJ.
Sicsú, J. 2006. "A Liberalização Financeira Brasileira No Período 1988–2002." In *Câmbio e Controles de Capitais*, edited by J. Sicsú and F. Ferrari, 222–245. Rio de Janeiro: Campus-Elsevier.
Stallings, Barbara, and Rogerio Studart. 2003. "Financial Regulation and Supervision in Emerging Markets: The Experience of Latin America since the Tequila Crisis." In *From Capital Surges to Drought*, edited by Ricardo French-Davis and Stephany Griffith-Jones, 292–316. Springer.
Teixeira, Luciene Pires, and Fátima Marília Andrade de Carvalho. 2005. "A Construção Civil Como Instrumento Do Desenvolvimento Da Economia Brasileira." *Revista Paranaense de Desenvolvimento* 109: 9–26.
Vreeland, James Raymond. 2003. *The IMF and Economic Development*. Cambridge; New York: Cambridge University Press.
———. 2007. *The International Monetary Fund: Politics of Conditional Lending*. New York, NY: Routledge.
Whitener, Brian. 2019. *Crisis Cultures: The Rise of Finance in Mexico and Brazil*. University of Pittsburgh Press.
Widmaier, Wesley W. 2004. "The Social Construction of the 'Impossible Trinity': The Intersubjective Bases of Monetary Cooperation." *International Studies Quarterly* 48: 433–53.
World Bank. 2022a. "Global Financial Development Database." Text/HTML. World Bank. https://www.worldbank.org/en/publication/gfdr/data/global-financial-development-database.
———. 2022b. *World Development Indicators*. Washington, DC: International Bank for Reconstruction and Development.

Chapter 3

Problems of Financialization

Chapter 2 documented the import of financialization into LAC from the Global North, gaining wide adoption in Latin America under the significantly different structural characteristics of emerging economies. This process unfolded through the region's three phases of economic development, catapulting the largely auxiliary financial sector into its current pivotal position in the economic system.

Our overriding questions concern the effects of financialization on social policy and on social inclusion in LAC nations. As straightforward as the questions are, there is no consensus on answers. Instead, a panoply of competing answers draws starkly different conclusions concerning these outcomes. Both standard liberal economic theory and critical views grounded in "subordinate financialization" and "dependent financialization" conclude that financialization, as a powerful external force, lies beyond the influence of national-level decision-makers. Financialization is a force to be celebrated or reviled, but independent of agentic control. The principal point of disagreement concerns the appraisal of the results of financialization. We focus our attention on how domestic elites embraced and negotiated this import into LAC.

In order to ground our understanding of financialization's policy and social consequences, we begin by establishing the theoretical underpinning for our expectations. In doing so, we hope to bridge the divide between competing literatures. The chapter proceeds as follows: we first review the principal theoretical approaches to explaining economic forces that gave rise to financialization; the following section introduces the problem presented by complexity to social theorizing; the next section proposes that an ideational explanation based on ideologies resolves the problem of complexity; we then introduce our notion of a market ideology as the principal vehicle for the transmission of financialization in LAC; two sections review the weaknesses in the two dominant approaches in studying financialization; finally, we introduce the implications for our theory and establish the bases for the empirical chapters that follow.

3.1 STRUCTURES AND IDEAS: MODELS OF POLICY CHANGE

Why do decision-makers at the domestic level of LAC governments accept financialization and the liberal economic theory at its foundation? The external context of economic outcomes and institutional constraints, strategic decisions by policymakers and other powerful interests, and dominant ideas must all play a role, but what is the prime mover? Perhaps external conditions dictate policy so that ideas simply follow context. Or do strategic actors seek the most advantageous economic package to maximize their advantage, choosing from a menu of possible policy options? Perhaps agents are in the driver's seat, driven by their ideas to adopt certain expectations and defining their interpretation of external context. In this section we outline in broad strokes the principal theories used in the social sciences to understand the sources of economic decision-making.

The explanation we adopt has real-world consequences, as economic decision-makers enact policies in accordance with their own theoretical views and because we subsequently judge the results of policies through the same theoretical lens. Mistaken views have dominated and distorted policy and evaluation.

Following Parsons (2007), we categorize two broad schools of thought that dominate the academic debate on the sources of economic policies as structural and ideational. Structural explanations are those that rely on the motive force of an external environment. This would include those typically regarded as rationalist, as these emphasize the predictability of rational actors navigating a given environment. Ideational explanations rely, as the name suggests, on the power of ideas and underscore the ambiguity of external conditions and their openness to interpretation. We depart from Parsons by folding his own category of institutional explanations—those that bestow causal force on the rules and procedures that govern political and economic interactions—under the structural rubric as these similarly emphasize the demands placed on actors to recognize and respond to their external environment. Parson's conception of psychological explanations that examine the power of universally "hard-wired" characteristics are less common but do make an appearance in the literature on financialization as discussed below.

3.1.1 Economy as Obstacle Course: Structure

Structural explanations are taken as sufficient for the causation of such conditions such as capital accumulation, class structure, political conditions, and power distribution. Traditionally Marxist accounts, of course, highlight these variables, beginning with the assumption that class interests are given and society is largely shaped by its productive forces. The turn toward neoliberalism in the last few decades of the twentieth century, in this view, is best seen not as a set of policy options aimed at solving problems, but as a class-based project adopted by a then-dominant capitalist class (Spronk and Webber 2015).

Non-Marxist theories might similarly emphasize the power of markets and capital but conclude that power is outside the control of any social class and that policy choices are between accommodating and defying market forces, with the only reasonable choice of taking advantage of the potential rewards offered by an international market (Friedman; Colburn). The "Washington Consensus," reached its status as consensus not by imposition by a powerful class in this view, but because reasonable observers can similarly read the writing on the wall. Such accounts capture underlying structural variables at the expense of overlooking politics as an important force and downplay more fine-grained mediating factors that condition the manner and timing of policy adoption.

Some theoretical approaches, on the other hand, adopt the same posture toward the international environment as a given set of material conditions but bring politics back into the picture by turning attention to the importance of domestic political institutions as crucial mediators conditioning policy outcomes. Material conditions that give rise to a crisis might demand economic reform, for example, but the timing and depth of reforms, or the failure to reform at all, are likely to be determined by the structure of government, the number, orientation, and relative power of political parties, and other institutional political factors (Alesina, Roubini, and Cohen 1997). Because these factors permute in myriad ways, a wide variety of outcomes is possible. The interplay of politics and economics produces unpredictable outcomes. This conclusion aligns with our view, but we will emphasize below that economic policies are the subject of real choices rather than products of institutional conjunctures.

A related line of approach is a rationalist one, which zooms in on the individual level of decision-making that takes place within a particular structural context, highlighting the rational capacities of agents. Often, the relevant actors are taken, sensibly, to be politically powerful individuals such as presidents, finance ministers, and other powerful figures. The reasoning behind these decisions might be political expediency; political figures might hope that successful economic reforms will increase chances of reelection or because they believe that economic reform is genuinely necessary for the national good, or some combination (Stokes 2001).

Rationalist theoretical approaches might also focus on the aggregate level of public opinion and its expectations for the outcomes—the distribution of winners and losers—of proposed reforms (Fernandez and Rodrik 1991). In either case, decisions can be affected by a variety of different economic and political inputs. Such theories add another layer of complexity to the analysis of economic policy outcomes, while still taking the material facts of economic conditions as given and simply to be navigated by institutions and actors.

As an example in the psychological vein, Kaplan (2013) hypothesizes that Latin American presidents and economic policymakers have developed a psychological propensity toward risk aversion as a result of their unhappy personal experiences with the economic crises of the latter twentieth century. This risk aversion manifests in a budget-cutting commitment to fiscal discipline common to executives of the left and right who have coalesced around a set of policy prescriptions that will prevent the recurrence of hyperinflation (p. 50–55). It was only when these governments were integrated into decentralized international securities markets that orthodox behaviors became the norm. This deeper integration creates tighter strictures on governments' options and leads to more scrupulous austerity policies than reliance on more concentrated lenders such as international banks (p. 173). As actors adopt ideas in response to the material conditions this account converges with other rational theories that subordinate ideas to one that simply reflects economic conditions.

3.1.2 Constructing the Course: Ideas

Ideational theories depart from the foregoing in turning attention to the economic and institutional conditions themselves, questioning their independent, material status. Such explanations reject the view of markets and finances as external to decision-makers and institutions the way an obstacle course is separate from an athlete. Rather, these explanations elevate ideas to the role of central player and posit that exterior structures are, at least partially and in consequential ways, socially constructed. Context does not carry with it straightforward and uncontroversial meaning but requires interpretation; an economic crisis is subject to various understandings. Collectively constructed ideas about appropriate social goals and policy methods for achieving them, these arguments claim, are essential for understanding policy outcomes (Abdelal, Blyth, and Parsons 2010). The interplay of and competition between these ideas determines what is desirable and even what is possible. Such ideational shifts occur as competition between viable policy paradigms is resolved in favor of one contestant, which assumes the status of the authoritative, expert view (Hall 1993). Neoliberalism assumed preeminence in Latin America as commitments to state-led economic models weakened and were displaced by neoliberal prescriptions through a process of "institutional isomorphism" (DiMaggio and Powell 1983), wherein external pressure by IFIs combines with internal advocacy of policymakers who have absorbed neoliberalism as the best option among alternative approaches (D. Pinheiro, Chwieroth, and Hicks 2015).

Policy ideas thrive in a cognitive layer that is partially independent of external, material factors. Decision-makers pursue policies that are not always rationally optimal responses to economic stimuli. Policies, instead, will be pursued regardless of their usefulness, sometimes being embraced more for their symbolic value than for their fiscal effectiveness. As Blyth puts it, "structures do not come with an instruction sheet" (2003). The meaning of economic events is instead determined by the prevailing set of ideas.

As globalization proceeded, a broad international consensus forms and creates pressures for adoption, while sets of policymakers implement its consensus in accordance with the possibilities of the national context of its history and structures (Fourcade-Gourinchas and Babb 2002). We can expect an alignment with the contours of market demands of international financial markets, especially in regions like Latin America with heavy concentrations of indebtedness.

A common view has it that U.S.-dominated financial institutions enforce low-spending orthodoxy (Stiglitz 2003). Ideationally oriented theoretical treatments appeal to the convergence of beliefs among international investors and domestic decision-makers to account for these events. Centeno (2007), for example, refers to "monopolies of thought and action" that create new rules for behavior arguing that aside from any material benefits of economic liberalism, as much adherence to the new rules can be attributed to "signaling" of commitment to orthodoxy (p. 80). The international context influences domestic-level policy decisions as policymakers signal to debt holders, sharing assumptions about what the amorphous financial markets will reward. Hay and Rosamond (2002) similarly discuss the "discourses" of globalization that create demands for dismantling welfare protections as a precondition for competing in a global economy despite any real evidence of the material need for budget restraint.

Signaling and discourse effects are evident in sovereign risk ratings. Such ratings are designed only to package information on the real-world structural soundness of an economy and the likelihood of its defaulting on loans. Rather than simple information about the material conditions of economies these ratings are aligned closely only with adherence to neoliberal policies and are unrelated to probability of default (Pinheiro 2021).

This outcome need not result from the concerted efforts of a small number of elites to impose their preferred policy paradigm, nor is it the imposition of international actors force-feeding austerity on nations from outside. Instead, it is the result of the meeting of beliefs of those agreeing as to what "the market" desires and the confluence of opinions on what makes an economy efficient. National-level elites may or may not subscribe to orthodox liberal economic ideas to recognize its significance and respond to it, and, as we have seen, even left-wing governments in Latin America have maintained a commitment to market orthodoxy.

Some scholars criticize ideationally based explanations as an overly simple indictment of a cadre of elites planning to extract wealth through manipulation of policy levers. Copley (2022), for example, critiques the suggestion that financialization is only the result of state capture by depersonalized financial interests. Instead, he emphasizes contestation and contingency in the search for practical solutions to economic problems as accounting for the emergence of financialization policies. In line with these explanations, Copley describes financialization as an unforeseen outcome of policymakers casting about for solutions to problems as they present themselves rather than the culmination of a premeditated plan to overhaul an economy. This critique leads to his rejection of ideationally based explanations as driven simply by elites pursuing their own material interests. Rather than a simple deployment of justifications by elites to material incentives, though, ideational arguments have it that actors respond to their shared understandings of what constitutes material reality.

By orienting our attention toward contingency, though, the argument highlights an important potential fault in ideational theories of global integration and austerity. Focusing on an irresistible global discourse exteriorizes the causal mechanisms as global-level forces beyond the reach of domestic-level actors. Contingency and contestation are always at the forefront of social activity.

Ideational theories do propose that globalization and neoliberalism are contingent political projects, and thus can be resisted and replaced with alternative policies (Hay and Rosamond 2002; Abdelal, Blyth, and Parsons 2010). They therefore carry the potential to connect the socially constructed structure of financialization with the participation of elites in the choice of policies and shaping of their implementation and distribution of advantages and disadvantages.

To avoid simply replacing a material structure with a socially constructed one, an ideational theory should integrate an agentic view of action which acknowledges the contested nature of policies. An agentic ideational theory stresses the contingency of policy implementation on several different factors, domestic and international, and acknowledges the interplay of ideas of actors on the one hand, and external institutional and economic conditions on the other. At the international and domestic levels institutional and economic conditions can shape policy outcomes, which in turn give rise to new beliefs, and vice versa. Central to such an account, though, is the set of policy options available to and implemented by actors at various levels, rather than simply the characteristics of structure.

Ideational theories, we conclude, go farthest in explaining the widespread adoption of the policy prescription of financialization but do not admit sufficient space for agentic interplay with ideational structures. A convincing explanation should account for a powerful, global-level ideational force without relieving domestic-level actors of responsibility for their participation in financialization, and without robbing them of power to change courses. We accomplish this first by introducing the problem presented by the complexity of socially constructed structures.

3.2 THE PROBLEM OF COMPLEXITY

Any exploration of social issues must contend with the fundamental observation that human behavior is inherently uncertain. The intractability of collective human behavior has struck scholars of many different backgrounds. Karl Popper (1984) demonstrates that appeals to the individual level cannot account for institutional outcomes. Our "social environment" is created by human action, but principally through an unconscious process, most often resulting in unintended and even unwanted outcomes. Even consciously designed institutions are subject to the same unpredictability in trajectory. Perhaps the most striking characteristic of social institutions is their resistance to individuals' intentions to direct them. Rather than beginning with the individual level and extrapolating to the social, causation travels both from the lower level to the higher, and from the higher to the lower level.

Starting with this basic observation, complexity theory has made significant inroads into social science, revealing the impossibility of designing simple linear models of human behavior. Social institutions, like other social systems, are complex systems in which higher-level activities of the system as a whole cannot be predicted based only on the qualities of the lower-level components. The interaction of the components creates a fully autonomous entity with its own characteristics. Emergence is thus an integral characteristic of complex systems (Holland 2014, p. 4). Emergent phenomena are hierarchically organized, with different rules governing behavior at different levels. These patterns persist even as the individual members of the group change, such that it is necessary to analyze the patterns of activity at each level independently of the other levels (Holland 1998, pp. 7–8).

More interesting still, social systems are complex adaptive systems. These complex systems are composed of agents that change their behavior as they learn and adapt to the behavior of other agents in the system. Causation thus flows from agents to system, and from system to agents. Individuals and small numbers of people have every bit of agency to make their own choices and determine their own actions but must contend with the actions of others, others' reactions to their own actions, and so on continuously.

The fundamentally unpredictable nature of these systems raises special difficulties for attempts to predict the behavior of social activity. Given the size of systems involved in markets and economies at the national and international levels, and the diversity of actors, complexity theory reminds us that we can count on dynamism and unexpected, even unlikely, events as the norm, rather than stability and predictability.

So, social structures are complex adaptive systems. Any theory of financialization, itself such a system, must therefore contend with this reality and account for how agents both respond to it and shape it. Additionally, such a theory must allow for the unpredictability and dynamism of such systems. "De-socialized" accounts of complex systems posit the separability of systems and agents, treating structures as external forces or as mechanisms to be manipulated. The connective tissue between systems and human agents, we argue, lies in the realm of ideologies. Below we discuss ideologies and introduce market ideology as the mode of transmission of financialization into LAC.

3.3 IDEOLOGY: CONNECTING COMPLEX STRUCTURES AND AGENTS

We argue that ideologies link structures and agents because these center the action-oriented nature of such beliefs. Ideologies provide the grounds through which agents interact with each other and the structure itself, in doing so both constituting the structure and grounding agents' interactions with each other.

Like financialization itself, defining ideologies can be contentious, as scholars disagree as to the precise outlines of ideologies and as to what should count as such. We shall adopt a fairly wide definition of the term emphasizing what ideologies do, though other scholars may prefer to categorize them differently. To begin, ideologies order the social world by giving meaning to basic concepts. Freeden refers to ideologies as "groupings of *decontested* political concepts" (1998, p. 81) in that they assert particular meanings for concepts in opposition to other ideologies. Ideologies further elevate the importance of some concepts by centering them at their core and assigning others adjacent and peripheral roles.

Ideologies also perform important legitimizing functions for particular social, political, and economic arrangements. By asserting appropriate understandings of the social, economic, and political world (by its own lights), ideologies establish roadmaps for preserving or altering the world in ways that achieve the optimal set of possible arrangements. Ideologies are fluid and particular to historical and national concepts and undergo constant reworking, in competition with other ideological groupings.

By ideology, then, we refer to a system of interconnected ideas that impose order on a complex world, defining concepts and positing connections between them, and establishing normative positions toward the concepts, legitimizing certain distributions and exercises of power and resources at the expense of others.

Of course, material structural changes in the world can themselves affect perceptions and lead to reevaluation and reformulation of ideas. But even in such cases the interpretations of structural conditions are inseparable from their ideational context. There is not a direct line from ideas to structure and back, but only between sets of ideas about the world. Instead of direct perceptions of external structures in their totality, our ideological predispositions shape perceptions of structure. Dominant ideational templates that dictate the authoritative understanding of how economies and markets operate emerge from continual interaction and negotiation between competing interpretations of the material world, a continual cycle of matching ideas about structure to other ideas about structure, with unpredictable outcomes.

Accounting for the complexity and unpredictability of the social world requires, as Blyth (2011) argues, a central place for ideas. Structural theories have suffered from the inability to mediate between agents and structures, ultimately devolving all explanatory lifting power to structures external to agents acting within them. Consequently, changes in the material environment cannot be explained except as exogenous shocks over which actors have little influence. The strength of an approach that focuses on ideologies as the operative ideational variables lies in its power to connect agents to the environmental structures in which they find themselves, and thus provides the link between structure and structural evolution. Structures alone do not dictate agents' actions, but nor do agents act in a free-floating vacuum without regard to material variables. Context and agents are important, and it is the ideas with which we interpret the world that provide this connective tissue.

3.3.1 Market Ideology

It is possible to separate globalization, neoliberalism, and financialization as distinctive processes undergirded by different ideologies. Steger (2008), for example, argues that globalization cannot be fully appreciated as simply a process contributing to global interconnectedness, but must be understood as being underpinned and propelled by a set of claims about the world providing important legitimizing roles for existing power structures and economic inequality. These claims declare the superiority of neoliberal economic policies and the desirability of integrating markets worldwide by promising widely dispersed benefits. The inevitability of this market integration and its leaderless, undirected nature comprise important aspects of the ideological claims of globalism, according to Steger. Given that the process of globalization does not exclusively lend itself to the neoliberal economic policy framework, Steger (2013) terms this ideology "market globalism" (p. 104) to distinguish it from other ideologies that seek alternative forms of global connection.

Commonly, though not without controversy, neoliberalism is taken to be the more fully developed ideology. Neoliberalism, conventionally understood as a revival of an older set of principles, has the longest genealogical history. Often used as a synonym for free market capitalism, neoliberalism provides an umbrella for a variety of views but can be described in a perspicuous list of traits. Turner (2011) treats neoliberalism as a full-blown ideology, boiling neoliberalism down to four constituent elements—the market, the minimal state, the rule of law, and private property. As a distinct descendant of liberalism, Turner traces its emergence to the reaction against collectivism and state interventionism in vogue in the post-World War II period in the United States, Britain, and Germany.

Differing in the names of basic concepts and the relative emphasis they place on each, scholars describe essentially the same complex of ideas. Looming large in all accounts of neoliberalism is the status of the state and its proper role. Neoliberalism is often encapsulated as being animated by an overriding suspicion of state power (Turner 2011, 15), while normative accounts from heterodox critics evoke a Marxian view of ideology, describing neoliberalism as a smokescreen wielded by political conservatives to legitimize social and economic inequality (see e.g. Chomsky 1998).

Relative to globalism and especially neoliberalism, "financialism" is a more recent entry into the catalog of ideologies, with inevitable departures from the others. Davis and Walsh (2017) distinguish financialization from neoliberalism by pointing out differences in emphasis between them concerning some key aspects of economic theory, focusing on their origins in their distinctive "epistemological and cultural foundations." Beyond an obvious fixation on financial markets, among the important differences in emphasis are the focusing of attention on the micro level of analysis, and a fixation on investors and stakeholders. The microlevel focus of financialism is revealed in its traditional assumption that market behavior reflects the cumulative decisions of a collection rational agents responding in similar and predictable fashion to external stimuli.

Some accounts of financialization define it synonymously with the shareholder value conception of control discussed in chapter 2. According to this view, shareholder value is not just an approach to management or business theory, but shareholder primacy is a normative set of ideas replete with wide-ranging assumptions concerning human behavior and the proper sphere of government with far-reaching consequences for entire economies (Bower and Paine 2017; Lazonick and O'Sullivan 2000) and institutions other than publicly traded companies. Financialized shareholder value tenets have crept into organizations that would appear unlikely homes for it, such as universities and privately owned firms (Eturk 2020).

In contrast to these attempts to narrowly conceive the definition of financialization, we see no reason to distinguish the neoliberal and financialized versions of ideology. We adopt the term market ideology as it suitably describes the same syndrome of ideas when used to support the appropriateness of financialization, neoliberalism, and Steger's "market globalization."

Globalization, neoliberalism, and financialization are analytically distinguishable, and the levels of each can differ in the same political and economic system. High levels of neoliberal policy framework implementation do not have to correlate with higher levels of financialized policy framework, for instance. They are woven together, though, as dimensions of an overarching and overlapping set of processes, driven by morphologically similar policies, rooted ultimately in a coherent set of ideas. In all cases, all are informed by neoliberal economic theory. Market ideology works as a label for the shared understanding underlying beliefs about the dominant modes of globalization, neoliberalism, and financialization. More than just coalescing on a basic model of the functioning of markets and on some basic policy recommendations, we can identify core assumptions about the economy—and a broader vision of the good society—that motivate the policies fundamental to market ideology. These propositions state that the economy is a separate system of rational actors seeking to maximize profits that is optimal and most efficient as a self-contained system free of outside interference. Rather than just the neoliberal economic tenets urging open markets and privatization, this is a view of the world and appropriate social and political arrangements that is marked by a skeptical attitude toward the state, seeking to minimize the role of the state in favor of liberating individual-level actors to engage in market transactions as freely as can be arranged.

3.3.2 Ideologies: Connecting Theory to Policy

The concepts of rational individuals engaging in market behavior that yields efficient markets absent government interference are typically articulated by academic economic theorists rather than politicians or the broad public. Ideas hatched in the halls of universities do not remain there, though, but surface as policy recommendations at the center of ideological projects.

We therefore distinguish economic theory, an area of academic and policy debates among those trained in specialized fields, and the ideologies derived from such academic theories, which references the more broadly shared assumptions rooted in theory. While theories are submitted to ongoing scrutiny, testing, and debate in academic publications, ideologies are programs of action providing rules of thumb for actors making decisions in the real world. Theories are thus always "ahead" of policy ideas, in that ideologies are the packaging of conventional wisdom about theory, perhaps even when the conventional wisdom is based in a flawed understanding of theory. The Washington Consensus, for example, assumed a life of its own as a summation of a particular brand of neoliberal policy paradigm rather unlike the Washington Consensus as originally formulated (Williamson 2004). Thus, neoliberal economic ideology, despite gaining wide acceptance in its prescriptions, is based on what we can call a "standard liberal economic theory" that will not gain the universal endorsement of economists in any of its theoretical underpinnings.

Ideologies link concepts and create order in a messy social world. Market ideology proposes the same solution for many problems; competitiveness requires cutting, reducing costs, and allowing the market to operate according to its natural efficiency. Rational agents thus maximize their self-interest, leading to efficiency and equilibrium. The important policy implications are the well-known suite of recommendations typically associated with neoliberalism, derived from shared ideas toward state intervention. In order to achieve optimal market efficiency, in addition to trade and monetary policy, social spending should be minimized as a distortion of market functioning.

3.3.3 Ideological Import and Diffusion

A key argument for our account is that financialization is an ideational import from the different economic circumstances of the United States, but that it was not simply force-fed by outside actors upon powerless Latin American nations. Instead, new policy plans are adopted as a response to real structural economic conditions and achieve paradigmatic status with consequences beyond the narrowly conceived issues they were intended to address. Financialization in the form of participation in international bond markets does carry particular weight in its influence on budgeting for social expenditures. This can appear only as an external structural constraint. Beyond such external pressures, though, we expect that internal financialization in the form of transformation of the domestic financial system will also significantly affect social spending as free market economic theory, as the progenitor of both, links policy mechanisms of financialization and austerity policies.

Berman (2011) models ideological change as a two-stage process, beginning with a "demand" stage, in which the currently hegemonic ideological dispensation is perceived to have failed. This leads to a "supply" stage in which competing ideologies and their proposed solutions are matched, and a new set of ideas gains a foothold, to become the new reigning ideology. This process is not a conscious, rationally directed process driven by a defined set of criteria in which ideological contenders are tried on like a new coat, judged by fit and cost.

Material structural conditions play a significant role in the judgment of prevailing ideological frameworks. In LAC, for example, hyperinflation and stagnant growth led to the reexamination of state-led ISI. This kind of "disequilibrium" can act as a catalyst for ideational change. On the other hand, sometimes the delegitimization of one ideology is not immediately followed by another dominant ideology. While the first stage is driven by the perceived failure of the existing ideas in material terms, the second phase does not necessarily arise from exogenous, structural sources. Instead, examining the role of agents and their skill in linking contexts and policy solutions is crucial for understanding why some sets of ideas gain wider acceptance over others (Berman 2013).

The ideational travel of market ideology links the internal and external dimensions of financialization, leading to an "Americanization" of economics around the world. As documented in chapter 2, a key transmission route of financialization in LAC has been economists trained abroad bringing neoliberal economic ideas to the policy-making process in their home state. A body of literature has emerged on the importance of epistemic communities in transforming neoliberal ideas into policy in developing economies. Babb (2004) documents the transition toward neoliberalism in Mexico as the profile of dominant elites shifted from law to U.S.-trained economists, accomplishing one of the most complete transitions of its type in Latin America, and Chwieroth (2007) establishes the important and independent role neoclassical economists have on capital accounts liberalization.

Emphasizing the contested nature of these shifts, Dezalay and Garth (2002) demonstrate how elite actors deploy contrasting "international strategies" in their domestic power struggles, appealing to international "expertises" to legitimize their own programs. The transformation of modern economics that began in the United States in the mid-twentieth century communicated the greatest authority of neoliberal economics in its superficial resemblance to natural sciences. Latin American elites educated at U.S. institutions became the most coherent group across the region in their shared economic ideas. As ideological imports to Latin America, neoliberal economic theories were deployed in a strategy that consciously focused on easily grasped policy recommendations communicated through the media. Dry academic theories became action-oriented policy prescriptions with the imprint of elite universities in the United States, promising an authoritative and scientific solution to the real economic dislocations that had shaken the region.

As the state-led model of economic growth experienced the crises discussed in chapter 2, the disequilibrium in the system opened the door to the supply stage into which market ideology stepped. The advantage of market ideology to policymakers and investors alike is to simplify the complexity of social systems by banishing uncertainty, transforming it into the analyzable, manageable risk akin to gambling. In the 1970s, market ideology served the role of challenging the predominant state-led development programs that crashed on the shoals of stagnation and hyperinflation. Only after a period of economic crisis and ideological upheaval did it attain status as common sense.

Market ideology propels changes that reach far beyond the economy, of course. As a set of ideas, it permeates society rather than remain within the circle of policymakers. Just as neoliberalism was created outside the borders of LAC but was nonetheless adopted domestically within LAC, the shared reproduction of market ideology travels from the economic and political sectors to all areas of life and at all levels of society.

Agents not only adapt to external changes in the economy but participate in the creation of financialization. Most obviously, perhaps, a culture of financialization is associated with the aggressively competitive ethos of Wall Street, but Haiven (2020) illustrates how this transformation ineluctably influences institutional governance outside the financial sector, as well as the world of art, from museums to literature.

A vibrant research stream has grown around the concept of the "financialization of daily life," which refers to the penetration of a financialized outlook into ever more aspects of life among individuals. In this vein, mundane, necessary activities normally undertaken for nonfinancial motives become suffused with considerations of their financial rationality or investment value (Simányi 2020).

Financialization changes the culture, but culture also changes the practice of financialization. Examining the changes to Caribbean culture through neoliberal economic restructuring, Freeman (2014) shows that the universality of neoliberal transformations in an era of globalization, its valorization of the flexible, self-made business-person for example, can only be interpreted through cultural specificities. The importance placed on reputation in the Caribbean, once a value at odds with colonial and capitalist structural modes, became adapted in the neoliberal era as an asset of middle-class entrepreneurs. By this mechanism, neoliberalism and financialization contribute to the emergence of a society marked by continual change and reworking not only of economic relations and material status but also of the understanding of the self.

Central to these analyses is the participation of ordinary citizens in the translation of what originated as foreign financial technologies into subjective understandings themselves. Market ideology, like other complex systems, therefore both shapes behavior and is shaped by agents' reactions to those behaviors.

An oft-noted problem (and sometimes objection) to ideational explanations is the immateriality of ideas and resulting difficulty in measuring any effects they may have. If ideas matter and have an independent effect, we can expect that the convergence around an agreed-upon set of ideologically derived assumptions about market efficiency drives a policy posture, converging at the international and domestic levels. This convergence takes place despite wide variations in economic conditions in the LAC nations. Signaling from national governments to international markets is not simply a rational response to external demands. Rather, an ideational account expects to find policy creep at the national level, with market ideology giving rise to inflation targeting, financial liberalization, and social spending cuts. An austerity mindset comes hot on the heels of financialization.

These observations are of particular importance for understanding how policy changes come about, and how the process of change might follow. Mehta (2011) explains that broad sets of economic, social, and political assumptions can grow from narrower policy solutions to particular problems to encompass assumptions about a wide range of public issues. As policy solutions to substantive problems appear to succeed, they suggest similar application on a wider scale. In the United States, for example, Keynesian economic policies expanded to become a philosophy that advocates for a mixed economy beyond the confines of Keynesian economic theory. The countercurrent toward neoliberal economics took a similar route to global dominance.

In recent years, though, the risks associated with unbridled neoliberalism and free market policies have become clear. The global financial crisis of 2008 and the Great Recession led more prominent economists and financial experts to rethink their standard theories. IFIs such as the IMF and World Bank have pushed the brakes on neoliberalism and charted new directions, and the Pink Tide in Latin America suggested the availability of alternatives. Given the recent turbulence in international financial markets and fresh scrutiny on the tenets of neoliberalism, can we expect a significant shift away from market ideology, and what would replace it?

Blyth (2011) points out that an ideational conception of social dynamics is necessarily an evolutionary one. The emergent nature of our interactions means that we cannot simply pull levers and push buttons to achieve intended outcomes, since such efforts will themselves be met with reactions to those very efforts, ending in unforeseen and likely unintended outcomes. Any equilibrium we observe is, therefore, contingent and subject to unpredictable disturbance and outcomes (pp. 98–99). While stability does occur, we can have no confidence in predicting its continuation but should expect continual change and unforeseen turns, as in evolution.

When assessing ideological change, therefore, we can be confident that change emerges, but as an uncertain and evolutionary process there can be no possibility of predicting which ideas will prevail. In the case of financialization and market ideology in LAC we witness disequilibrium as a result of economic crises and the challenge to dominant modes of thinking but cannot determine the ultimate outcome until after the fact.

In the next sections we provide an overview of how de-socialized structural theoretical approaches produce blind spots in policy-making and empirical assessment. Below we describe how the de-socialized model of economics in conventional liberal economics leads to an austerity mindset that extends beyond the servicing of financial interests. The next section will discuss the different mistakes in assessment of financialization which, though made by critical theorists, is nonetheless rooted in the same de-socialized model of financialization.

3.4 BLINDSPOT: MARKET IDEOLOGY

Chapter 2 documented the intellectual bases of modern financialization in such theories as the portfolio theory of the firm, the shareholder value conception of control, and the notion of value at risk. These abstruse approaches to economics yielded profound changes in the understanding of the functioning of markets and the behavior of financial and governmental institutions. Below we review how the self-consciously simplified and stylized theoretical treatment of economic theories underpinning market ideology overlook the inherent complexity and unpredictability of economic and financial systems.

At least since the first half of the twentieth century and the early days of modern economics critics have given voice to some version of the countervailing view that economics is fundamentally uncertain. Uncertainty arises from many actors at the individual and group levels guessing at the intentions and future actions of other actors, underscoring its basically social character. For as long as economists presumed that rationality would yield efficiency in markets, it has garnered skepticism. As early as 1935 the Austrian economist Oskar Morgenstern pointed toward the paradox inherent in the assumptions behind economic equilibrium. Economists dismiss uncertainty by relying on the theoretical endowment to actors of unlimited power to predict the behavior of other actors, which, even if possible, would lead to a never-ending loop of reactions to others' presumptive choices (Fox 2011, p. 49).

While there are countless unpredictable events that may befall us, making uncertainty unavoidable, in the classical liberal imagination such uncertainty allows room for creativity, innovation, and luck, providing space for the freedom of individuals to pursue their own interests. The state, therefore, should refrain from attempts to regulate uncertainty and should allow individuals to manage uncertainty according to their own lights. This conception of the connection between freedom and uncertainty thus engenders skepticism toward the possibilities and wisdom of regulation and state power (O'Malley 2012). This understanding of risk and uncertainty implies that there can be no security except that provided by private actors. Risks can be managed through calculation and uncertainty only through individual imagination and intuition. There is freedom in the unknown, the freedom for rational private actors to take their own actions to hedge against risks and to rely on their own creativity and imagination to navigate uncertainty. Decentralized markets composed of dispersed agents, in this view, are the most efficient means of managing risk.

As Best (2008) points out, through microlevel rationality in the form of financial elites, uncertainty may be minimized to such an extent that it need not invite greater regulation of the financial industry. Indeed, regulation is counterproductive and self-defeating given that self-interested rational agents will simply compensate for their consequences and evade their intended effects. Thus, uncertainty in the market has been banished. The very exit of the state from the market, therefore, removes uncertainty. Further, the management of risk in this fashion will carry benefits more widely by maximizing economic efficiency. Without predicting the behavior of individuals, the outcomes become knowable in advance.

Blyth (2011, p. 98) notes that while we presume to design the social world, given its emergent characteristics created by our unguided actions, "our control of the consequences of those designs might be, despite our intelligence, much less than we think." Complexity implies that economic systems evolve independent of directed action. Ford (2015, p. 87) describes the "policymakers paradox," the especially difficult problem that confronts decision-makers in social systems: there is no surefire way to know in advance whether a given action will have any effect on the behavior of the system, or whether any effects it might have will be desirable or undesirable. The paradox is apparent in such an economic model when it comes to state regulation, but put aside when it comes to the individual level of rational individual levels actors, who are stipulated to overcome the problem through risk management.

This error has been particularly evident in the wake of the financial crisis of 2008. Among the major mysteries surrounding the meltdown was how so many experts and financial elites could have been taken by surprise by such a momentous event. From the standard view of markets as in principle efficient and in equilibrium, unforeseen events such as the financial crisis are explained in terms of market failures, rather than inherent features of uncertain complex systems (Palley 2014, ix).

Uncertainty is fundamental to complex social systems like economies and financial markets. Conventional economic thinkers are aware of this, of course. Friedrich Hayek pointed out the complexity of economies, after all. The standard conclusion of that observation, though, is to wield complexity as a critique of socialist economic planning (Kilpatrick 2001). It is an unwarranted step, though, from rejection of state planning to confidence that rational agents at the individual level lead to predictable, much less optimal, results. Such a theory poses a false dilemma between centralized state planning and the minimal state of laissez-faire market principles.

Basu (2003) demonstrates the fallaciousness of separating the economy from government, a mistake that gives rise to an understanding of "government intervention" as an activity by outside agents interfering in the natural operations of the market. Instead, the agents in an economy are embedded in a web of social and institutional connections. Fligstein (2001) focuses our attention on the fact that in contrast to the tenets of traditional liberal economics, there is no single way to efficiently organize economic institutions. Instead, a variety of different approaches to market organization are compatible with profit-making, and the standard economic view focusing on actors' concern for efficiency is only partially correct. A fuller understanding of an economic system requires an account of the interdependent web of actors, including the government, labor, and other social groups and the social relations between them. This fuller picture reveals the fact that too narrow a focus on efficiency hides from attention the fact that these actors at times seek stability as a concurrent goal. Efficiency itself, in fact, is inseparable from this larger context, making a notion such as the shareholder conception of value a socially determined concept (Fligstein 1993).

Economists outside the mainstream liberal school have long pointed out the importance of the social aspects and subjective beliefs in the determination of economic outcomes, but the intellectual wave cresting in the 1970s in the United States thoroughly embraced the theories of efficient markets and state retrenchment. These ideas were transmitted to Latin America, principally through elite-level policy makers trained in economics there.

A de-socialized market theory, by reducing the nature of markets to a collection of rational figures who are expected to behave in precisely the same way, removes the role of individual-level idiosyncrasies, emotional states, or goals. This view of economic behavior posits the homogeneity of economic actors. The resulting view is of an economy as an enormous machine, the behaviors of which are preprogrammed (Arthur 2015). Anomalous outbursts of irrationality may cause minor fluctuations, but the market can be expected to return to equilibrium when these deviations from rationality are punished by the market. This further leads to an understanding of the market itself as having emotional states and desires that are taken to reflect the same assumptions of standard economic theory concerning the minimal role of the state in regulatory roles. In effect, standard economic theory has dealt with complexity by assuming it away.

3.5 BLINDSPOT: CRITICAL APPROACHES

We turn now to financialization studies and the implications of a de-socialized, structural view of international finance for the assessment of the results of financialization. Critical theorists will likely agree that financialization has roots in a view of economics that does not conform to reality, thus distorting economic policy. However, this should not lead us to the conclusion that domestic-level actors are implicated in a structure beyond their own interpretation and participation. The same blind spot as that found in policymaking decisions has, we argue, led to scholars of financialization to seek outcomes in social inclusion that confirm a skeptical view of financialization in LAC.

Subordinate or dependent financialization, while evocative descriptions that capture dynamics that we have described in the spread of neoliberal theories from more advanced to developing economies, nonetheless point toward a view of the international financial system as a fixed set of relations with rigid roles assigned for advanced capitalist nations, international financial actors, and developing nations. Bonizzi, Kaltenbrunner, and Powell (2020) state, for example, that financialization in emerging economies "emerges from and is fundamentally shaped by the subordinate nature of their integration into the world economy," a fact that "may serve to cement or even deepen their subordination in the global hierarchy of nations" (p. 184). Lapavitsas and Soydan (2022) underscore the focus in financialization studies on identifying the "social, economic, and institutional determinants of the conduct of economic agents" which leads to a portrayal of finance as the single most salient characteristic of economies, and therefore a negative estimation of financialization as a whole. Studies on dependent financialization, approaching the question from the dependency school, introduce analysis of domestic elites as beneficiaries of financialization, but nonetheless account for their actions as determined by their structurally given interests (see e.g. Reis and de Oliveira 2021).

We have pointed out the elites have absorbed a de-socialized market model based on market ideology and implemented policies not directly connected to finance through cuts to social spending. This need not represent a uniform response that leaves no room for domestic-level maneuvering. There is, rather, room for choices made at the national level even as less developed, subordinate economies are pressured by external forces.

Debates over neoliberal globalization can provide an instructive view of how a similar theoretical contest was ultimately decided in favor of neither a positive nor negative assessment, but one that privileges a heterogenous process in which national actors charted a variety of paths to global integration.

As neoliberalism spread in the wake of the demise of the Bretton Woods system, conventional wisdom had it that ensuring efficiency in a fast-paced and competitive world market required scaling back the state, provoking a "race to the bottom" that would slash public spending and welfare provisions, leaving the most vulnerable in society to the mercy of indifferent international markets. A movement toward a single global market, in this view, will make national differences in policy preferences untenable and impose the same market-friendly (and presumably budget-hostile) set of constraints on all states that wish to avoid being left behind in the race for prosperity. Globalization itself implies the erosion of the national and particular and emergence of a single, unified economy operating on the same logic. The welfare state, in this "hyperglobalization" model, would figure among the primary casualties of an era of international neoliberalism.

The hyperglobalization thesis did not accurately predict the contours of neoliberal policy implementation. Foreign capital does not travel as easily and quickly as would be necessary to reliably produce the race to the bottom (Hay 2000). Instead, initial expectations that globalization and neoliberalism would require such a race likely produced early movements toward convergence. Martin-Mayoral and Sastre (2017) show a trend toward reductions in spending during the 1990s and divergence thereafter, as governments experimented with different approaches to social policy in response to disappointing results from economic orthodoxy of the Washington Consensus period. In terms of effects on social inclusion Huber and Stephens (2012) find that market liberalization is not associated with any direct impact on inequality and poverty.

Implementation of neoliberal reforms is variegated and responsive to a complex web of national-level variables. Several contextual features have been shown to be significant in the translation of international neoliberalism to the national level. Scholars have identified a multitude of political and social variables that can shape the implementation of neoliberalism; regime type, party ideology, and the relative strength of various types of social actors, the popularity of presidents, and others all can influence the implementation of neoliberal policies and budget priorities. Governments can even respond to international economic competition by increasing social spending as a means of shoring up security in the face of threats of instability in the event of sudden changes in the global economic order. A multitude of different actors and processes determine social policy, and their arrangements vary significantly from one country to the next, producing distinctive results (see e.g. Bonvecchi and Scartascini 2020).

Evidence shows that welfare expenditures diverged between developed and less developed economies as a result of globalization, with less developed economies devoting less to welfare (Rudra 2002), and that democracies in the developing world are less likely to enact severe cuts in social spending (Rudra and Haggard 2005; Huber, Mustillo, and Stephens 2008; Kaufman and Segura-Ubiergo 2001). In fact, left governments did maintain the broad policy outlines of neoliberal orthodoxy. Nonetheless, the predicted demise of welfare protections was not borne out, and a host of domestic-level factors mediate the global forces of integration, such that neoliberalism does not result in uniform policy outcomes around the world.

Although initially the diffusion of neoliberal policy ideas might have been expected to globalize a single logic of austerity capitalism and welfare retrenchment, that view was not borne out in all cases but was heavily conditioned by the array of social and political actors pressing for and against welfare priorities. In a globalized context economic policy-making becomes a complex act of negotiating between domestic and international actors (Babb 2004). It is evident that neoliberal globalization does not take the same form across cases.

Thus, multitudes of variables mediate liberalization. As for the effects on other social and political dimensions, such as social spending, inequality, and welfare outcomes, perhaps unsurprisingly, the answer is not straightforward. Higher or lower levels of development, the strength of the rule of law, human capital, and other characteristics of an economy will all have independent effects on the outcomes of financialization (Cerra et al. 2022, p. 288).

Empirical observation would suggest, then, that while global economic forces are potent, they are not determinative in producing outcomes. Indeed, given its complexity, it cannot be determinative. Therefore, we find that critical views, too, are theoretically laden. A significant part of the disconnect between theory and observation lies in the conceptualization of financialization as a unified and mechanistic structure, rather than a widely varying, contextualized social process. The reality of a phenomenon as complex as financialization is beholden to no theory.

3.6 IMPLICATIONS

Debates over financialization have suffered from a neglect of the complexity of the process of financialization. Standard economic approaches suffer theoretically induced errors surrounding financialization, leading each to miss important aspects of on-the-ground reality in LAC. Neoliberalism and financialization are advertised as rational approaches making economies efficient and broadening opportunities. As told by market ideology this is a universal story applying to all nations, written in the universal language of mathematics.

But the cognitive connections between economic theory and policy made by market ideology do not limit itself to economic and financial liberalization; it expands to apply its logic to other areas such as social spending, in pursuit of its efficiency maximization tenets. If, on the other hand, only structural conditions are salient, then domestic effects should not be driven by market logic but only reflect the constellation of material variables, the obstacle course faced by policymakers. These structural conditions are, of course, very different between the United States and LAC, and among the nations of LAC, and yet we find similar results across these distinctive cases.

The skeptical lens of subordinate or dependent financialization rightly centers attention on the outcomes felt by people on the ground rather than on macroeconomic indicators. It is appropriate to be reminded that the judgment of the importance of inequality, poverty, and inclusion, and their sources and treatments, is heavily influenced by the theoretical ideas that we bring to our interpretation. Nonetheless, critical approaches similarly emphasize the universality of financialization as an external, material force of overwhelming power, thus sidelining the mediating and participatory role of domestic conditions and agents at the national level.

Based on our theoretical critique of the orthodox liberal economic theory on which financialization is derived and on heterogeneous empirical outcomes of neoliberal globalization, we expect that each side in this polarized debate is half right. Financialization does have an independent negative effect on social policy detached from any rational economic necessity but is unlikely to yield uniformly negative impacts on social inclusion across cases in LAC.

Our suggested approach, then, is to discard the strictly structural and mechanistic conception of markets in favor of the more realistic understanding that markets are social, made of agents acting and reacting to each other in institutionally and socially diverse contexts, without predictable consequences. The standard neoliberal economic model as well as critical views have both failed to integrate this view, producing complementary but particular blind spots. An integrated, holistic, approach toward economics and markets as intertwined social systems points toward the possibility of different approaches to economic management and development, and the conclusion that there is not a universally applicable model for policy nor a universal critique of financialization as an integrated concept; there are many financializations with many outcomes.

CONCLUSION: TESTING THEORY

This chapter reviewed the dominant explanations for how financialization gained purchase in the policy realm. We find that there have been two broad theoretical approaches to explanations. Structuralist theories appeal to impersonal forces to explain policy adoption, either directly or mediated through rationalist, institutionalist, or psychological lenses. Ideational theories draw attention to ideas as the driving force for policy change. Both fall short as they fail to account for the complexity of social systems, producing incomplete explanations of financialization. We attempt to offer a more nuanced understanding by centering our explanation on a market ideology, which connects agents and structures through belief-oriented action. We maintain that such a view better integrates the actions of domestic-level social planners and their ability to shape policy. Thus, we hypothesize that financialization will exert downward pressure on fiscal spending, but the embrace of financialization will lead to varying effects on social inclusion. The following chapters test these propositions by examining the relationships between levels of financialization and domestic social spending in chapter 4, and the implications for social inclusion in chapter 5.

BIBLIOGRAPHY

Abdelal, Rawi, Mark Blyth, and Craig Parsons, eds. 2010. *Constructing the International Economy*. Cornell Studies in Political Economy. Ithaca, NY: Cornell University Press.

Alesina, Alberto, Nouriel Roubini, and Gerald D Cohen. 1997. *Political Cycles and the Macroeconomy*. Cambridge, MA: The MIT Press. https://mitpress.mit.edu/books/political-cycles-and-macroeconomy.

Arthur, W. Brian. 2015. *Complexity and the Economy*. Oxford ; New York: Oxford University Press.

Babb, Sarah. 2004. *Managing Mexico: Economists from Nationalism to Neoliberalism*. 2. print., 1. paperback print. Princeton Paperbacks. Princeton, NJ: Princeton University Press.

Basu, Kaushik. 2003. *Prelude to Political Economy: A Study of the Social and Political Foundations of Economics*. Paperback. Oxford: Oxford University Press.

Berman, Sheri. 2011. "Ideology, History, and Politics." In *Ideas and Politics in Social Science Research*, edited by Daniel Béland and Robert Henry Cox, 105–26. Oxford; New York: Oxford University Press.

———. 2013. "Ideational Theorizing in the Social Sciences since 'Policy Paradigms, Social Learning, and the State': Ideational Theorizing in Political Science." *Governance* 26 (2): 217–37. https://doi.org/10.1111/gove.12008.

Best, Jacqueline. 2008. "Ambiguity, Uncertainty, and Risk: Rethinking Indeterminacy[1]." *International Political Sociology* 2 (4): 355–74. https://doi.org/10.1111/j.1749-5687.2008.00056.x.

Blyth, Mark. 2003. "Structures Do Not Come with an Instruction Sheet: Interests, Ideas, and Progress in Political Science." *Perspectives on Politics* 1 (4): 695–706. https://doi.org/10.1017/S1537592703000471.

———. 2011. "Ideas, Uncertainty, and Evolution." In *Ideas and Politics in Social Science Research*, edited by Daniel Béland and Robert Henry Cox, 83–101. Oxford University Press.

Bonizzi, Bruno, Annina Kaltenbrunner, and Jeff Powell. 2020. "Subordinate Financialization in Emerging Capitalist Economies." In *The Routledge International Handbook of Financialization*, edited by Philip Mader, Daniel Mertens, and Natascha van der Zwan, 177–87. Routledge International Handbooks. London New York: Routledge.

Bonvecchi, Alejandro, and Carlos G. Scartascini. 2020. *Who Decides Social Policy? Social Networks and the Political Economy of Social Policy in Latin America and the Caribbean*. Latin American Development Forum. Washington, DC: World Bank Group. https://doi.org/10.1596/978-1-4648-1572-0.

Bower, Joseph L., and Lynn S. Paine. 2017. "The Error at the Heart of Corporate Leadership." *Harvard Business Review*, May 1, 2017. https://hbr.org/2017/05/the-error-at-the-heart-of-corporate-leadership.

Centeno, Miguel Ángel. 2007. "Isomorphic Neoliberalism and the Creation of Inevitability." In *Globalization and Uncertainty in Latin America*, edited by Fernando López-Alves and Diane E. Johnson, 77–95. New York: Palgrave Macmillan. https://doi.org/10.1057/9780230603554_4.

Cerra, Valerie, Barry J. Eichengreen, Asmaa El-Ganainy, and Martin Schindler, eds. 2022. *How to Achieve Inclusive Growth*. 1st ed. Oxford; New York: Oxford University Press.

Chomsky, Noam. 1998. *Profit Over People: Neoliberalism and Global Order*. Seven Stories Press.

Chwieroth, Jeffrey. 2007. "Neoliberal Economists and Capital Account Liberalization in Emerging Markets." *International Organization* 61 (Spring): 443–63.

Copley, Jack. 2022. *Governing Financialization: The Tangled Politics of Financial Liberalization in Britain*. 1st ed. Oxford: Oxford University Press.

Davis, Aeron, and Catherine Walsh. 2017. "Distinguishing Financialization from Neoliberalism." *Theory, Culture & Society* 34 (5–6): 27–51. https://doi.org/10.1177/0263276417715511.

Dezalay, Yves, and Bryant G. Garth. 2002. *The Internationalization of Palace Wars: Lawyers, Economists, and the Contest to Transform Latin American States*. The Chicago Series in Law and Society. Chicago: University of Chicago Press.

DiMaggio, Paul J., and Walter W. Powell. 1983. "The Iron Cage Revisited: Institutional Isomorphism and Collective Rationality in Organizational Fields." *American Sociological Review* 48 (2): 147. https://doi.org/10.2307/2095101.

Eturk, Ismail. 2020. "Shareholder Primacy and Corporate Financialization." In *The Routledge International Handbook of Financialization*, edited by Philip Mader,

Daniel Mertens, and Natascha van der Zwan, 43–55. Routledge International Handbooks. London New York: Routledge.

Fernandez, Raquel, and Dani Rodrik. 1991. "Resistance to Reform: Status Quo Bias in the Presence of Individual-Specific Uncertainty." *American Economic Review* 81 (5): 1146–55.

Fligstein, Neil. 1993. *The Transformation of Corporate Control*. 1. paperback ed. Cambridge, MA: Harvard University Press.

———. 2001. *The Architecture of Markets: An Economic Sociology of Twenty-First-Century Capitalist Societies*. Princeton, NJ: Princeton University Press.

Ford, Christopher A. 2015. "Musings on Complexity, Policy, and Ideology." In *World Politics at the Edge of Chaos: Reflections on Complexity and Global Life*, edited by Emilian Kavalski, 79–109. Suny Series, James N. Rosenau Series in Global Politics. Albany: State University of New York Press.

Fourcade-Gourinchas, Marion, and Sarah L. Babb. 2002. "The Rebirth of the Liberal Creed: Paths to Neoliberalism in Four Countries." *American Journal of Sociology* 108 (3): 533–79. https://doi.org/10.1086/367922.

Fox, Justin, ed. 2011. *The Myth of the Rational Market: A History of Risk, Reward, and Delusion on Wall Street*. 1st Harper Business pbk. ed. New York: Harper Business.

Freeden, Michael. 1998. *Ideologies and Political Theory: A Conceptual Approach*. 1. issued in paperback. Oxford: Clarendon Press.

Freeman, Carla. 2014. *Entrepreneurial Selves: Neoliberal Respectability and the Making of a Caribbean Middle Class*. Next Wave: New Directions in Women's Studies. Durham, NC: Duke University Press.

Haiven, Max. 2020. "Culture and Financialization: Four Approaches." In *The Routledge International Handbook of Financialization*, edited by Philip Mader, Daniel Mertens, and Natascha van der Zwan, 347–57. Routledge International Handbooks. London New York: Routledge.

Hall, Peter. 1993. "Policy Paradigms, Social Learning, and the State: The Case of Economic Policymaking in Britain." *Comparative Politics* 25 (3): 275–96.

Hay, Colin. 2000. "Contemporary Capitalism, Globalization, Regionalization and the Persistence of National Variation." *Review of International Studies* 26 (4): 509–31. https://doi.org/10.1017/S026021050000509X.

Hay, Colin, and Ben Rosamond. 2002. "Globalization, European Integration and the Discursive Construction of Economic Imperatives." *Journal of European Public Policy* 9 (2): 147–67. https://doi.org/10.1080/13501760110120192.

Holland, John H. 1998. *Emergence: From Chaos to Order*. Helix Books. Reading, Mass: Addison-Wesley.

———. 2014. *Complexity: A Very Short Introduction*. 1st ed. Oxford: Oxford University Press.

Huber, Evelyne, Thomas Mustillo, and John D. Stephens. 2008. "Politics and Social Spending in Latin America." *The Journal of Politics* 70 (2): 420–36. https://doi.org/10.1017/S0022381608080407.

Huber, Evelyne, and John D. Stephens. 2012. *Democracy and the Left: Social Policy and Inequality in Latin America*. University of Chicago Press.

Kaplan, Stephen B. 2013. *Globalization and Austerity Politics in Latin America*. Cambridge University Press.

Kaufman, Robert R., and Alex Segura-Ubiergo. 2001. "Globalization, Domestic Politics, and Social Spending in Latin America: A Time-Series Cross-Section Analysis, 1973–97." *World Politics* 53 (4): 553–87.

Kilpatrick, Henry E. 2001. "Complexity, Spontaneous Order, and Friedrich Hayek: Are Spontaneous Order and Complexity Essentially the Same Thing?" *Complexity* 6 (4): 16–20. https://doi.org/10.1002/cplx.1035.

Lapavitsas, Costas, and Aylin Soydan. 2022. "Financialisation in Developing Countries: Approaches, Concepts, and Metrics." *International Review of Applied Economics* 36 (3): 424–47. https://doi.org/10.1080/02692171.2022.2052714.

Lazonick, William, and Mary O'Sullivan. 2000. "Maximizing Shareholder Value: A New Ideology for Corporate Governance." *Economy and Soceity* 29 (1): 13–35.

Martín-Mayoral, Fernando, and Juan Fernández Sastre. 2017. "Determinants of Social Spending in Latin America During and after the Washington Consensus: A Dynamic Panel Error-Correction Model Analysis." *Latin American Economic Review* 26 (1): 10. https://doi.org/10.1007/s40503-017-0053-6.

Mehta, Jal. 2011. "The Varied Roles of Ideas in Politics: From 'Whether' to 'How.'" In *Ideas and Politics in Social Science Research*, edited by Daniel Béland and Robert Henry Cox, 23–46. Oxford; New York: Oxford University Press.

O'Malley, Pat. 2012. *Risk, Uncertainty and Government*. Routledge-Cavendish. https://doi.org/10.4324/9781843146025.

Palley, Thomas I. 2014. *Financialization: The Economics of Finance Capital Domination*. Houndmills, Basingstoke, Hampshire: Palgrave Macmillan.

Parsons, Craig. 2007. *How to Map Arguments in Political Science*. Oxford; New York: Oxford University Press.

Pinheiro, Diogo, Jeffrey M. Chwieroth, and Alexander Hicks. 2015. "Do International Non-Governmental Organizations Inhibit Globalization? The Case of Capital Account Liberalization in Developing Countries." *European Journal of International Relations* 21 (1): 146–70. https://doi.org/10.1177/1354066114523656.

Pinheiro, Diogo L. 2021. "Sovereign Risk Ratings in Latin America: Measures of Economic Conditions or Policy Paradigm Compliance?" *Journal of Global South Studies* 38 (2): 343–73. https://doi.org/10.1353/gss.2021.0032.

Popper, Karl. 1984. "The Autonomy of Sociology." In *Popper Selections*, edited by David Miller, 345–56. Princeton, NJ: Princeton University Press.

Reis, Nadine, and Felipe Antunes de Oliveira. 2021. "Peripheral Financialization and the Transformation of Dependency: A View from Latin America." *Review of International Political Economy*, December, 1–24. https://doi.org/10.1080/09692290.2021.2013290.

Rudra, Nita. 2002. "Globalization and the Decline of the Welfare State in Less-Developed Countries." *International Organization* 56 (2): 411–45.

Rudra, Nita, and Stephan Haggard. 2005. "Globalization, Democracy, and Effective Welfare Spending in the Developing World." *Comparative Political Studies* 38 (9): 1015–49. https://doi.org/10.1177/0010414005279258.

Simányi, Léna Pellandini. 2020. "The Financialization of Everyday Life." In *The Routledge Handbook of Critical Finance Studies*, edited by Christian Borch and Robert Wosnitzer, 1st ed., 278–99. Routledge. https://doi.org/10.4324/9781315114255-18.

Spronk, Susan, and Jeffery R Webber, eds. 2015. "Introduction - Systemic Logics and Historical Specificity: Renewing Historical Materialism in Latin American Political Economy." In *Crisis and Contradiction: Marxist Perspectives on Latin America in the Global Political Economy*, 1–28. Leiden: Brill.

Steger, Manfred. 2013. *Globalization: A Very Short Introduction*. Oxford University Press. https://doi.org/10.1093/actrade/9780199662661.001.0001.

Steger, Manfred B. 2008. "Globalization and Ideology." In *The Blackwell Companion to Globalization*, edited by George Ritzer, 367–82. Oxford: Blackwell Publishing Ltd. https://doi.org/10.1002/9780470691939.ch18.

Stiglitz, Joseph E. 2003. *Globalization and Its Discontents*. New York, NY: W. W. Norton & Company.

Stokes, Susan C. 2001. *Mandates and Democracy: Neoliberalism by Surprise in Latin America*. Cambridge University Press.

Turner, Rachel S. 2011. *Neo-Liberal Ideology: History, Concepts and Policies*. Edinburgh: Edinburgh University Press.

Williamson, John. 2004. "The Strange History of the Washington Consensus." *Journal of Post Keynesian Economics* 27 (2): 195–206.

Chapter 4

Bond Markets and Their Implications for Social Spending

In chapter 3 we introduced the idea of market ideology that has accompanied the process of financialization in LAC. Financial development is only a part of the story of financialization. We argued that understanding the effects of financialization requires attention to its ideational dimension, encapsulated by what we call market ideology. This set of ideas carries assumptions about the role of the state and the market vis-a-vis public policy.

We now shift our focus to financialization's effects on public policy. The facet of financialization that likely has the greatest impact on public policy is that which most directly impacts state funding: a government's reliance on the bond market for funds. Unsurprisingly, some researchers have gone as far as operationalizing financialization specifically as the share of external debt that is in the hands of bond markets (Kaplan 2013; Kaplan and Thomsson 2017). The purpose of this chapter, then, is the estimate the impact of this form of financialization on a government's ability to spend on critical policy areas for social development. A wide-ranging literature has investigated the determinants of several different forms of social spending in Latin America (Brown and Hunter 1999; Huber and Stephens 2001; 2012; Jensen 2011; Kaufman and Segura-Ubiergo 2001; Tenorio 2014; Wibbels 2006), but to our knowledge no systematic attempt has been made to understand the impact of financialization on those forms of social spending.

Understanding the role of financialization in changing the dynamics of social spending requires us to ask three interrelated questions. First, what is the direct impact of the changing composition of government debt on spending patterns? That is, if financing is done primarily through bond markets and institutional investors, does that lead to differences in spending on healthcare, education, and welfare? Of course, the fact that there might be differences may not, by itself imply a direct connection between financialization and spending. Or, alternatively, we could even be discussing a scenario of reverse causation. That is, it is possible that a country spends so much on social matters that it becomes more likely to default on its debt, leading to difficulties in obtaining market financing. This possibility leads to the next two key questions in this chapter. Does the market "punish" countries that spend more on things like healthcare and education? Here we answer this question by looking at how Sovereign Risk Ratings issued by credit rating agencies are influenced by levels and changes of spending. And that leads us to the last key question in this chapter: is this potential "punishment" evidence based, or is it a reflection of a series of assumptions embedded in a sort of neoliberal policy paradigm (Babb 2013; Hall 1993)? More precisely, are countries that spend more on the select types of social spending discussed here more likely to default on their debts?

The chapter proceeds with a discussion of how global financial markets have come to dictate public policy formulation in LAC nations.

4.1 BACKGROUND

"Wall Street wants blood." That statement was one of the defining stories of late 1990s Brazilian politics (*ISTOÉ* 2000; Elio Gaspari 2000). But that remark was not uttered by protestors or radical left-wing agitators. Rather, it was allegedly said by Pedro Parente, then second in command to the Brazilian Finance Minister, in a meeting with other cabinet members. "Contagion" from the 1997 Asian financial crisis and the 1998 Russian financial crisis deeply affected other developing countries. As discussed in chapter 2, Brazil had just managed to get inflation under control by adopting many of the recommendations of the International Monetary Fund and the so-called "Washington Consensus": opening up of financial markets, removal of capital controls, reliance on foreign investment to sustain stable exchange rates, and general austerity. In response to the two aforementioned crises, the IMF's recommendation was more of the same: Stanley Fischer, then first deputy managing director of the IMF, and Michel Camdessus, managing director, repeatedly suggested that the solution to the crisis was to raise interest rates to instill "confidence" in the local currency, and added austerity to be able to sustain those high-interest rates. Brazil, then under the control of PSDB, a formerly center left party that fully embraced neoliberalism, followed those recommendations. The cabinet meeting in which Parente reportedly remarked that "Wall Street wants blood" was specifically called to discuss budget cuts. Parente had reported that Pedro Malan, then finance minister, wanted to include a program from the Ministry of Education that sent researchers and graduate students abroad to train at foreign universities. Mendonça de Barros, president of the national development bank BNDES, protested, claiming that the program was relatively cheap (the proposed cuts would save about US$ 80 million, a fraction of a percent of the government budget) and that the cuts would be personally devastating to the hundreds of researchers who would suddenly find themselves stranded in a foreign country, with the stipends they relied on to live deeply cut or frozen. "Wall Street wants blood," then, wasn't a protestation against the whims of the market. It was an argument in favor of deep budget cuts; Brazilian researchers abroad might become the symbolic "blood" offered as sacrifice to Wall Street and serve as proof of how serious the government was in its intentions to cut spending (Elio Gaspari 2000).

Pedro Parente himself never confirmed this story, which was made public by Mendonça de Barros. That he revealed this to the press was seen as part of an internal struggle within the Fernando Henrique Cardoso government, with "desenvolvimentistas" like Barros on one side, and "monetaristas" like Parente and Malan on the other. Brazil's reliance on foreign financing, then, tilted the scales toward the "monetaristas," those who privileged austerity and deregulation as government policies. This story highlights a key moment in the process of financialization in Brazil: the more reliant governments became on financing by markets, rather than state to state or multilateral loans, the more "investor confidence" mattered. The geopolitics of government finance became less about alliances and multilateral relations and more about shoring up investor confidence that the government was willing and able to meet its financial obligations. Bond markets became all powerful, and rating agencies that informed regulation in those markets were all powerful. As a prominent *New York Times* columnist put it:

> There are two superpowers in the world today in my opinion. There is the United States and there's Moody's Bond Rating Service. The United States can destroy you by dropping bombs, and Moody's can destroy you by downgrading your bonds. And believe me, it's not clear sometimes who's more powerful. (Friedman 1996)

This quote is illustrative of the fundamental shift in how government financing works when bond markets become the main way in which governments obtain funding. Fear of a default by a government can be as harmful as a default itself. Financialization, to the extent that it is related to this shift in government financing, can be a powerful force toward government austerity. This is hardly surprising: a significant literature establishes the ties between financialization and austerity (Kaplan 2013). But while financialization and austerity have been linked together in the existing academic literature on globalization and neoliberalism, much less has been written about the particular forms that this austerity takes. What sorts of government spending get cut, and what sorts are left untouched? Are there forces that resist this move toward austerity? And what, in particular, are the impacts of financialization on different forms of government social spending? The goal of this chapter is to further develop the argument developed in the previous chapter by focusing on how financialization affects specific forms of government spending: spending on healthcare, education, social security, as well as its impact on overall spending. We also aim to bridge some of the gap between the existing literature on financialization and austerity and the literature on neoliberalism and social spending. In the next subsection, we will discuss these literatures. After that we will show, using quantitative data, how financialization has a significant impact on spending on healthcare and education (though not on social security and welfare spending), an impact that is mitigated by an active labor movement.

4.2 EXISTING PERSPECTIVES ON SPENDING AND FINANCIALIZATION

Austerity has long been recognized as one of the central features of neoliberalism (Babb 2005; 2013; Kaplan 2018). It is, therefore, unsurprising that many different factors tied to the rise of neoliberalism are also tied to the rise of austerity. Defenders of austerity programs insist that it is just a matter of sound economics, the sort frequently described as "supply side." As a result, several commentators have described the emergence of austerity as a political force in Latin America being a consequence of "good economics" arriving at the region (Harberger 1996). Such deterministic accounts generally ignore the vast literature on the political, cultural, and economic forces at play in shaping economic policy.

The existing literature on the rise of austerity politics in Latin America tends to point to a number of different factors: the increasing influence of U.S.-trained economists (Chwieroth 2009; Kogut and Macpherson 2011), the increased reliance on the International Monetary Fund in times of crises (Vreeland 2003; 2007), a generalized race to the so-called bottom as a result of the removal of capital account controls (Rodrik 2006), and similar processes (Wibbels 2006). While these claims are supported by some empirical studies of some cases, we would like to argue that ultimately, these changes can be traced back to the rise of institutional finance as a major player in government funding. Not that this insight is particularly revolutionary: a significant literature already discusses the role of financialization in getting some of these previously mentioned factors in place: financialization has affected the odds that U.S.-trained economists are nominated to government positions (Dezalay and Garth 2002; Kaplan 2018), vulnerability to external economic shocks (Abu-El-Haj 2007) and so on. Not many studies, however, have measured the direct impact of financialization on austerity, and, more specifically, different types of government spending. Here, we turn to trying to understand the role of financialization on key measures of spending that affects the welfare of a population: spending on education, health care, social security, and total government spending.

The bulk of the existing literature on welfare spending focuses on international economic ties and domestic politics (Rudra 2002; Tenorio 2014). In particular, it has focused on the "compensation" versus "competition" hypotheses debate on the international economic front, which highlights the extent to which international economic forces exert downward pressure on spending, and the extent to which unions (Rudra 2002), left-wing governments (Huber, Mustillo, and Stephens 2008) or protests (Tenorio 2014) force governments to spend more to make up for the increase in market volatility during recent decades. On the domestic economic front, the emphasis has been on the way that certain key manufacturing sectors (Rudra 2002) or unemployment (Noy 2011) shape spending. Comparably less has been said about the spread of certain models of state intervention in the economy and their effects on spending.

4.3 PREDICTING SOCIAL SPENDING

In chapter 3 we presented in broad strokes the argument concerning how ideational processes in the form of market ideology drive financialization. This chapter focuses on these ideational processes on an international scale. It is based on the idea that states come to increasingly resemble one another in their policy choices (Meyer and Rowan 1977) through the spread of particular models that gained legitimacy on a global scale, not because these ideas naturally propagate as some sort of ether, but because these ideas are tied to, and direct, the potential flow of significant resources. The ideas associated with portfolio investment and finance become the dominant ideas because finance becomes the dominant force in the shaping of emerging market government spending. For the most part, this particular type of analysis has been conducted before with regards to de jure policy adoption, privatization and deregulation (Henisz, Zelner, and Guillén 2005), financial liberalization (Pinheiro, Chwieroth, and Hicks 2015), and in particular on the spread and possible retrenchment of the so-called Washington Consensus (e.g. Babb, 2012), among other topics. Welfare and social security programs have notably come under close scrutiny, and been the subject of extensive cuts, in much of the developed world (Blyth 2002), but attempts to understand the way that certain ideas shape government spending in Latin America are relatively new.

In order to understand the way that ideas from without the region end up taking hold within the region, our analysis here proceeds by proposing three different sets of hypotheses. The first set of hypotheses follows much of the established literature in trying to understand the determinants of social spending, with an added emphasis on the role of financialization. In a world of perfectly rational actors with converging interests, who a government owes money to should matter quite a bit less than how much it owes. As such, this first set of hypotheses explores whether we should expect differences in terms of spending for nations where their external debt is owed mostly to other state actors and multilateral organizations or to atomized securities markets and institutional investors. The second set of hypotheses focuses on where those differences may come from. Specifically, the emphasis is on whether rating agencies, which are embedded in regulations and guide investment by institutional actors, have particularly negative views of the types of social spending discussed here. A growing literature focuses on the political determinants of country risk ratings (Biglaiser and DeRouen 2007; Gültekin-Karakaş, Hisarcıklılar, and Öztürk 2011; Pinheiro 2020; 2021), but it has to this point focused mostly on the adoption of policies related to the Washington Consensus. Less attention has been paid to whether credit rating agencies are particularly harsh on certain types of spending. The third and final set of hypotheses deals with whether there is evidence that these forms of social spending should be singled out as predictive of fiscal troubles. That is, are CRAs being rational actors when they punish those forms of spending, or are they enacting a particular worldview that is independent of evidence?

The first set of models we will cover in this chapter is about understanding the factors that shape social spending. As such, this first set of hypotheses will cover existing research regarding spending, as well as adding a set of hypotheses regarding financialization and spending. The most prominent set of political hypotheses in the literature concerns measures of partisan rule. Scholars have hypothesized that democracy augments popular pressures on government and social spending since at least Pampel and Williamson's late 1980s work (Pampel and Williamson 1988). Moreover, a substantial literature argues that that democracy boosts social spending (Brown and Hunter 1999; Huber and Stephens 2012; Kaufman and Segura-Ubiergo 2001). Indeed, the idea and actuality of democracy as a developmental driver of welfare state has gained globally extensive support for developing nations (Boix 2001; Haggard and Kaufman 2008).

More recently, Huber, Mustillo, and Stephens (2008) find that it is the legacy of democracy that has a particularly important impact on different forms of spending. That is, it is not necessarily the presence or absence of a democratic government in a given year that shapes spending, but the cumulative effect of years of democratic governance. As a result, we hypothesize:

Hypothesis 1: Democracies will be relatively reluctant to cut spending and likely to increase it.

In addition to a democracy effect, Tenorio (2014) has found that Latin American democracies are particularly sensitive to general strikes and labor activism. As such, we would expect that the greater the number of general strikes in a given democracy, the more a government will spend on social security and welfare:

Hypothesis 2: the greater the number of general strikes, the more the government will spend on social programs and in general.

With regards to partisan politics, Huber and Stephens' 2012 book offers perhaps the more exhaustive exploration of the impact of the Latin American left on social spending. That book follows their previous work on the topic, Huber et al. (2008). They found no evidence of an impact of left-leaning governments. They argue that left-right balance affects how governments spend money in Latin America, but not necessarily their amount. Likewise, Noy (2014) found little evidence of left-wing effect on welfare effort. Left-leaning governments affect how progressive spending is, and generally privilege spending on equality-enhancing programs, especially related to education. But while those findings seem to hold for several types of spending, another very influential article on the matter, by Kauffman and Segura-Ubiergo (2001), found that executives that have been historically tied to labor have a significant and positive impact on disaggregated measures of social spending, especially health, education, and social security. Additionally, Carnes and Mares find that left-wing executives have a significant impact on non-contributory forms of social security (Mares and Carnes 2009), which started to become particularly popular in Latin America during the 1990s, and Morgan and Kelly (2013) find that left-leaning governments impact inequality through spending on human capital (Morgan and Kelly 2013). As a result, we cautiously propose the following hypothesis, fully expecting that our results may not be consistent across the varieties of spending we analyze here:

Hypothesis 3: left-leaning executives will lead to greater government spending.

With regards to political and economic issues, we have two important, existing competing orientations, a Competition Thesis and a Compensation Thesis. The Competition Thesis—coined in a 1989 paper by Garrett in *International Organization* and supported by findings in 2001 papers by Garrett and Mitchell (2001) and Burgoon (2001)—emphasizes the shifting payoff structure of a rapidly globalizing world that pressure for leaner states and at the service of leaner and more competitive economies. As regards increased exposure to international flows of goods and services, the Competition Thesis proposes that increased trade openness pressures and warrants more laissez-faire economic policy (i.e. policy that is restrictive on taxes, restrictive on fiscal deficits, and restrictive on spending that promotes these targeted outcomes). There is some support for this perspective in the existing literature for Latin American nations (e.g. Kaufman and Segura-Ubiergo 2001). Based on the discussion we offer the following hypothesis:

Hypothesis 4a: The more a nation is subjected to international competition, as measured by international trade as a percentage of GDP, the more likely it is to reduce social spending.

The Compensation Thesis states that the more a nation becomes exposed to the volatility of the global market, the greater its need for and provision of government-provided safety net. For rich democratic nations, many papers have found strong evidence that greater trade openness stimulates social spending (Garrett 1998, Hicks 1999; Rodrik 1998). Although a few have found the opposite (e.g. Burgoon 2001) little or no support has been found for the compensation hypothesis for Latin America. However, support for its operation as an indicator of *developmentally* regarded source of welfare state or evolution has been found for the rich democracies (Cameron 1978; Hicks 1999) and worldwide (e.g. Boix 2001; Haggard and Kaufman 2008).

We offer this "compensation" alternative to our "competition" hypothesize:

Hypothesis 4b: The more a nation is subjected to international competition, as measured by international trade as a percentage of GDP, the more likely it is to increase social spending.

As previously discussed, one of the key characteristics of the end of the embedded liberalism era of the Bretton Woods era was that state-to-state lending and borrowing started to play a much smaller role in the global economy. Government financing, then, became dominated by bond markets, private investors, and a ubiquitous "market," the "Wall Street" that occasionally "wants blood" from the start of this chapter. This leads to a qualitatively different sort of relationship between lender and borrower: one where the expectations of a potential default on one's debt can be as devastating for a country's ability to borrow as a default itself. This becomes evident when we look at the way that these financial markets are currently regulated. In the United States, for example, institutional investors face several regulations as to how much "risk" they can take on. But "risk" here has a specific meaning. The Securities and Exchange Commission (SEC) has designated several private firms as "National Recognized Statistical Research Organizations" (NRSROs), which include firms such as Fitch and Standard and Poor. These NRSROs have the power to designate a particular bond or financial instrument as either "investment grade" or "speculative grade." The requirements and limits placed on how institutional investors handle "investment grade" instruments are much less severe and restricted than those placed on "speculative grade," with some investors being outright banned from holding "speculative grade" instruments. As such, governments interested in financing deficits through bond markets need to show those in this market that they are "safe" investments and being deemed as a risky investment carries with it significant consequences, as institutional investors are then affected by these stricter regulations. This, by itself, already should have significant impacts on spending decisions by governments. But existing research has also shown that these credit ratings aren't significantly, or even partially, driven by a government's economic fundamentals. Rather, they are driven by ideological adherence to the neoliberal policy paradigm (Pinheiro 2021), denominated as market ideology in chapter 3. Existing research also shows that in anticipation of concerns by NRSROs, even left-wing governments will appoint economists who will please the "market" and signal a commitment to debt repayment, especially in economic downturns.

Owing money to bond markets, then, is substantially different than owing money to other governments. And as a result, we should expect that *who* a government owes money to will have at least as significant an impact on social spending decisions as *how much* they owe. This leads to the following hypothesis:

Hypothesis 5: the higher the proportion of a government's debt that is in the form of bonds issued to private investors, the more that government will cut spending, as a way to satisfy different private market actors

In other words, a government that has a majority of its debt tied to financial markets will have a greater incentive to adopt the prescriptions of the neoliberal policy paradigm, as even the appearance of divergence can lead to capital flight, downgrading by NRSROs, and general suspicion by investors.

Economic contexts and conditions, both relatively domestic and relatively international, are broadly implicated in the determination of social policy expenditure (Hicks 1999; Huber and Stephens 2001; Huber, Mustillo and Stephens 2008). Both levels of economic *development and rates of economic growth* provide resources for financing of social legislation. Indeed, economic development is a core traditional development measure broadly found to augment social spending and state scale both in the rich democracies (e.g.

Cameron 1988; Pampel and Williamson 1989, Ch. 3; Hicks 1999, Huber and Stephens 2001) and worldwide (e.g. Pampel and Williamson 1989, Ch. 4; Boix 2001; Haggard and Kaufman 2008).

We hypothesize as follows:

Hypothesis 6: levels of economic development positively affect social spending; and

Hypothesis 7: rates of economic growth positively affect social spending.

The dependent population, or share of economic dependents in a population, exerts pressures on social spending. However, more specificity is needed. In particular, the proportion of young in a population (who tend not to be economically active) will tend to place downward pressure on social security and welfare spending to the extent that it restricts the proportion of the population that is economically active. Similarly, the proportion of elderly in a population (i.e. elderly who tend not to be economically active) will tend to increase social spending to the extent that it adds to the burdens of low-income households, increasing poverty, or generates demand for spending on public pensions. Positive effects of these groups, especially the elderly, are common in theory and findings on the causes of social spending literature. We hypothesize:

8a—the proportion of "elderly" in a population is positively associated with social spending.

8b—the proportion of "youth" in a population is negatively associated with social spending

In addition to the above hypotheses, we also control inflation, government debt service, and share of urban population.

4.3.1 How the Markets View Social Spending

The rise of bond markets in financing government deficits happened in a fairly short time. With the emergence of the Bretton Woods accords in the mid to late 1940s, international financing of governments happened primarily through state-to-state negotiations or through multilateral organizations like the International Bank for Reconstruction and Development (IBRD) (Block 1977). The end of the Bretton Woods accords came in 1973, fluctuations that were once absorbed by central banks and diluted by capital controls were "privatized." Now, fluctuating exchange rates and mobile capital could wipe out or generate profits in an instant. By 1976, 60 percent of all foreign debt was owed to private financial sources (Frenkel and O'Donnell 1994). But the rise of private markets did not mean an absence of regulations. Rather, these markets were regulated through the emergence of Sovereign Risk Ratings. From the 1970s onwards, then, a number of regulatory schemes were introduced in response. In 1973, Rule 15c3-1 designated certain CRAs as NRSROs. These included Moody's, Standard and Poor, and Fitch—the three largest agencies in the field. This rule essentially created a barrier to entry into the ratings market, as the NRSRO designation referred to the agencies whose ratings could be used to satisfy regulatory requirements (Partnoy 1999; 2006). In 1975, the SEC amended that rule to make it so that capital "haircut" requirements varied according to the risk grade assigned by NRSROs (Cantor and Packer 1997). In the 1980s, the role of the NRSROs was further strengthened, as changes in regulations now made disclosure requirements, margin lending, and exposure limits all dependent on those risk ratings.

Risk ratings, then, have become the key aspect of determining what is risky or not, with immense potential to deepen economic crises—a sell-off of a country's bonds can be made far more severe if institutional investors are forced to offload their share because of regulatory requirements. A substantial literature tries to understand what shapes the ratings given to different countries (Afonso 2003; Bouchet, Fishkin, and Goguel 2018), and unsurprisingly, there is some evidence of different forms of bias in these ratings (Gültekin-Karakaş, Hisarcıklılar, and Öztürk 2011; Kiff, Nowak, and Schumacher 2012; Pinheiro 2020; 2021). There is evidence, for example, that neoliberal policy adoption is rewarded by these agencies (Biglaiser and DeRouen 2007), even when it does not correspond to a reduction in the risk of investing in a particular country (Pinheiro 2021). However, these studies have looked at specific forms of neoliberal policy adoption, such as deregulation and privatization, and not austerity. So here the emphasis is on whether these credit rating agencies evaluate the riskiness of a country solely based on adoption of general austerity measures that have been known to be tied to financialization (Kaplan 2013), or if these agencies, and by extension the market, also care about the specific types of spending. This leads us to our first hypothesis regarding how credit rating agencies view spending:

Hypothesis 10—The greater the overall government spending of a country, the riskier that country will be considered

Investors in the bonds of a particular country should be primarily concerned with one thing: that country's ability to pay what they owe when those financial instruments reach maturity. A country that spends too much will be at a greater risk of default, as high spending can lead to deficits and an inability to pay on time. But if overall spending should be correlated negatively with the risk rating of a country, there is no evident reason we should expect markets to care about how much a government spends on particular areas, such as healthcare or education. Unless, of course, there is evidence that certain types of spending are more resistant to austerity. Which brings us to the next set of hypotheses.

4.3.2 Government Spending and Default

In theory, the key thing that should matter to financial markets regarding government bonds is the government's ability to repay in full and on time. As such, the only reason investors should have to care about the composition of a government's spending (rather than its overall size) is if they have reason to believe that certain types of spending are particularly "sticky" and unlikely to be cut. And here neoliberal economists tend to see social spending as potentially troublesome: from Chile's privatization of its social security system (Montecinos 1998), there has been some concern that the unpopularity of cuts to popular programs may make it more likely that governments will default in the future. This is in part corroborated by the existing literature on how different forms of social pressure bolster social spending (Kaufman and Segura-Ubiergo 2001; Tenorio 2014). This leads us to the following hypothesis:

Hypothesis 11—Sovereign risk ratings will be negatively correlated with different dimensions of social spending

This brings us to the third set of models to be estimated here: is there any evidence that social spending indeed makes it more likely that a nation will default on its debt? If we find in the previous set of models that indeed rating agencies have a negative view of social spending, that may very well be an evidence-based reaction to rampant social spending. But that connection has to be established. And, in fact, this may very well be where financialization serves as a sort of Trojan horse for the importation of key ideas from outside Latin America. If, rather than an empirically established relationship, the dominant view of social spending as contributing to defaults is an evidence-free assumption, we'd be able to establish how the sort of neoliberal consensus regarding austerity and government involvement in certain areas became the dominant view in Latin America: this is not a rational reaction to economic shocks, it is an imposition of a policy paradigm through the regulation of access to credit.

Hypothesis 12: Any negative impacts of social spending on a country's risk rating will be tied to evidence of social spending increasing the likelihood of default.

4.3.3 Methods

On the methodological front, we use error correction models that include both year and country fixed effects to address unmeasured heterogeneity. This has been the standard in recent work on social security in Latin America (see Kauffman and Segura-Ubiergo 2001; Noorudin and Simmons 2006; and Tenorio 2014). The key advantage to this method is that we are able to estimate both short-term and long-term effects of each variable, while also addressing the potential problems associated with co-integration of variables. Besides being the standard in much of the recent literature on social security spending (Kauffman and Segura-Ubiergo 2001; Noorudin and Simmons 2006; and Tenorio 2014), testing using methods discussed by Westerlund and Edgerton (2008) provides some evidence of the appropriateness of ECM here given co-integration, though as Beck and Katz (2011) suggest, our time horizon is too short to conclusively establish co-integration. However, we are still comfortable in using ECM, since as Beck and Katz argue in the case of social security data in time horizons similar to ours, "if the series are stationary but adjust very slowly, the EC (or equivalent ADL) model is a good place to start, and if the series are integrated, either the EC model will work (the series are said to be co-integrated) or the residuals will appear highly correlated." (2011, pp. 343–344).

With regards to our error correction models, it is important to highlight that the short-term impacts of a given variable come from the yearly change in that variable, while the long-term impacts come from the lagged version of that variable. The measure of long-term impact of a variable is not given by the regression coefficient directly, but instead by the Long Run Multiplier (LRM), which is calculated as the coefficient for the lagged variable divided by the negative coefficient of the lagged dependent variable and presented in an additional column in table 4.1. Standard errors and significance are then obtained through the Bewley transformation method (De Boef and Keele 2008). These models are estimated using country- and year-fixed effect variables, to capture country-specific and year-specific variations.

4.3.4 Data

The bulk of our data comes from the 2016 Huber, Stephens, Mustillo, and Pribble datasets, the Banks dataset, and the World Bank's World Development Indicators, Database of Political Institutions and Global Financial Development Database (Beck et al. 2001; Huber et al. 2008; World Bank 2022a; 2022b). To the extent that they differ, we note the differences below.

4.3.4.1 Dependent Variables

Our first set of models have four different dependent variables, all from the Huber et al dataset: government spending on healthcare as a share of GDP, government spending on education as a share of GDP, government spending on Social Security and Welfare as a share of GDP, and total government spending as a share of GDP.

The second set of models estimate the impact of different variables on a country's sovereign risk rating. We transformed existing letter ratings into numbers (see figure 4.1 below) and averaged the risk rating given to each country.

Finally, the last set of models predicts two different types of economic crises: defaults and banking crises. The data comes from Reinhart and other sources (Reinhart et al. 2021).

4.3.4.2 *Independent Variables*

Political variables: The democracy variable is built the same way as Huber, Mustillo, and Stephens constructed it, as a cumulative measure of years under democracy since 1945. A measure of leftist partisanship of the chief of government is taken from the World Bank's DPI, and used in cumulative form as well.

S&P	Fitch	Moody's	
AAA	23 AAA	24 Aaa	21
AA+	22 AA+	23 Aa1	20
AA	21 AA	22 Aa2	19
AA-	20 AA-	21 Aa3	18
A+	19 A+	20 A1	17
A	18 A	19 A2	16
A-	17 A-	18 A3	15
BBB+	16 BBB+	17 Baa1	14
BBB	15 BBB	16 Baa2	13
BBB-	14 BBB-	15 Baa3	12
BB+	13 BB+	14 Ba1	11
BB	12 BB	13 Ba2	10
BB-	11 BB-	12 Ba3	9
B+	10 B+	11 B1	8
B	9 B	10 B2	7
B-	8 B-	9 B3	6
CCC+	7 CCC+	8 Caa1	5
CCC	6 CCC	7 Caa2	4
CCC-	5 CCC-	6 Caa3	3
CC	4 CC	5 Ca	2
C	3 C	4 C	1
D	2 DDD	3	
SD	1 DD	2	
	D	1	

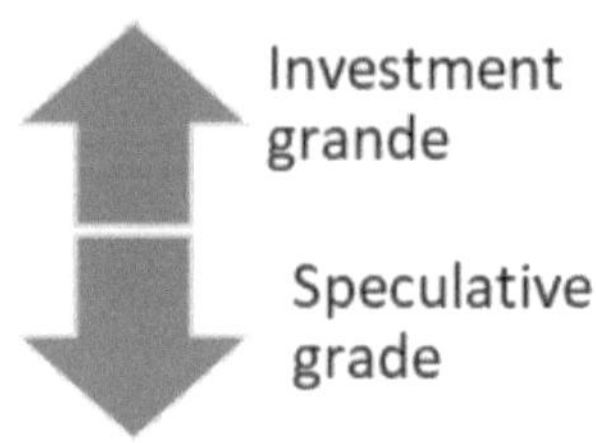

Figure 4.1 Converting Sovereign Risk Ratings to Numbers. *Source*: Data Sourced from Pinheiro (2021).

General Strikes: General strikes, which Tenorio (2014) refers to as "organized labor protests" comes from the Banks dataset.

GDP per capita at 2010 constant dollars levels lagged one year: Obtained from the World Development Indicators. Serves as an indication of the relative wealth of particular nations. Here we use the natural log of the GDP per capita.

Demographic data: Demographic data used both for the per capita measures above and for the share of the population who live in urban areas and of different age ranges all come from the World Bank's World Development Indicators.

Economic control variables: Inflation, trade, and external debt as percentage of GDP all come from the World Bank's WDI.

Financialization: Following Kaplan, we measure financialization as a share of the government's debt that is tied to bonds and other securities. That is, the share of the external debt that is tied to international financial markets rather than bilateral or multilateral loans. This is estimated by using the World Bank's measure of Outstanding International Public Debt Securities and dividing it by the total external debt.

4.3.5 Results

Table 4.1 presents the results of the error correction models for different measures of spending estimated for this chapter. Variables preceded by a "D." indicate short-term effects of that variable, while those with an "L." refer to long-term effects. The long-term effects, as well as their significance level, are presented in a separate column.

The first and most important finding is that in most of our models, who a country owes money to has a significant, negative long-run impact on social spending. This is the case even when controlling for the amount of debt a country has. In fact, our models indicate external debt is positively associated with higher spending, long term, indicating that austerity isn't necessarily a response to indebtedness. Austerity, instead, seems to be tied to the role of bond markets in government financing. But that austerity is not consistent across the board: it is not significant when it comes to social security, and overall government spending actually increases, according to our models.

With regards to control variables, it is unsurprising that GDP per capita is associated, in both the short and the long term, with increased levels of government spending: the only coefficient that is not significant is for the short-term effects of GDP per capita variations on health care spending. Demographic variables, for the most part, seem to have negative long-term impacts on spending. While this may seem surprising for some of the

Table 4.1 Results of Error Correction Models

	Health Spending		*Education Spending*		*Social Security*		*Total Public Spending*	
VARIABLES	*LRM*		*LRM*		*LRM*		*LRM*	
Lagged Dependent Variable	−0.423***		−0.530***		−0.302***		−0.451***	
	(0.057)		(0.059)		(0.075)		(0.079)	
L.GDP Per Capita	1.603**	3.791***	−1.188*	−2.244***	0.990	3.283**	−6.471	−14.361***
	(0.717)	(0.669)	(0.651)	(0.666)	(1.322)	(1.288)	(4.988)	(4.829)
D.GDP Per Capita	0.826		0.711		2.133		−9.906	
	(1.248)		(1.287)		(1.954)		(8.251)	
L.Trade percentage of GDP	0.003	0.006	0.004	0.008	−0.019*	−0.063***	0.076**	0.169***
	(0.007)	(0.007)	(0.006)	(0.006)	(0.011)	(0.010)	(0.036)	(0.040)
D.Trade percentage of GDP	0.000		−0.012		0.020		0.023	
	(0.008)		(0.008)		(0.013)		(0.047)	
L.percentage Urban Population	0.023	0.055*	0.118***	0.222***	−0.050	−0.164***	0.184	0.408
	(0.032)	(0.033)	(0.031)	(0.032)	(0.047)	(0.047)	(0.272)	(0.269)
D.percentage Urban Population	−1.313***		−1.120***		−0.720		3.180**	
	(0.348)		(0.325)		(0.525)		(1.612)	
L.percentage population over 65	0.509**	1.203***	−0.255	−0.481*	1.167**	3.869***	0.454	1.007
	(0.258)	(0.254)	(0.275)	(0.275)	(0.501)	(0.546)	(1.842)	(1.843)
D.percentage population over 65	−3.073		−4.895**		−2.156		14.891	
	(1.979)		(1.927)		(2.691)		(15.589)	
L.percentage Population 0–14	−0.020	−0.047	−0.171**	−0.324***	−0.001	−0.004	1.071	2.376***
	(0.076)	(0.075)	(0.071)	(0.067)	(0.110)	(0.110)	(0.938)	(0.895)

D.percentage Population 0–14	−1.123**		−0.570		−2.036**		2.684	
	(0.525)		(0.450)		(0.798)		(2.974)	
L.cumulative Democracy	−0.118	−0.279**	0.037	0.070	−0.198	−0.656***	−0.323	−0.717
	(0.107)	(0.109)	(0.108)	(0.108)	(0.185)	(0.176)	(0.759)	(0.753)
D.cumulative Democracy	−0.026		0.267		−0.308		0.103	
	(0.155)		(0.170)		(0.271)		(1.011)	
L.cumulative Left Rule	0.137	0.324***	0.139	0.262***	0.213	0.705***	1.397**	3.101***
	(0.109)	(0.107)	(0.098)	(0.095)	(0.141)	(0.147)	(0.555)	(0.592)
D.cumulative Left Rule	0.077		0.240**		−0.038		0.643	
	(0.138)		(0.119)		(0.161)		(0.580)	
L.percentage of external debt in Bonds and other Securities	−0.012**	−0.028***	−0.007	−0.013***	0.001	0.002	0.047	0.104***
	(0.005)	(0.005)	(0.004)	(0.004)	(0.008)	(0.008)	(0.032)	(0.031)
D.percentage of external debt in Bonds and other Securities	−0.003		−0.009		−0.005		0.129***	
	(0.006)		(0.006)		(0.010)		(0.041)	
L.Inflation	−0.000	−0.000	0.000	0.000	−0.000	−0.001*	−0.060**	−0.133***
	(0.000)	(0.000)	(0.000)	(0.000)	(0.000)	(0.000)	(0.028)	(0.031)
D.Inflation	−0.000		0.000*		−0.000		−0.018	
	(0.000)		(0.000)		(0.000)		(0.026)	
L.External Debt percentage of GNI	−0.001	−0.003	−0.005**	−0.009***	−0.005	−0.016***	−0.032*	−0.071***
	(0.002)	(0.002)	(0.002)	(0.002)	(0.004)	(0.004)	(0.018)	(0.017)
D.External Debt percentage of GNI	−0.002		−0.007*		−0.007		−0.031	
	(0.004)		(0.004)		(0.006)		(0.023)	

(*continued*)

Table 4.1 Continued

	Health Spending		*Education Spending*		*Social Security*		*Total Public Spending*	
VARIABLES	*LRM*		*LRM*		*LRM*		*LRM*	
L.Strikes	0.035	0.083	0.141**	0.266***	0.041	0.137	–0.298	–0.661*
	(0.060)	(0.060)	(0.064)	(0.064)	(0.101)	(0.100)	(0.383)	(0.381)
D.Strikes	0.005		0.054		0.056		-0.043	
	(0.050)		(0.050)		(0.084)		(0.294)	
Constant	–19.006***	–44.949***	13.020**	24.586***	–13.045	–43.248***	6.572	14.586
	(6.452)	(6.400)	(6.348)	(6.294)	(11.487)	(11.092)	(66.277)	(66.320)
Observations	227	227	226	226	217	217	168	168
R-squared	0.417	0.939	0.525	0.887	0.366	0.938	0.472	0.953
N	227	227	226	226	217	217	168	168
r2	0.417	0.939	0.525	0.887	0.366	0.938	0.472	0.953
chi2	157.4	2807	246.4	1771	122.4	4881	138.6	3912

Standard errors in parentheses
*** p<0.01, ** p<0.05, * p<0.1
Source: Authors' estimates

variables, like education or social security spending, very young or very old populations also affect the age dependency ratio, and a smaller share of the population that is of economically active age will negatively impact a government's tax revenue, and, consequently, their ability to spend.

Openness to trade has a negative long-run impact on spending on social security and total spending. This indicates that unlike what the literature has found for European nations, in Latin America it is the competition hypothesis that seems to hold: the bigger the share of international trade in the economy, the lower the spending on social security and total spending.

On the political side, our results are also unsurprising: democracies tend to spend more, with significant effects in education and social security, and left-wing government has a significant long-run impact across three of the four types of spending analyzed here. Differences with previous research that found limited effects of left-wing parties may be due to the fact that as our sample includes more recent years, the full effect of the rise of the so-called pink wave. Likewise, our results also show the importance of labor activism, with the number of strikes per year having a long-term positive effect on all four types of spending.

This brings us to the second set of models. Here the main question is why owing money to private actors in financial markets would lead to greater pressure toward austerity than owing money to other states or multilateral institutions. Table 4.2 contains the results of error correction models trying to estimate the average sovereign risk rating for particular countries (where a higher grade means a safer investment). Here most of the results for control variables are unsurprising. A previous history of defaults, left-wing rule and trade openness all lead to long-term negative effects on risk ratings, while higher GDP and a longer history of democracy lead to higher ratings. Also unsurprisingly, overall spending also has a long-term negative effect on risk ratings. What is more surprising, however, is that higher spending on education and social security, but not health, also leads to lower ratings. That is, credit agencies punish countries that spend more on education and social security, regardless of overall spending.

The question then becomes if this punishment is evidence based. Table 4.3 presents odds ratios for the equations trying to predict both sovereign default and banking crises. External debt is the main predictor of both, and interestingly share of debt held in bonds reduces the likelihood of defaults but increases the likelihood of banking crises. But more importantly, there is no evidence that different types of social spending are associated with either defaults or banking crises.

Table 4.2 Predictors of Sovereign Risk Ratings

	Education Spending Impact on Avg. Ratings		*Health Spending Impact on Avg. Ratings*		*SS Spending Impact on Avg. Ratings*		*Total Spending Impact on Avg. Ratings*	
VARIABLES	*LRM*		*LRM*		*LRM*		*LRM*	
Lagged Dependent Variable	−0.228***		−0.211***		−0.144***		−0.209***	
	(0.047)		(0.047)		(0.046)		(0.052)	
D.Cumulative Years in Default	−0.322***		−0.307***		−0.263***		−0.293***	
	(0.059)		(0.060)		(0.057)		(0.073)	
L.Cumulative Years in Default	−0.143**	−0.628***	−0.123**	−0.584***	-0.127**	-0.883***	-0.032	-0.154*
	(0.061)	(0.058)	(0.061)	(0.059)	(0.059)	(0.062)	(0.085)	(0.083)
D.GDP per capita	3.512***		3.445***		3.204***		4.196***	
	(0.529)		(0.528)		(0.512)		(0.604)	
L.GDP per capita	0.727**	3.189***	0.732**	3.469***	0.541*	3.753***	0.639*	3.050***
	(0.300)	(0.299)	(0.307)	(0.318)	(0.289)	(0.298)	(0.336)	(0.371)
D.Trade as percentage of GDP	0.009**		0.010**		0.011***		0.007	
	(0.004)		(0.004)		(0.004)		(0.004)	
L.Trade as percentage of GDP	−0.003	−0.013***	−0.003	−0.012***	−0.002	−0.013***	−0.003	−0.013***
	(0.002)	(0.003)	(0.002)	(0.002)	(0.002)	(0.002)	(0.003)	(0.003)
D.Cumulative Democracy	0.004		−0.012		−0.021		0.016	
	(0.069)		(0.070)		(0.066)		(0.070)	
L.Cumulative Democracy	0.125***	0.549***	0.117**	0.557***	0.082*	0.566***	0.170***	0.813***
	(0.044)	(0.043)	(0.046)	(0.044)	(0.042)	(0.041)	(0.047)	(0.048)
D.Cumulative Left Rule	−0.012		−0.023		−0.016		−0.001	
	(0.061)		(0.060)		(0.059)		(0.061)	
L.Cumulative Left Rule	−0.050	−0.221***	−0.063	−0.296***	−0.052	−0.361***	−0.041	−0.194***
	(0.057)	(0.057)	(0.050)	(0.049)	(0.047)	(0.046)	(0.055)	(0.053)

D.percentage of external debt in Bonds and other Securities	0.003		0.003		0.002		0.007	
	(0.003)		(0.003)		(0.003)		(0.004)	
L.percentage of external debt in Bonds and other Securities	−0.005**	−0.022***	−0.005**	−0.023***	−0.004*	−0.026***	−0.004	−0.018***
	(0.002)	(0.002)	(0.002)	(0.002)	(0.002)	(0.002)	(0.002)	(0.003)
D.Inflation	0.000***		0.000**		0.000**		0.003	
	(0.000)		(0.000)		(0.000)		(0.002)	
L.Inflation	−0.000	−0.000	−0.000	−0.000	−0.000	−0.000	−0.001	−0.002
	(0.000)	(0.000)	(0.000)	(0.000)	(0.000)	(0.000)	(0.002)	(0.002)
D.External Debt percentage of GNI	−0.007***		−0.007***		−0.008***		−0.007***	
	(0.002)		(0.002)		(0.002)		(0.002)	
L.External Debt percentage of GNI	−0.001	−0.007***	−0.001	−0.007***	−0.001	−0.008***	−0.003	−0.012***
	(0.001)	(0.001)	(0.001)	(0.001)	(0.001)	(0.001)	(0.002)	(0.002)
D.Education Spending	−0.045*							
	(0.027)							
L.Education Spending	−0.019	−0.085***						
	(0.021)	(0.021)						
D.Health Spending			−0.033					
			(0.029)					
L.Health Spending			−0.003	−0.016				
			(0.018)	(0.018)				
D.SS Spending					−0.011			
					(0.015)			
L.SS Spending					−0.013	−0.093***		
					(0.010)	(0.012)		

(continued)

Table 4.2 Continued

	Education Spending Impact on Avg. Ratings		*Health Spending Impact on Avg. Ratings*		*SS Spending Impact on Avg. Ratings*		*Total Spending Impact on Avg. Ratings*	
VARIABLES	*LRM*		*LRM*		*LRM*		*LRM*	
D.Government Spending							−0.012**	0.020***
							(0.006)	(0.007)
L.Government Spending							−0.017***	−0.079***
							(0.006)	(0.006)
Constant	−5.778**	−25.336***	−5.976**	−28.323***	−4.290	−29.743***	−5.572*	−26.610***
	(2.714)	(2.718)	(2.766)	(2.858)	(2.614)	(2.668)	(3.122)	(3.426)
Observations	196	196	198	198	193	193	172	172
R–squared	0.713	0.960	0.710	0.960	0.709	0.964	0.664	0.956
N	196	196	198	198	193	193	172	172
r2	0.713	0.960	0.710	0.960	0.709	0.964	0.664	0.956
chi2	449.4	5093	432.4	4871	443.8	5338	253.2	3777

Standard errors in parentheses
*** $p < 0.01$, ** $p < 0.05$, * $p < 0.1$
Source: Authors' estimates

Table 4.3 Predictor of Crises

	(1)	(2)	(3)
	Default		Crisis Index
VARIABLES		/	
F.rr_debt_default_ext2			
lgdppc2010	1.478		0.878
	(1.544)		(0.185)
TradeofGDPNETRDGNFSZS	0.904**		0.987*
	(0.043)		(0.007)
cumdemoc	10.353*		1.090
	(13.822)		(0.216)
cumleftdpi	0.865		1.099
	(0.832)		(0.188)
sharebonddebt	0.926**		1.013*
	(0.031)		(0.007)
rr_inflationannual	1.000		1.000
	(0.001)		(0.000)
externaldebtstocksofgnidtdoddect	1.161***		1.008**
	(0.045)		(0.004)
cseduc	0.739		0.941
	(0.422)		(0.092)
cshlth	1.128		0.959
	(0.461)		(0.072)
csssw	0.892		0.958
	(0.234)		(0.052)
time	1.276		0.925
	(0.627)		(0.096)
time2	0.982		1.014
	(0.062)		(0.013)
time3	1.000		0.999
	(0.002)		(0.000)
deficitifs	0.796**		0.975
	(0.092)		(0.016)
/		.	
		(.)	
lnsig2u		0.000	
		(0.000)	
F.rr_bcdi_index			.
			(.)
/lnalpha			0.000
			(0.000)
Constant	0.001		
	(0.009)		
Constant F.rr_bcdi_index			10.101
			(18.457)
Observations	140	140	140
Number of imfcode	11	11	11

(continued)

Table 4.3 Continued

	(1)	(2)	(3)
	Default		*Crisis Index*
VARIABLES		/	
N	140	140	140
r2	.	.	.
chi2	30.21	30.21	47.72

seEform in parentheses
*** $p < 0.01$, ** $p < 0.05$, * $p < 0.1$
Source: Authors' estimates

4.4 CONCLUSION

In this chapter we have analyzed the impact of financialization on different aspects of government spending and deregulation. The impact of financialization on different dimensions of social spending is a novel area of research. Here, we show that financialization leads to long-term declines in spending on health, education, and overall spending. These pressures likely happen because markets punish governments that spend too much on social programs, out of fear that cutting those programs would prove too unpopular. But evidence shows that social spending is not directly related to either defaults or banking crises. This suggests that financialization instead serves as a way through which external policy paradigms take hold over Latin American politics.

The models predicting sovereign risk ratings show that credit rating agencies consistently penalize spending of most kinds: only health spending is not statistically significant, but its LRM is still negative, barely missing significance in a one-tailed test. This indicates a remarkable consistency in the views that shape CRA reports. Unsurprisingly, then, the bond markets that so heavily count on sovereign risk ratings serve as a source of negative pressure on social spending. Here it is worthwhile discussing how the particular pattern of results fits in with the perspective that financialization promoted a particular form of austerity. Education and healthcare are deeply affected by financialization, while social security is not. To understand this particular pattern, two possibilities are suggested by the literature. The first is that social security reform, with its well-defined set of beneficiaries, may face much greater public scrutiny in the event of proposed cuts (Tenorio 2014). The second, and perhaps equally important reason is that as Latin American nations originally set up their retirement and pension systems in a pay-go structure, any reforms or cuts to social security entitlements may take years, if not decades to manifest themselves. Chile's famous example of privatizing its social security system led to a significant increase in government spending during the transition, and it wasn't until the late 1980s that government spending on social security returned to 1980s levels (Mesa-Lago 2008).

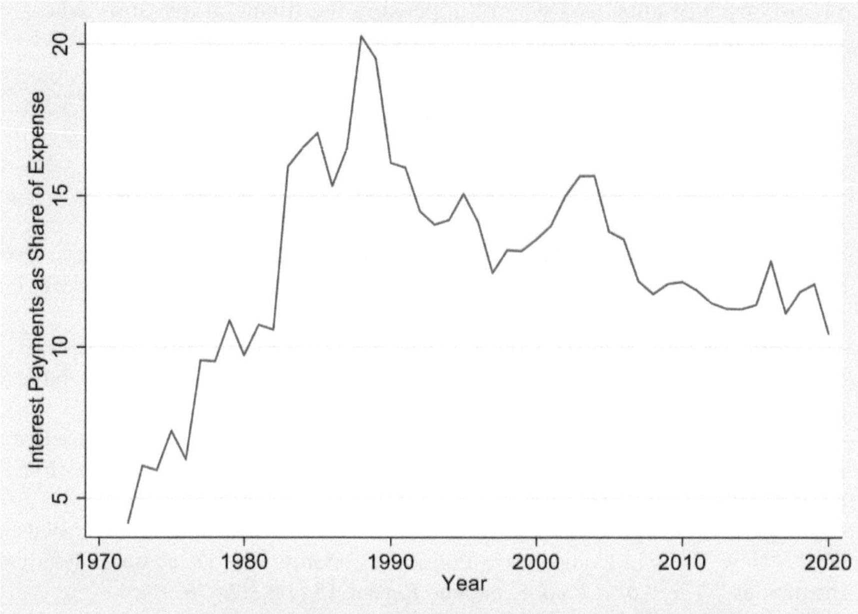

Figure 4.2 Average Interest Payments as Share of Government Expense. *Source*: Data Sourced from World Bank (2022a).

Finally, at first sight, we have a result that seems at odds with the narrative of financialization and austerity shared so far: our models indicate financialization seems to have a long term, positive association with overall government spending. But there is a clear explanation for that result: the emergence of bond markets as the main financiers of governments in the region during the 1980s coincides with a surge in interest payments by central governments. Figure 4.2 shows the average for interest payments as a share of total government spending for the region:

Interest payments went from an average of just under 5 percent of all spending in the early 1970s to around 20 percent by the late 1980s. And it is perhaps here that one of the ideological components of financialization becomes clear: as the demands of bond markets demand higher interest rates and a potential deterioration of government accounts, economists at the IMF and elsewhere came up with a new method of calculating government deficits: in the late 1980s and early 1990s the measure of "primary deficit," calculated as government deficit excluding interest repayments, became widely used (Blejer and Cheasty 1992). Overall deficits mattered less than primary deficits in the eyes of institutions like the IMF. Governments are supposed to balance their budgets but cutting elsewhere, but not cutting interest repayments.

Taken all together, this paints a very clear picture of the impact of financialization on governments: discretionary spending on social needs is to be the main target of cuts, as a way of appeasing the financial investors who are key in funding the government.

BIBLIOGAPHY

Abu-El-Haj, J. 2007. "From Interdependence to Neo-Mercantilism." *Latin American Perspectives* 34 (5): 92–114.

Afonso, A. 2003. "Understanding the Determinants of Sovereign Debt Ratings: Evidence for the Two Leading Agencies." *Journal of Economics and Finance* 27 (1): 56–74.

Babb, Sarah. 2005. "The Social Consequences of Structural Adjustment: Recent Evidence and Current Debates." *Annual Review of Sociology* 31 (1): 199–222. https://doi.org/10.1146/annurev.soc.31.041304.122258.

———. 2013. "The Washington Consensus as Transnational Policy Paradigm: Its Origins, Trajectory and Likely Successor." *Review of International Political Economy* 20 (2): 268–97.

Beck, Thorsten, George Clarke, Alberto Groff, Philip Keefer, and Patrick Walsh. 2001. "New Tools in Comparative Political Economy: The Database of Political Institutions." *The World Bank Economic Review* 15 (1): 165–76.

Biglaiser, Glen, and K. DeRouen. 2007. "Sovereign Bond Ratings and Neoliberalism in Latin America." *International Studies Quarterly* 51 (1): 121–38.

Blejer, Mario, and Adrienne Cheasty. 1992. "How to Measure the Fiscal Deficit." *Finance and Development* 29 (3): 40–42.

Block, Fred L. 1977. *The Origins of International Economic Disorder : A Study of United States International Monetary Policy from World War II to the Present.* Berkeley: University of California Press.

Blyth, Mark. 2002. *Great Transformations : Economic Ideas and Institutional Change in the Twentieth Century.* Cambridge; New York: Cambridge University Press.

Boix, Carles. 2001. "Democracy, Development, and the Public Sector." *American Journal of Political Science* 45(1): 1–17.

Bouchet, Michel Henry, Charles A. Fishkin, and Amaury Goguel. 2018. "Country Risk in the Age of Globalization: Cycles and Dynamics. A Review of Literature." In *Managing Country Risk in an Age of Globalization,* edited by Michel Henry Bouchet, Charles A. Fishkin and Amaury Goguel, 53–92. Palgrave Macmillan.

Brown, David S., and Wendy Hunter. 1999. "Democracy and Social Spending in Latin America, 1980–92." *American Political Science Review* 93 (04): 779–90.

Burgoon, Brian. 2001. "Globalization and Welfare Compensation: Disentangling the Ties That Bind." *International Organization* 55 (03): 509–51.

Cameron, David R. 1978. "The Expansion of the Public Economy: A Comparative Analysis." *American Political Science Review* 72 (04): 1243–61.

Cantor, R., and F. Packer. 1997. "Differences of Opinion and Selection Bias in the Credit Rating Industry." *Journal of Banking & Finance* 21 (10): 1395–1417.

Chwieroth, J.M. 2009. *Capital Ideas: The IMF and the Rise of Financial Liberalization.* Princeton University Press.

Dezalay, Yves, and Bryant G. Garth. 2002. *The Internationalization of Palace Wars : Lawyers, Economists, and the Contest to Transform Latin American States*. The Chicago Series in Law and Society. Chicago: University of Chicago Press.

Elio Gaspari. 2000. "Wall Street Não Quer Sangue, Quer Dinheiro." *Folha de Sao Paulo*, May 24. https://www1.folha.uol.com.br/fsp/brasil/fc2405200024.htm.

Frenkel, Roberto, and Guillermo O'Donnell. 1994. "The 'Stabilization Programs' of the International Monetary Fund and Their Internal Impacts." In *Money Doctors, Foreign Debts, and Economics Reforms in Latin America from the 1890s to the Present*, edited by Paul W. Drake, 159–74. Wilmington, DE: Scholarly Resources Inc.

Friedman, Thomas L., dir. 1996. *Interview with Thomas Friedman*. PBS.

Garrett, Geoffrey, and Deborah Mitchell. 2001. "Globalization, Government Spending and Taxation in the OECD." *European Journal of Political Research* 39 (2): 145–77.

Gültekin-Karakaş, Derya, Mehtap Hisarcıklılar, and Hüseyin Öztürk. 2011. "Sovereign Risk Ratings: Biased Toward Developed Countries?" *Emerging Markets Finance and Trade* 47 (Sup2): 69–87. https://doi.org/10.2753/REE1540-496X4703S204.

Haggard, Stephan, and Robert R. Kaufman. 2008. *Development, Democracy, and Welfare States: Latin America, East Asia, and Eastern Europe*. Princeton University Press. https://books.google.com/books?hl=en&lr=&id=9hNpt49NHQcC&oi=fnd&pg=PR12&dq=Haggard+and+Kaufman,+2008&ots=6JtDRx-6J8&sig=OzXgBJV0oTU7HtyAh48pLRTF9Y0.

Hall, Peter A. 1993. "Policy Paradigms, Social Learning, and the State: The Case of Economic Policy Making in Britain." *Comparative Politics* 25 (3): 275–96.

Harberger, Arnold C. 1996. "Good Economics Comes to Latin America." In *The Post-1945 Internationalization of Economics*, edited by A. W. Coats, 301–11. Durham, NC: Duke University Press.

Henisz, Witold J., Bennet A. Zelner, and Mauro F. Guillén. 2005. "The Worldwide Diffusion of Market-Oriented Infrastructure Reform, 1977–1999." *American Sociological Review* 70 (6): 871–97.

Hicks, Alexander M. 1999. *Social Democracy & Welfare Capitalism: A Century of Income Security Politics*. Cornell University Press. https://books.google.com/books?hl=en&lr=&id=Ya5n2SntjRwC&oi=fnd&pg=PR9&dq=alexander+hicks+1999&ots=pj99WQvojU&sig=b6XA8_MrKhqlbiCGZt9IkV-GqZc.

Huber, Evelyne, Thomas Mustillo, and John D. Stephens. 2008. "Politics and Social Spending in Latin America." *The Journal of Politics* 70 (02): 420–36.

Huber, Evelyne, and John D. Stephens. 2001. *Development and Crisis of the Welfare State: Parties and Policies in Global Markets*. University of Chicago press. https://books.google.com/books?hl=en&lr=&id=Xppszgpm-boC&oi=fnd&pg=PR9&dq=huber+and+stephens&ots=BXDX7RDWrU&sig=xoXeaQfqB94YV5K8gmQiBCqwJCY.

———. 2012. *Democracy and the Left: Social Policy and Inequality in Latin America*. University of Chicago Press.

Huber, Evelyne, John D. Stephens, Thomas Mustillo, and Jennifer Pribble. 2008. *Social Policy in Latin America and the Caribbean Dataset, 1960–2006*. University of North Carolina.

ISTOÉ. 2000. "Afasta de mim esta torta," May 29. https://istoe.com.br/37776_AFASTA DE MIM ESTA TORTA/.

Jensen, Carsten. 2011. "Two Sides of the Same Coin? Left-Wing Governments and Labour Unions as Determinants of Public Spending." *Socio-Economic Review*, mwr015.

Kaplan, Stephen B. 2013. *Globalization and Austerity Politics in Latin America*. Cambridge University Press.

———. 2018. "Fighting Past Economic Wars: Crisis and Austerity in Latin America." *Latin American Research Review* 53 (1): 19–37. https://doi.org/10.25222/larr.292.

Kaplan, Stephen B., and Kaj Thomsson. 2017. "The Political Economy of Sovereign Debt: Global Finance and Electoral Cycles." *The Journal of Politics* 79 (2): 605–23. https://doi.org/10.1086/688441.

Kaufman, Robert R., and Alex Segura-Ubiergo. 2001. "Globalization, Domestic Politics, and Social Spending in Latin America: A Time-Series Cross-Section Analysis, 1973–97." *World Politics* 53 (04): 553–87.

Kiff, John, Sylwia Barbara Nowak, and Liliana B. Schumacher. 2012. "Are Rating Agencies Powerful? An Investigation into the Impact and Accuracy of Sovereign Ratings." SSRN Scholarly Paper ID 1997736. Rochester, NY: Social Science Research Network.

Kogut, Bruce, and J. Muir Macpherson. 2011. "The Mobility of Economists and the Diffusion of Policy Ideas: The Influence of Economics on National Policies." *Research Policy* 40 (10): 1307–20.

Mares, Isabela, and Matthew E. Carnes. 2009. "Social Policy in Developing Countries." *Annual Review of Political Science* 12: 93.

Mesa-Lago, Carmelo. 2008. *Reassembling Social Security: A Survey of Pensions and Health Care Reforms in Latin America: A Survey of Pensions and Health Care Reforms in Latin America*. Oxford University Press. https://books.google.com/books?hl=en&lr=&id=2nGWZc0qncAC&oi=fnd&pg=PR13&dq=Mesa-Lago,+2008&ots=GIAzdaqnZ2&sig=bkxRG6KyLKfk2s4JJP4FbSAL49I.

Meyer, John W., and Brian Rowan. 1977. "Institutionalized Organizations: Formal Structure as Myth and Ceremony." *American Journal of Sociology* 83(2): 340–63.

Montecinos, Verónica. 1998. *Economists, Politics and the State: Chile 1958–1994*. CEDLA Amsterdam. http://www.sidalc.net/cgi-bin/wxis.exe/?IsisScript=SIBE01.xis&method=post&formato=2&cantidad=1&expresion=mfn=014026.

Morgan, Jana, and Nathan J. Kelly. 2013. "Market Inequality and Redistribution in Latin America and the Caribbean." *The Journal of Politics* 75 (03): 672–85.

Noy, Shiri. 2011. "New Contexts, Different Patterns? A Comparative Analysis of Social Spending and Government Health Expenditure in Latin America and the OECD." *International Journal of Comparative Sociology* 52 (3): 215–44.

Pampel, Fred C., and John B. Williamson. 1988. "Welfare Spending in Advanced Industrial Democracies, 1950–1980." *American Journal of Sociology* 93(6): 1424–56.

Partnoy, F. 1999. "The Siskel and Ebert of Financial Markets: Two Thumbs down for the Credit Rating Agencies." *Washington University Law Quarterly* 77: 619–712.

———. 2006. "How and Why Credit Rating Agencies Are Not Like Other Gatekeepers." In *Financial Gatekeepers: Can They Protect Investors?* edited by Yasuyuki Fuchita and Robert E. Litan, 59, 83–86.

Pinheiro, Diogo L. 2020. "The Origins of Sovereign Risk Ratings: Explaining the When and Why." *Comparative Sociology* 19 (3): 388–414.

———. 2021. "Sovereign Risk Ratings in Latin America: Measures of Economic Conditions or Policy Paradigm Compliance?" *Journal of Global South Studies* 38 (2): 343–73.

Pinheiro, Diogo L., Jeffrey M. Chwieroth, and Alexander Hicks. 2015. "Do International Non-Governmental Organizations Inhibit Globalization? The Case of Capital Account Liberalization in Developing Countries." *European Journal of International Relations* 21 (1): 146–70.

Reinhart, C., K. Rogoff, C. Trebesch, and V. Reinhart. 2021. "Global Crises Data by Country." *Behavioral Finance & Financial Stability*. https://www.hbs.edu/behavioral-finance-and-financial-stability/data/Pages/global.aspx.

Rodrik, Dani. 2006. "Goodbye Washington Consensus, Hello Washington Confusion? A Review of the World Bank's *Economic Growth in the 1990s: Learning from a Decade of Reform*." *Journal of Economic Literature* 44 (4): 973–87. https://doi.org/10.1257/jel.44.4.973.

Rudra, Nita. 2002. "Globalization and the Decline of the Welfare State in Less-Developed Countries." *International Organization* 56 (02): 411–45.

Tenorio, Barbara Zarate. 2014. "Social Spending Responses to Organized Labor and Mass Protests in Latin America, 1970–2007." *Comparative Political Studies* 47(14), 1945–1972.

Vreeland, James Raymond. 2003. *The IMF and Economic Development*. Cambridge ; New York: Cambridge University Press.

———. 2007. *The International Monetary Fund: Politics of Conditional Lending*. New York, NY: Routledge.

Wibbels, E. 2006. "Dependency Revisited: International Markets, Business Cycles, and Social Spending in the Developing World." *International Organization* 60 (02): 433–68.

World Bank. 2022a. "Global Financial Development Database." Text/HTML. World Bank. https://www.worldbank.org/en/publication/gfdr/data/global-financial-development-database.

———. 2022b. *World Development Indicators*. Washington, DC: International Bank for Reconstruction and Development.

Chapter 5

Financialization, Social Policy, and Social Inclusion

In chapter 4 we learned about the effects of international bond markets on government social spending in LAC. Typically, the size of international debt securities relative to GDP has resulted in a long-term decline in government health and education spending but not in aggregate social welfare outlay.

These findings support our thesis that the politics of austerity has gone hand in hand with market ideology and financialization in the region. They also illustrate how global finance has shaped the composition of social spending in the region. However, these results do not test the social outcomes of financialization, an important issue, especially since financial markets and services have become instruments of public policy and development. Further, we noted in chapter 3 that the expansion of global markets has produced heterogeneous social results.

This chapter examines financialization's impact on extreme poverty and income inequality. By focusing on poverty and inequality, we gain purchase on social inclusiveness of financialization in LAC, one of the most unequal regions of the world. Financial inclusiveness or access to financial services and products has become a common concern among mainstream development experts. Our interest here is how welfare gains from financialization are distributed across different segments of society. We investigate how private sector credit and international private debt securities have affected absolute inclusion, approximated by extreme poverty and relative inclusion levels, measured by the Gini coefficient. We bring private sector credit back into our empirical investigation since credit has become a vehicle for fulfillment of social rights and basic needs, highlighted in chapter 2. Finally, we explore how the levels of poverty and inequality correlate with access to vaccines and excess COVID-19 deaths in the region.

The chapter begins by outlining the rationale for our approach to evaluating financialization's social effects.

5.1 POVERTY, INEQUALITY, AND INCLUSION

Greek mathematician Euclid purportedly told King Ptolemy I that there isn't a "royal road to geometry." Neither there appears to exist a royal road to the evaluation of programs, policies, and social arrangements (Sen 2000a). Our concern for efficiency, equity, effectiveness, or another issue may dictate our path, which has a bearing on the information included and, no less crucially, excluded from the assessment process. We should offer a justification for our approach to evaluate the social consequences of financialization, which has become an intensely polarizing issue.

So, why poverty? The notion that less poverty is better for society has existed since the eighteenth century (Ravallion 2016). To be sure, the premodern Chinese, Greek, and Indian civilizations also viewed poverty as undesirable, but the concern was for transient poverty and its threat to the regime's stability; eradicating poverty is a modern idea. Enlightenment thinkers, such as Adam Smith, Jean-Jacques Rousseau, Nicolas de Condorcet, and Immanuel Kant, broke away from the Mercantilist view that poverty was essential for society and its economic development. The two world wars, the Great Depression and the collapse of colonialism in the Global South, brought further shifts in the sociological imagination about poverty as a social problem that needs to be eradicated; and that the level of poverty should be the yardstick of society's progress.

Ending extreme poverty has been a symbolic goal, finding expression in the United Nations Sustainable Development Goals, whose first aim is to end extreme poverty in all forms by 2030. However, the COVID-19 pandemic has erased two decades of gain in reducing extreme poverty (U.N. 2021). An estimated 119–124 million people were pushed below the international extreme poverty line of $1.90 a day in 2020. In LAC, extreme poverty increased to levels last seen 20 years ago (ECLAC 2022b). Extreme poverty rose to 13.80 percent in 2021 from 13.10 percent in 2020, even though the overall poverty rate declined to 32.10 percent from 33.0 percent during the same period.

Moreover, maximizing the well-being of the least well-off is morally and ethically desirable (Pogge 2009; Rawls 1971; Sen 2000a). As Sen argues, the pursuit of social justice cannot be indifferent to the people's actual lives. Poverty impinges on people's substantive freedom and ability to lead the life of their choice.

Entwined with poverty is the issue of economic inequality. The current level of global inequality, the sum of between- and within-country inequalities, mirrors those witnessed at the peak of Western imperialism in the early twentieth century (Chancel et al. 2022). The within-country inequality accounted for almost two-thirds of global inequality in 2020. While the wealthiest 10 percent of the global adult population currently captures 52 percent of the worldwide income, the bottom 50 percent receives about 8.5 percent of the income.[1]

The LAC reflects the global pattern of inequality (Chancel et al. 2022). While the richest 10 percent of the population captures 55 percent of the national income in LAC, the bottom 50 percent earned 10 percent of it in 2021. The pattern points to a dual society in LAC, where one group enjoys a level of prosperity comparable to high-income countries and the other reels under extreme poverty. The region's downward trend in income inequality since 2002 came to a halt in 2022, with deterioration impacting the poorest sections more (ECLAC 2022a).

Rising inequality poses a serious economic, social, political, and moral challenge (Alesina and Rodrik 1994; Blanchard and Rodrik 2021; Ravallion 2005; Solt 2008; Stiglitz 2015). Economic inequality has implications for current and future levels of poverty. It can restrict social mobility, especially at the bottom of the income distribution. It can also be detrimental to economic stability and growth. Moreover, a high level of inequality can hamper collective action and imperil spending on common goods such as education and infrastructure.

Further, inequality weakens social cohesion and increases crime and many other social problems. Greater economic inequality can drive a steep political wedge as higher levels of inequality erode political interests among the electorate, dampen political discourse, and discourage electoral participation among all but the most affluent section of the electorate. Overall, inequality reduces social welfare since the utility derived from additional units of income is lower for the well-off.

The issue of poverty and inequality should not remain confined to income or wealth, which are important means for avoiding destitution. Poverty should be understood in terms of one's ability to partake in the community (Atkinson and Marlier 2010; Nussbaum 2000; Sen 2000a). Often, poverty and other forms of deprivation stem from social arrangements that exclude certain groups from socioeconomic activities. In LAC, various institutional mechanisms of inclusion and exclusion, rooted in privileges, identity, geography, and other factors, have sustained historically high levels of economic inequality (ECLAC 2022a).

We examine financialization's impact on extreme poverty and income inequality within the social inclusion framework, to which we will return later. Financial inclusion, that is, access and use of formal financial services, has been an important concern among scholars and policymakers alike.

Financial inclusion arguably has the potential to reduce poverty, smooth consumption, and manage financial risk as it enables people to save and invest in the future.[2] Rojas-Suárez (2016) shows that financial inclusion has been particularly challenging in Latin America because of income volatility of low-income households, lack of competition among financial institutions, low levels of trust in financial institutions, the mismatch between financial products and needs of low-income households, and paucity of knowledge about financial products.

Our interest here is in the benefit sharing—how financialization's welfare gains are shared in heterogeneous society—dimension of social inclusion. While economic resources such as income and wealth are important for understanding the material conditions of people's life, they do not reflect the non-economic dimensions of well-being. A comprehensive understanding of welfare should pay attention to peoples' health, education, capabilities or freedom to live the life of one's choice, and ability to participate in economic, political, and cultural activities. We only very briefly explore the health aspect within the limited context of COVID-19 vaccine availability and excess mortality. Further, our aim here is to evaluate how welfare benefits of financialization are shared across society. We do not attempt to provide theoretical explanation of poverty and inequality.

In the next section, we take a closer look at social inclusion and exclusion, its rise in social policy literature, economic growth and development discourse, and how extreme poverty and inequality relate to social inclusion and benefit sharing.

5.2 SOCIAL INCLUSION AND SOCIAL POLICY

If the Great Wars, Great Depression, and end of colonialism cemented the plan for poverty eradication, the economic and political transformations of the late twentieth century brought about new notions of deprivations such as social in/exclusion, new poverty, and underclass (Silver 1994). Globalization, liberalization, the knowledge economy, demographic shifts, spatial or geographical transitions, migration, climate change, and democratization are among the many factors that catapulted social inclusion onto the global agenda (Rodgers 1995; Silver 2015; World Bank 2013).

An idea derived from the concept of social exclusion, social inclusion first emerged in the social policy discourse in France, where the term was applied to a plethora of issues including, but not limited to, groups excluded from social insurance, people bypassed by economic growth and recovery process, and weakening social bonds. Social exclusion has roots in French revolutionary history and Republican thought (Sen 2000b; Silver 1994). The need for inclusion arguably arises from the demand for fraternity in the French Revolution and the related development in the eighteenth century; concern for equality demands the elimination of poverty. Exclusion implied the erosion of solidarity, a break in social bonds between individuals and society. As Silver (2015) points out, inclusion, with its "positive and affirmative" (p. 3) connotation, has to come to replace exclusion in policy discourse.

The allure of social inclusion goes beyond the French social policy discourse, however. Social inclusion has been the mainstay of the New Labor's Third Way attempt to modernize social institutions in Britain (Giddens 2000; Levitas 2005). The Copenhagen Declaration on Social Development identified social exclusion, poverty, and unemployment as urgent problems requiring attention (U.N. n.d.). The rhetoric of social inclusion has become infused in the social policy agenda in Thailand and South Korea (Jayasuriya 2006), India (Mehrotra 2016), and Brazil (Power 2001). If the Social Panorama of Latina America is any indicator, social inclusion and social exclusion have been recurring themes in the development discourse in the region since the mid-2000s (de Roldán 2012).

Social inclusion is intrinsically valuable (Sen 2000b). The ability to voluntarily partake in social, political, and economic life is important on its own; therefore, it can be a part of capability poverty. There is also instrumental value to social inclusion. Exclusion limits the opportunities available to people to live the life of their choice. Exclusion can lead to other forms of deprivation. Take the example of poverty levels in Brazil, Chile, Colombia, Ecuador, Mexico, Peru, and Uruguay. Poverty tends to be concentrated among the marginalized indigenous population and Afro-descendants' relative to the dominant group (non-indigenous and non-African descendants) in the seven countries (ECLAC 2022a). Further, sociologists emphasize the importance of inclusion for social cohesion and solidarity. Exclusion erodes collective values, destroys social fabric, and ruptures social and symbolic bonds binding individuals to society (Silver 2015). From climate change and forced displacement to rising hunger and violence against women, many of the threats to human security in the Anthropocene era demand greater solidarity (UNDP 2022). Social inclusion is indispensable to human well-being, social justice, and sustainable growth. The exclusion of individuals and groups comes at a high social, political, and economic cost to society (World Bank 2013).

Amid economic transformation and the neoliberal critique of the welfare state as economically detrimental and morally corrosive, social inclusion gained prominence in the social policy discourse. Globalization, neoliberalism, and the knowledge economy have fundamentally altered the welfare state's economic, ideological, and political foundations (Mishra 2000; Rodrik 2005). A system designed to provide a cushion against short-term unemployment and old age, the traditional social protection framework is ill-equipped to address the insecurities because of long-term job loss, displacement, obsolescence of skills, and new poverty (Hacker 2019).

The idea of social inclusion is often invoked to recast the traditional social policy into a supply-oriented welfare state variously described as a "developmental welfare state" (Midgley and Tang 2001; Riesco 2009), "active welfare" (Esping-Andersen 2002) or Third Way-welfare state modernization (Giddens 2000). Social inclusion—and not, if only a heuristic device, decommodification, or ability to maintain socially acceptable living standards independent of the market—should be the cornerstone of the welfare state in the post-Cold War era.[3] Social welfare policy can not remain divested from macroeconomic and employment policies. It should work to lower barriers and bolster opportunities for people to meet their welfare needs within the economy successfully. It should aim to address inequality of opportunity that could result from, among other things, social exclusion.

There is also a growing recognition of social inclusion's importance for economic growth and development. The 2030 agenda for sustainable development emphasizes social inclusion for the peace and prosperity of people and the planet.[4] The Commission on Growth and Development (2008) identifies social inclusion, along with accumulation, macroeconomic stability, and innovation, as a critical ingredient for sustained economic growth. This powerful economic tool has lifted millions out of poverty and transformed societies. Economic growth becomes sustainable only when its benefits are widely shared across social groups and regions. The economic success of Japan, East Asia, and Southeast Asia could well be attributed to their socially inclusive approach to development (Sen 2000b). Primary education, healthcare, and other social services helped lower the barriers to opportunities that otherwise may not have been available to a large section of the population. On the other hand, social exclusion hampers human capital development.

The altered social, economic, technological, and ideological landscape may have created the condition for embracing social inclusion in social policy and development discourse. The theoretical justification for the shift toward social inclusion has been anchored in the capability approach developed by Amartya Sen (2000a) and Martha Nussbaum (2000). In brief, the capability approach is a normative framework that places people's actual lives at the center of development policies or public policies. It claims that freedom to achieve well-being is of primary moral importance (Robeyns 2005). From this perspective, well-being or more generally, quality of life should be judged in terms of people's functioning (various doings or activities and beings or states achieved) and capabilities (freedom to enjoy various functioning). Further, the capabilities approach distinguishes between the means (necessary resources such as income) and ends (capabilities). The capability approach is sensitive to how different circumstances or conversion factors—personal conversion factors (health, sex), social conversion factors (identity, social norms), and environmental conversion factors (climate and geography)—influence the transformation of goods and services into functioning. Attention to opportunity and freedom can enrich analyses and understanding of challenges societies face (Dreze and Sen 2013).

Social exclusion directly affects capabilities or freedom to live the life one desires. Exclusion could take an active form that is deliberate and targeted, as in the case of redlining. When unintended, the social exclusion could also be passive. For example, the lack of credit in rural areas could be considered as passive exclusion, an unintended outcome of financialization.

By turning the spotlight on actual outcomes and effective opportunities for valuable functioning, the capabilities approach reconfigures inequality in ways that as Giddens (2000) maintains, are more appropriate for the post-Cold War era, when globalization and technology have created new sets of winners and losers with vastly different life chances. From the capability approach's perspective, neither utility (pleasure, happiness, or satisfaction) nor primary goods (rights, opportunities and power, income, and wealth) are the appropriate space to evaluate justice. Instead, the focus should be on the effective opportunity people have. It calls for focus on the uneven distribution of freedom and opportunities that provide fresh insight into advantages people may enjoy. In many development contexts, some have the chance for education and healthcare, while others don't. Also, inequality of opportunity impacts the ability to partake in social change. Social movements and public action can affect the government's agenda and priorities.

We want to acknowledge some of the drawbacks of the social inclusion framework that we rely upon for evaluating the social consequences of financialization. First, the language of social inclusion conjures up a vision of a good society that encourages the status quo (Levitas 2005). Social inclusion can serve many political purposes; it helps to distract from rising inequality, unemployment, class conflicts, and family breakdown (Jayasuriya 2006; Silver 1994). The talk of inclusion has facilitated the transformation of social citizenship into, what Jayasuriya calls, market citizenship where social association is mostly understood in terms of access to and participation within the market. In India, Jayala (2009) asserts the talk about inclusive growth, inclusive government, and, one may add, the current avatar of inclusiveness, *sabka saath*, *sabka vikas* (development for all) have best been "energizing slogans" (p. 363) without much actual value.

Similarly, Petras and Veltmeyer (2003) dismiss Lula's Third Way inclusion agenda as an attempt to incorporate grassroots empowerment with disempowering economic projects. Lula's Third Way policies offered limited political incorporation in the name of equality. It neglects class, state, and structural issues perpetuating and sustaining inequality.

5.2.1 Social Inclusion and Benefit Sharing

Despite its proliferation, social inclusion remains a vague term. Silver (1994; 2015) aptly points out that the conception of social inclusion changes with political philosophy. For example, Republicanism equates social inclusion with social solidarity to achieve collective goods. Exclusion is inherent in nation, race, locality, and cultural identity that define boundaries between groups. It draws attention to the culture of poverty, long-term unemployment, and the trend toward flexible specialization. Liberals envision social inclusion as state-guaranteed individual liberty, property rights, and freedom to assemble and form groups, including a network of voluntary civil associations. Finally, social democracies emphasize the social rights of citizens to a decent standard of living. Further, the meaning of inclusiveness also varies with social context and country. Consider the case of India, where social inclusion warrants a particular focus on marginalized social groups such as the scheduled castes or Dalits, scheduled tribes or indigenous populations, and minorities (Ahluwalia 2011).

Social inclusion is often narrowly defined (e.g. Ianchovichina and Gable 2012; Ianchovichina and Lundstrom 2009) in regard to labor market participation and productive employment opportunities. Inclusiveness implies "equality of opportunity in terms of access to markets, resources, and unbiased regulatory environment for businesses and individuals" (Ianchovichina and Gable 2012, 150). It often aims to move people out of low-productivity sectors or bring individuals left out of the economic growth process into the labor market. What matters for inclusion is the level of absolute poverty in society, not inequality. The focus should be on social policies such as education that enhance human capital, and not income redistribution to the excluded groups. Markets should drive the inclusion process, with the government playing the role of facilitator.

A second approach broadly conceptualizes social inclusion as a complex process with economic, social, and political dimensions. Social inclusion entails participation in all forms of social life, not just labor market participation, which is crucially important for welfare. It demands attention to how widely the benefits and opportunities are shared across all groups in a society. At the societal level, inclusion requires the broadening of social ties as well as strengthening social cohesion, integration, and solidarity. Not only poverty but inequality too matters for inclusion; inequality of outcome cannot be overlooked entirely for supposed efficiency and incentive to work because today's result has implications for future opportunities. In this view, social policy is vital for inclusion as it can lower barriers to opportunities, foster human capital, and enable risk-sharing and risk-taking. From this perspective, empowerment in social and political life is essential because it allows citizens to voice their preferences, foster accountability, and improve governance. As Cerra (2022) summarizes, 1) benefit sharing, 2) opportunity to access public services, 3) participation in economic life, and 4) empowerment in social and political life are the four broad objectives of inclusion.

Our approach here aligns with the broader understanding of social inclusion. We focus on benefit sharing. First, benefit sharing requires poverty reduction. We noted earlier that poverty is a significant source of exclusion, as a lack of resources can inhibit people from participating in society. Further, benefit sharing implies attention to inequality. Benefit sharing does not mean complete equality of outcome because of moral hazard and other perverse incentives. But Ahluwalia (2011) cautions an increase in inequality may not be accepted if it is accompanied by only modest improvement in the living standard of the poor. Moreover, inequality of outcome bears on the inequality of opportunity.

Following Cerra (2022), we use the international poverty benchmark of $1.90 a day and the Gini coefficient as measures of inclusiveness. Extreme poverty is the absolute measure of inclusiveness, focusing on the bottom of the income distribution. The Gini coefficient is the relative measure of inequality that covers the population more broadly. We address the issue of measurement in greater detail later. In passing, extreme poverty is especially high in rural areas, among the young population and ethnic and racial minorities (ECLAC 2022b). In addition, poverty and inequality have implications for access to healthcare, which is fundamental to inclusiveness.

5.3 TRENDS IN RELATIVE AND ABSOLUTE INCLUSION

We begin with a review of the overall trend in income inequality in LAC, one of the world's most unequal regions. Since economic disparity has been an enduring concern of LAC, our focus here will be on relative inclusion or income inequality.

Figure 5.1 illustrates the trend in the aggregate Gini index before tax and transfer of LAC countries since 1980. The average Gini index fell to a historic low of 46.03 in 2015 before rising again. The change, however, has not been uniform. From the lost decade of the 1980s to the Pink Wave and beyond, both economic and political forces seem to have tempered the trajectory of income inequality in the region. Inequality persisted throughout the 1980s when the region reeled under debt crises, high inflation, and faltering economic growth. On average, the mean Gini index grew by 0.03 points during

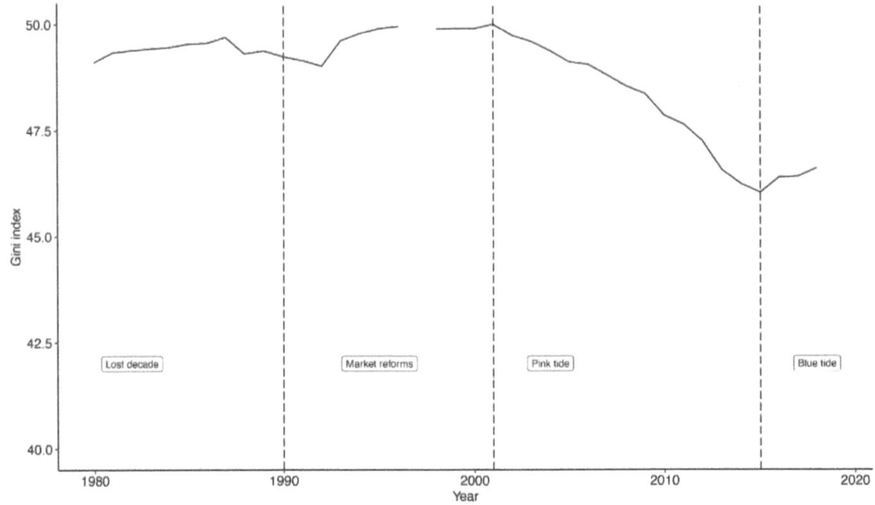

Figure 5.1 Trend in Average Gini Index. *Source*: Data Sourced from Solt (2019).

the period. We find considerable variations in the level of inequality among the countries, with the Gini index highest in Brazil (60.86) and lowest in Argentina (40.66). The income share of the poorest segment and the middle class decreased during the lost decade (Gasparini and Lustig 2011; Londoño and Székely 2000).

Inequality continued to rise during the 1990s when governments turned to market reforms. The region experienced 0.07 points increase in the average Gini between 1990 and 2002. But not all countries share the regional trend of the annual increase in average Gini index. Nicaragua, Brazil, Belize, Peru, Panama, Grenada, Guatemala, and El Salvador experienced a decline in inequality, much of the gain accruing in the late 1990s. These trends are consistent with earlier findings (e.g. Gasparini et al. 2011) based on household survey data.[5] The rise in inequality during the market-reform phase of the 1990s is attributed to an increase in the relative return to tertiary education.

The Gini index on average, dropped about 0.30 points between 2002 and 2015. The decline in inequality was widespread. Lopez-Calva and Lusting (2010) also point to an overall decline in income inequality in the region. The authors show that inequality declined in countries with different levels of historical inequalities, macroeconomic conditions, demography, inclusiveness of social policies, and ideological inclination of ruling parties. A favorable international economic environment, booming commodity prices, and a strong labor market helped bring inequality down. Left-leaning governments lowered inequality faster than the non-leftist governments, increasing the income share of the first seven deciles at the expense of the richest 10 percent of the income distribution. The graph shows that the declining inequality trend has been reversed during the Blue Tide. There has been a 1.04 points increase in the annual Gini index, driven mainly by increases in Brazil, Chile, Peru, and Costa Rica.

Let's turn our attention to the trend in aggregate absolute poverty between 1981 and 2019, summarized in figure 5.2. The average poverty headcount ratio in the region fell from 17.50 percent in 1981 to 3.07 percent in 2019. Like aggregate inequality, the decline in the proportion of people living below the international poverty line of $ 1.90 per person per day has not been smooth. The poverty rate was especially volatile during the lost decade of the 1980s when the poverty rate peaked at 27.40 percent before falling again. A similar pattern of volatility also marked the 1990s. On average, the annual change in the mean poverty rate decreased by 0.21 points in the 1990s. During the Pink Tide, the region witnessed a systematic decline in extreme poverty. The annual change in the average poverty rate fell by 0.64 points between 2001 and 2015. The downward trajectory has continued during the Blue Tide but at a slower pace. The average change in the yearly poverty rate was −0.09 between 2016 and 2019.

We noted earlier that inequality and poverty are intimately linked to each other. Unsurprisingly, poverty and inequality in the LAC generally follow similar patterns (Londoño and Székely 2000). The pace of poverty reduction tends to be lower in countries with higher income inequality; the growth elasticity of poverty reduction decreases as the income distribution becomes

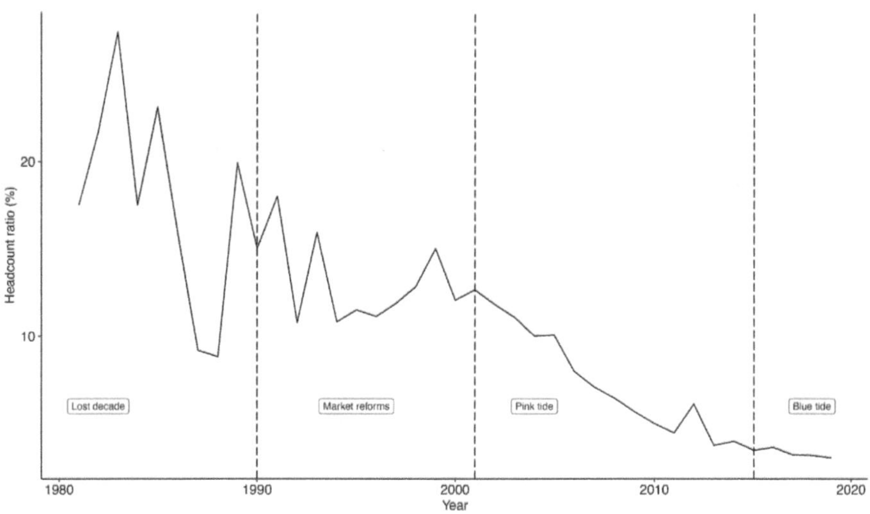

Figure 5.2 Trend in Average Extreme Poverty. *Source*: Data Sourced from World Development Indicators (2019).

more uneven. In Latin America, a buoyant economy and social policy have helped to bring about a systematic decline in absolute poverty between 1992 and 2010 (Gasparini and Cruces 2013). The growth effect, that is, an increase in income at the same rate across the entire population distribution, accounted for a 5 percent drop in absolute poverty in the 1990s. Social policy contributed to a 1 percent increase in the rate during the same period. In contrast, economic growth and social policy facilitated a systematic decline in the absolute poverty rate in the 2000s. While the growth factor contributed to a 6 percent decrease in poverty, redistribution accounted for 4 percent of the decline.

5.4 FINANCIALIZATION AND SOCIAL INCLUSION

How has financialization changed relative and absolute inclusion in LAC? Figure 5.3 graphs the linear association between the two dimensions of financialization under consideration with the level of extreme poverty and the Gini index. Panels A and B in figure 5.3 illustrate how private credit as a percent of GDP correlates with extreme poverty and with Gini coefficient, respectively. Private credit has a statistically significant positive association with Gini coefficient. In contrast, the poverty level and Gini index have statistically significant negative associations with international debt securities in panels C and D, respectively.

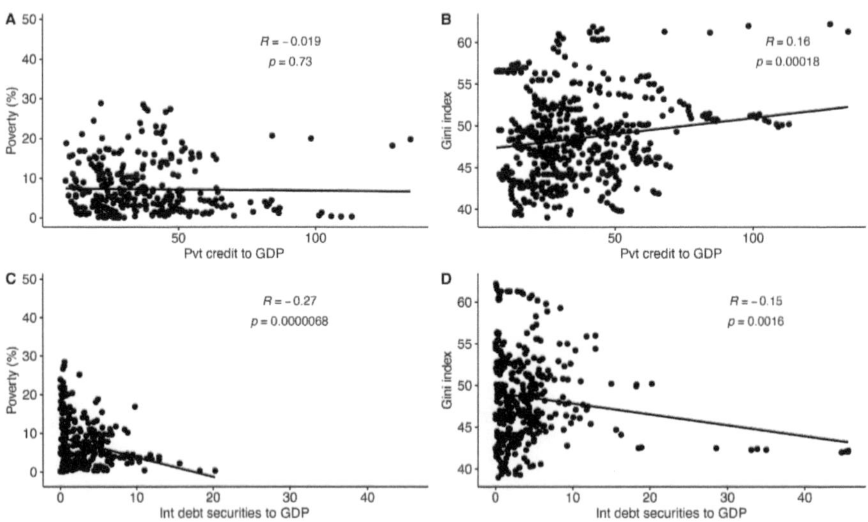

Figure 5.3 Financialization, Poverty, and Inequality. *Source*: Data Sourced from Solt (2019) and World Development Indicators (2019).

Financialization's impact on poverty and inequality has generated much debate in the literature.[6] One set of theoretical models posits that financial development ameliorates poverty and inequality by boosting economic growth. The financial system plays a pivotal role in the efficient functioning of the economy. First, it provides a mechanism for spatial and intertemporal allocation of resources. Second, financial intermediaries reduce the cost of acquiring and processing information to evaluate firms, managers, and markets. Third, creditors and shareholders enhance corporate governance by monitoring how firms manage their resources and future investments. Fourth, they are essential for managing risk and facilitating exchange. Finally, these functions influence saving, investment, and technological innovation that bolster long-term growth. Economic growth is always good for the poor (Dollar, Kleineberg, and Kraay 2016). The empirical analysis of 121 countries over the past four decades suggests that the income of the bottom 20 percent and 40 percent of the income distribution rises proportionally with mean average income as the economy grows. Thus, the policies and institutions that boost growth also enhance social inclusion.

Furthermore, financial development that lowers transaction and information costs benefits the poor. Financial imperfections such as transaction and information costs are especially binding on the poor without a steady income stream, collateral, credit history, and political connections. The occupations requiring high levels of investments are out of the reach of the poor in the absence of credit (Banerjee and Newman 1993). So, "poor agents choose working for a wage over self-employment, and wealthy agents become entrepreneurs who monitor workers" (p. 274). Credit constraints also limit the ability of the relatively poor to invest in human capital (Galor and Zeira 1993). Under the assumption of indivisibility in human capital, the initial distribution of wealth affects who has access to resources to invest in human capital. Capital accumulation in the economy implies that more funds would be available to the poor for investment purposes (Aghion and Bolton 1997). The redistribution of wealth from rich lenders to poor and middle-class borrowers brings about greater equality of opportunity and can accelerate the trickle-down process. Therefore, financial development can reduce poverty and inequality by easing credit constraints.

Another set of theoretical models (e.g. Greenwood and Jovanovic 1990) postulates a curvilinear relationship between financial development, economic progress, and inequality. Financial intermediation and growth are intricately linked. Financial intermediaries improve capital allocation and enhance economic growth benefiting the poor, irrespective of society's level of economic development. The distributional effect of financial development and therefore its net impact on the poor depends on the level of economic development (Claessens and Perotti 2007). In the early stages of development, the rich gain from financial development since only they can afford access. But the benefits of financial development are more diffused across society as more people access financial markets at higher levels of development.[7] The empirical evaluation of financial development's effect on inequality in 91 countries does not support the inverted-U hypothesis (Clarke, Xu, and Zou 2003).

A third set of theoretical models casts doubt on the claim that financialization mitigates poverty and inequality. An economic explanation based on growth and credit constraint neglects the political economy's role in financial development. The level of historical inequalities (Claessens and Perotti 2007), political and other interest groups (Acemoglu and Robinson 2013; Rajan and Zingales 2003), and institutional environment (López-De-Silanes, Buscaglia, and Loayza 2002) are crucial for understanding the nature of financialization in emerging economies.

From the political economy perspective, financialization could well end up enforcing historical cleavages instead of reducing inequality and poverty. Access to the financial system tends to be skewed in favor of the rich and the urban populace in emerging economies. Without a credit history, collateral, or secured income stream, the poor mainly rely on informal networks and family connections for capital. Even risk-free and low-cost payment services are available, if at all, at a higher cost to low-income groups. Lack of trust in financial institutions, inadequate knowledge about financial products, the mismatch between financial products and the needs of lower-income households, and behavior biases keep poorer segments outside the financial system. If usage of financial services is any indicator, LAC has lagged behind countries with similar economic backgrounds (Frisancho and Vera-Cossío 2020; Rojas-Suárez 2016). Only 40 percent of the residents owned an account in a formal financial institution in LAC, compared to 90 percent in OECD countries. The number is still lower (35 percent) for the poorest quintile of the population. Further, only 5 percent of the poorest quintile of the household borrow from formal financial institutions. Lenders charge higher interest rates to poorer borrowers.

Economic inequality begets political inequality. It can skew the distribution of political influence, allowing the opportunistic elite to capture the reform process and regulatory apparatus. When the institutional environment, such as the judicial system, property rights, and enforcement of contracts, is weak, the regulatory barriers to access finance are exceptionally high to the benefit of the elite. Large, family-owned business groups tend to dominate the financial markets through the joint control of financial institutions and corporations.

There are other reasons why financialization exacerbates inequality and poverty. Financialization has changed income distribution. It has increased capital's share of income and decreased labor's portion of income (Palley 2013). The shift in income toward profit and interest has disproportionately benefited the more affluent households. Further, as Stiglitz (2012) argues, the rent-seeking behavior of the financial sector, coupled with lax regulations, has added to the widening economic disparities. Finally, financial globalization has been accompanied by frequent crises (Reinhart and Rogoff 2009). Such crises have come in all shapes and sizes. The costs of these financial crises have been "socialized often in a highly regressive fashion" (Claessens and Perotti 2007, 765). The burden of the crises and subsequent structural reforms is typically higher for poor and marginalized groups in LAC (Gautam 2015).

The complexity of financialization makes uncovering the nexus between financial development and social inclusion all the more difficult. Many factors affect growth and inclusion simultaneously (Cerra, Lama, and Loayza 2022). Moreover, financialization manifests through different channels with varying consequences for poverty and inequality. Consider the example of microcredit, a vital development tool expanding credit to the poor. While not as transformative as initially thought, microcredit has a modest positive effect on the average borrower (Banerjee, Karlan, and Zinman 2015). Similarly, international remittances have also improved the living standards of the poor in LAC (Acosta et al. 2008). The study shows each percentage increase in remittances to GDP ratio decreases the region's poverty headcount ratio of 0.4 percent. On the other hand, as we saw earlier, economic crises have had a debilitating effect, especially on the poor and marginalized groups. Finally, financial development has been notoriously hard to measure because of the different channels of financialization (Ang and McKibbin 2007; Levine 2004; Seven and Coskun 2016). For example, private credit to GDP ratio, which is the most common measure of financialization, captures the depth of the financial system but not its width or inclusiveness. It is a proxy for the bank-based financial system and provides little information for the securities market or market-based financial system.

We are agnostic about the direction of the hypotheses.

5.4.1 Inequality Beyond Financialization

Since Simon Kuznets'(1955) inverted-U hypothesis, income inequality often has been explained as a function of economic development measured by per capita income. There exists a curvilinear relationship between economic progress and income inequality. Inequality first increases, then peaks and eventually falls as countries transition from low to high level of income. Kuznets' path-breaking work based on the small set of developed (the United States and the United Kingdom) and developing (India, Puerto Rico, and Sri Lanka) has been subjected to much scrutiny.[8] The empirical support for the

Kuznets curve has been mixed. For example, Brazil's long-term inequality mimics the Kuznets curve—rising from the early 1900s, reaching a high plateau during the 1970s–1990s, and declining thereafter (León 2021). However, there are other countries in LAC, Asia, and even Europe where the pattern of inequality does not resemble the Kuznets curve (Acemoglu and Robinson 2002). The rising inequality in OECD countries points to the great U-turn of the Kuznets curve in advanced economies.

How globalization and technology have altered income distribution has garnered much attention in the recent discussion on inequality. As Atkinson (2018) points out, much of the explanation draws on what Dutch economist Jan Tinbergen described as the race between the growing demand for skilled workers and the expansion of the educated population. Globalization shifts the demand in favor of relatively highly educated workers, and as the demand for skilled workforce outstrips the supply, the wage premium for skilled laborers increases. Similarly, technological advancements in areas such as information and communication technology also favors educated and skilled workers. An increased wage premium partially contributed to the rise in inequality in the 1990s, as governments in the region turned toward market reforms and opened up their economies (Cornia 2010; Gasparini and Lustig 2011; López-Calva and Lustig 2010). A decline in the skill premium was accompanied by declining inequality in the 2000s.

However, Thomas Piketty (2020) cautions against over-emphasizing the role of the impersonal market and technological forces in shaping inequality. "Inequality is neither economic or technological: it is ideological and political" (p. 7). In the long run of history, the struggle for ideas matters for inequality across different epochs. From the premodern societies before the eighteenth century to the contemporary hyper-capitalist period, societies come up with their justifications for prevalent inequality, lest the entire edifice of the society collapse. The premodern ternary societies justified their inequalities along the lines of the functions performed by different groups necessary for the community's survival. Today's hyper-capitalist society pins its inequalities on meritocracy, glorifying the winners in the economic system and vilifying "the losers for the supposed lack of merit, virtue and diligence" (p. 710). The inequality regimes comprising the different discourses and institutional arrangements provide justification and structure for the economic, social, and political inequalities. Historical experiences such as colonization, the notion of fairness, membership in political community, and ownership of property are some factors that temper the inequality regimes, influencing the structure of contemporary inequalities. Consider Brazil, South Africa, and the United States, where the legacy of slavery, colonization, and racial discrimination weighs heavily on the high levels of inequality.

Indeed it is not an accident that LAC has one of the world's most unequal regions. The process of colonization gave rise to extractive economic and political institutions, which enabled a handful of elites to maximize their benefits at the expense of most of the populace. The institution and social structures concentrate power in the hands of a few; land, education, and political power remain out of the reach of much of society. The extractive institutions, which took root in Latin America and Africa, are not immutable. But the trend creates a vicious cycle and persists over time.

Branko Milanovic (2016) notes that in the premodern era inequality increased or decreased because of exogenous shocks or malign forces such as wars, civil conflicts, epidemics, and new discoveries. Both benign social and economic forces (e.g. politics, labor unions, education levels, aging population, and technological changes) and malign forces enabled the Great Flattening of income inequality in the richer countries during much of the twentieth century. Government's approach toward minimum wage, labor unions, and progressive social policies help us understand the rise of inequality through the 1980s and 1990s and its fall in the 2000s in Latin America (Cornia 2010; Gasparini and Lustig 2011).

5.5 DATA AND ESTIMATION

Our primary outcomes of interest are income inequality and extreme poverty, which are common proxies for relative and absolute inclusiveness, respectively. We also want to explore their association with access to COVID-19 vaccination and excess mortality in the region.

A standard measure of income inequality is the Gini coefficient.[9] A Gini coefficient of one denotes perfect inequality and zero perfect equality. The Gini coefficient is an easy-to-understand summary measure of inequality. It allows countries to be ranked by their level of inequality, irrespective of the size of their population and economy. The evolution of income inequality over time can be monitored using the Gini coefficient. The Gini coefficient is an appropriate indicator of inequality if the focus is on the middle sector of the distribution (Pettinato 2002). It sheds little light on how inequality is concentrated between and within the different groups, unlike, say 90/10 decile ratio. Further, the choice of data can have a bearing on our conclusion about the level and trend of inequality, especially in cross-national analyses (Atkinson and Brandolini 2001). First, there are no universally accepted criteria for estimating Gini. Some countries (e.g. Asia and Africa) use consumption, and others (Latin America) rely on income in their calculation of Gini. Second, the scope and timing of the household survey can vary from country to country. For example, Argentina's household survey is limited to urban areas. Others, like Brazil, conduct national surveys. Each country uses different types of surveys, different types of coverage, different timing of surveys, and different procedures to gather and process information.

The Standardized World Income Inequality Database or SWIID (Solt 2008) attempts to overcome some of the problems with cross-country data. SWIID provides Gini estimates based on disposable (post-tax and transfer) and market income (pre-tax and transfer). The trend in inequality is more driven by pre-tax income or market income than post-tax income. We, therefore, focus here on market-based Gini coefficients. By doing so, we can also examine the effect social policies have on inequality.

Our second dimension of inclusiveness is extreme poverty. We use the $1.90 poverty headcount ratio from the World Development Indicators (World Bank n.d). The $1.90 poverty measure is calculated as the average of the national poverty of 15 of the world's poorest countries. We choose to focus on extreme poverty because it is the first of the SDGs.[10] Moreover, the extreme poverty level has increased during the pandemic for the first time in 27 years in LAC.

The idea of inclusion goes beyond monetary measures such as inequality and poverty calculated based on income. Inclusion also entails access to public goods and services. Health, education, and financial services are also vital measures of inclusion. We explore how extreme poverty and inequality correlate with access to vaccines and excess mortality.

To account for potential factors confounding the relationship between inclusion and financialization as defined above, we control for a set of economic and political variables commonly suggested in the literature. Following Dollar and colleagues (2016) we include annual GDP growth in the right-hand side of the equation. Prior empirical studies (Beck, Demirguc-Kunt, and Levine 2004; Claessens and Perotti 2007; Seven and Coskun 2016) also suggest growth-boosting macroeconomic policies such as low-inflation, international trade, size of government, and human capital boost income share of the poorest and reduce poverty. We use the logged annual growth rate in implicit GDP deflator as a proxy for inflation, logged sum of exports and imports as percentage of GDP to capture economic openness, logged government final consumption as percentage of GDP as control for macroeconomic conditions, and logged average years of schooling in 1960 as a proxy for initial human capital in the economy. We also include the logged level of GDP per capita and its square to account for the inverted-U relationship between the level of economic development and inequality.

Government welfare spending could also have implications for relative (inequality) and absolute (poverty) inclusion.[11] We include three measures of social spending—aggregate welfare spending, education, and health. We also include lagged levels of Gini and poverty for theoretical and methodological purposes. The lagged values help to test how poverty and inequality persist over time. The polity score of democracy is also included to account for political regimes. Finally, we include country and decadal dummies to account for spatial and temporal heterogeneities. The summary statistics are found in Table 5.1.

Our estimation strategy relies on the instrumental variable technique. Financialization may drive change to income distribution and poverty, but the latter may also spur the development of financial intermediaries. A variable or instrument that highly correlates with income distribution/poverty can be hard to find. Another strategy in the literature (e.g. Rudra 2002) is to use higher moments as instruments. When no outside data is available as an instrument, the third moment of the data can be exploited as an instrument (Lewbel 1997). The quality of the instrument depends on the skewness of the data. Only when these instruments are weak do we use the lagged value of data as instruments. Lagged values are natural candidates for instruments in the TSCS setup.[12]

Other methodological issues associated with the panel data are heteroscedasticity, spatial and contemporaneous correlation, and autocorrelation. Based on Beck (2001) and Beck and Katz (1995), we correct for panel heteroscedasticity and spatial correlation. We use the first difference of the dependent variables to address for serial correlation. In addition, we use a

Table 5.1 Summary Statistics

Variables	*N*	*Mean*	*Std. dev*	*Min*	*Max*
Ln Gini	765	3.884	0.0953	3.664	4.130
Ln Poverty rate	414	1.666	1.223	−2.303	3.888
Ln Credit (% GDP)	852	3.465	0.541	1.886	4.899
Ln Int. sec. (% GDP)	511	0.472	1.609	−6.381	3.817
Ln Edu. (% GDP)	839	1.310	0.419	−0.916	2.208
Ln Health (% GDP)	837	0.811	0.657	−2.303	2.708
Ln Welfare (% GDP)	754	0.967	1.017	−2.303	2.821
Ln Avg. sch yrs.	1,000	1.172	0.485	−0.218	2.013
Ln GDP growth	927	1.164	0.877	−4.414	2.980
Ln Global (% GDP)	1,026	0.705	0.355	0.0732	2.298
Ln Inflation	865	4.272	1.186	−7.502	8.531
Ln Gov. con (% GDP)	963	2.549	0.386	1.074	3.772
Political regime	936	0.632	0.482	0	1

Source: Authors' estimates

dynamic approach and include lagged dependent variables on the right-hand side. The general empirical specification is the following:

$$\Delta Y_{i,t} = \beta_0 + \beta_j Y_{i,t-1} + \beta_k Fin^{\#}_{i,t-1} + \beta_l SP_{i,t-1} + \beta_l X_{i,t-1} + \beta_m Sch_i + \beta_n Con_i + \beta_o Dec_i + \varepsilon_{i,t} \quad (1)$$

where $\Delta Y_{i,t}$ is the annual change in logged Gini coefficient (relative inclusion) and extreme poverty (absolute inclusion) in country i in year t. $Y_{i,t-1}$ is the lagged levels of Gini coefficient and extreme poverty. $Fin^{\#}_{i,t-1}$ represents the vector of lagged financialization variables: credit-to-GDP and international private debt securities outstanding. It is the predicted value estimated in the first stage, using the instruments for all the endogenous variables. $SP_{i,t-1}$ represents the vector of lagged social spending variables: social security welfare, health, and education spending. $X_{i,t-1}$ represents the vector of control variables: inflation, government consumption, annual GDP rate, GDP per capita, GDP capita square (to account for Kuznet curve for income inequality). Sch_i is the average schooling in years in 1960, Con_i indicator for country, and Dec_i decadal dummies.

5.5.1 Results

Table 5.2 summarizes the results of the 2SLS estimates for the growth in Gini coefficient. Our principal independent variable of interest is private credit-to-GDP. Following Lewbel (1997) we utilize higher moments of private credit to GDP ($(X - \bar{X})^2$) as an instrument in the first stage for lack of valid alternative instruments. The t statistics for our instrument in the first states were 23.72, 9.62, and 10.31, respectively, for models 1, 2, and 3 in table 5.2. We notice that the coefficient on private credit is positive and statistically significant across the three models. It supports the view that private credit increases the growth of Gini coefficient, but the magnitude of change is not large. A 1 percent increase in private credit results in around 0.005 percent increase in Gini coefficient. Social security and welfare spending also had a statistically significant negative effect on the growth of Gini. A percent increase in social welfare spending leads to a modest 0.004 percent decrease in Gini growth. The coefficients on inflation in all three models are positive and statistically significant. A one percent increase in inflation results in a 0.001 percent increase Gini growth.

We turn our attention to estimates obtained from estimating equation 1 when the principal independent variable of interest is international private debt securities. We use the second lag as an instrument for international debt securities in the first stage. The coefficients on international private debt securities in the three models in table 5.3 are negative but statistically significant only in Model

Table 5.2 Private Credit and Gini Market Income

	(1)	(2)	(3)
Variables	*Δ Gini*	*Δ Gini*	*Δ Gini*
Credit	0.00491*	0.00454*	0.00598**
	(0.00270)	(0.00215)	(0.00246)
Social security	−0.00361**		
	(0.00166)		
Health		−0.000411	
		(0.00149)	
Education			0.00166
			(0.00251)
Lag Gini	−0.104**	−0.124***	−0.0898**
	(0.0451)	(0.0385)	(0.0356)
Average school yrs.	0.00431	0.00557	0.00582
	(0.00574)	(0.00659)	(0.00609)
Inflation	0.00147**	0.00121***	0.00123**
	(0.000592)	(0.000406)	(0.000535)
Gov. consumption	−6.74e-05	0.00431	−0.000199
	(0.00426)	(0.00301)	(0.00379)
Globalization	−0.0147*	−0.00987	−0.00170
	(0.00769)	(0.00930)	(0.00957)
GDP growth	−0.000666	−0.000688	−0.000997
	(0.000934)	(0.000752)	(0.000609)
GDP capital	−0.0163	−0.0182	−0.0142
	(0.0181)	(0.0125)	(0.0173)
GDP capita square	0.000149	8.82e-05	0.000122
	(0.000341)	(0.000304)	(0.000428)
Political regime	0.00131	0.00216	0.00196*
	(0.00106)	(0.00156)	(0.000990)
1990s	−0.00719***	−0.00834***	−0.00708***
	(0.00167)	(0.00227)	(0.00159)
2000s	−0.0104***	−0.0119***	−0.0102***
	(0.00226)	(0.00315)	(0.00207)
Constant	0.573	0.672**	0.480
	(0.342)	(0.240)	(0.281)
Observations	281	288	284
R-squared	0.487	0.519	0.489
Country FE	YES	YES	YES

Robust standard errors in parentheses
*** p<0.01, ** p<0.05, * p<0.1
Source: Authors' estimates

6. The coefficients for GDP growth are negative and statistically significant ($\beta = -0.001$, $p < 0.05$) in all three models in table 5.2. A 1 percent growth in GDP leads to about a 0.001 percent decline in the Gini coefficient.

Next, we examine financialization's influence on growth in absolute poverty. In table 5.4, models 7 through 9 present estimates for change in absolute

Table 5.3 International Debt Securities Outstanding and Gini

	(4)	(5)	(6)
Variables	Δ Gini	Δ Gini	Δ Gini
International debt securities	−0.000494	−0.000623	−0.000963*
	(0.000519)	(0.000485)	(0.000548)
Social security	−0.00141		
	(0.00194)		
Health		0.00201	
		(0.00137)	
Education			−0.00235
			(0.00259)
Lag Gini	−0.0261	−0.0165	−0.0184
	(0.0184)	(0.0209)	(0.0217)
Average school years	−0.00367	−0.00846*	−0.00849*
	(0.00403)	(0.00404)	(0.00413)
Inflation	0.000199	−0.000145	0.000200
	(0.000240)	(0.000386)	(0.000391)
Gov. consumption	−0.00493	−0.00462	−0.00298
	(0.00308)	(0.00282)	(0.00193)
Globalization	−0.00408	−0.00184	−0.00478
	(0.00636)	(0.00665)	(0.00710)
GDP growth	−0.00159**	−0.00172**	−0.00159**
	(0.000655)	(0.000669)	(0.000683)
GDP capital	−0.00423	0.00580	0.0146**
	(0.00712)	(0.0104)	(0.00542)
GDP capita squared	0.000436	8.28e-05	−7.98e-05
	(0.000253)	(0.000324)	(0.000215)
Political regime	−0.000522	0.000703	0.000739***
		(0.000542)	(0.000234)
1990s	−0.00788***	−0.00851***	−0.00783***
	(0.00183)	(0.00193)	(0.00159)
2000s	−0.0100***	−0.0107***	−0.0107***
	(0.00329)	(0.00334)	(0.00319)
Constant	0.0974	−0.0119	−0.0971
	(0.106)	(0.134)	(0.102)
Observations	261	265	261
R-squared	0.513	0.530	0.541
Country FE	YES	YES	YES

Robust standard errors in parentheses
*** $p < 0.01$, ** $p < 0.05$, * $p < 0.1$
Source: Authors' estimates

poverty when the principal variable of interest is private credit. We use the higher moment of private credit to GDP ($(X - \bar{X})^2$) as an instrument in the first state. The t statistics for our instrument in the first states were 6.90, 5.27, and 4.39 for models 7, 8, and 9 in table 5.3. Both total social security and

Table 5.4 Private Credit and Extreme Poverty

	(7)	(8)	(9)
VARIABLES	*Δ Poverty*	*Δ Poverty*	*Δ Poverty*
Lag P190	−0.429***	−0.448***	−0.488***
	(0.0997)	(0.134)	(0.111)
Credit	−0.143	−0.251	−0.280
	(0.326)	(0.517)	(0.392)
Social security	0.168***		
	(0.0542)		
Health		−0.00539	
		(0.131)	
Education			−0.299*
			(0.138)
Average school years.	−0.658*	−0.578	−0.626***
	(0.337)	(0.345)	(0.0546)
Inflation	−0.443***	−0.420***	−0.418***
	(0.109)	(0.0892)	(0.107)
GDP growth	−0.0310	−0.0296	−0.0275
	(0.0220)	(0.0263)	(0.0249)
Gov. consumption	0.0527	0.134	0.146
	(0.124)	(0.167)	(0.164)
Globalization	0.626	0.430**	0.450**
	(0.360)	(0.166)	(0.203)
Political regime	−0.276**	−0.241*	−0.357**
	(0.0910)	(0.125)	(0.152)
1990s	0.0346	−0.00633	0.00811
	(0.158)	(0.238)	(0.182)
2000s	−0.0782	−0.0958	−0.0566
	(0.180)	(0.202)	(0.171)
Constant	3.735**	3.868**	4.702***
	(1.266)	(1.530)	(1.103)
Observations	151	153	152
R-squared	0.382	0.335	0.354
Country FE	YES	YES	YES

Robust standard errors in parentheses
*** $p < 0.01$, ** $p < 0.05$, * $p < 0.1$
Source: Authors' estimates

welfare spending ($\beta = 0.17$, $p < 0.01$) and education spending ($\beta = -0.30$, $p < 0.1$) have a statistically strong impact on change in the absolute poverty rate. The coefficients on democracy are statistically significant in all three models. The growth in absolute poverty is 0.3 points lower in democracies compared to non-democracies.

Table 5.5 presents the estimates for the effect of international private debt securities on absolute poverty growth. We use the higher moment of private credit to GDP ($(X - \bar{X})^2$) as an instrument in the first state. The t statistics for our instrument in the first states were 4.70, 4.64, and 5.00, respectively, for models 10, 11, and 12 in table 5.5.

We find that private debt securities have a negative effect on the growth of absolute poverty. The coefficient is statistically significant in ($\beta s = -0.10$, $p < 0.05$) in the three models. A 1 percent increase in private debt securities decreases poverty by 0.1 percent. Both social security and welfare spending

Table 5.5 International Debt Securities Outstanding and Extreme Poverty

	(10)	(11)	(12)
VARIABLES	*Δ Poverty*	*Δ Poverty*	*Δ Poverty*
Lag P190	−0.369***	−0.323**	−0.357***
	(0.104)	(0.121)	(0.0771)
International debt securities	−0.0661**	−0.105**	−0.0711***
	(0.0226)	(0.0344)	(0.0195)
Social security	0.162**		
	(0.0639)		
Health		0.0926*	
		(0.0439)	
Education			−0.275
			(0.161)
Average school years.	−1.045***	−0.983***	−0.758***
	(0.140)	(0.281)	(0.142)
Inflation	−0.397***	−0.356***	−0.227*
	(0.0762)	(0.0932)	(0.120)
GDP growth	−0.0191	−0.0188	−0.0211
	(0.0161)	(0.0253)	(0.0157)
Gov. consumption	0.0820	0.165*	0.187***
	(0.110)	(0.0813)	(0.0416)
Globalization	−0.0151	−0.0938	−0.0942
	(0.0512)	(0.124)	(0.194)
Political regime	−0.128	−0.0252	−0.0642
	(0.105)	(0.153)	(0.162)
1990s	0.0755*	0.0187	−0.00545
	(0.0375)	(0.0540)	(0.0555)
2000s	0.0241	0.0352	−0.0473
	(0.0621)	(0.0265)	
Constant	3.827***	3.382***	3.004***
	(0.531)	(0.798)	(0.680)
Observations	150	154	150
R-squared	0.337	0.200	0.298
Country FE	YES	YES	YES

Robust standard errors in parentheses
*** $p < 0.01$, ** $p < 0.05$, * $p < 0.1$
Source: Authors' estimates

($\beta = 0.17$, $p < 0.05$) and health spending ($\beta s = 0.10$, $p < 0.1$) achieved statistical significance in models 10 and 11.

5.5.2 Inclusion and the Pandemic

In figure 5.4 the idea of social inclusion extends to universal healthcare (UHC), which finds expression in target 3.8 of SDG. Specifically, SDG target 3.8 aims to promote UHC along with access to healthcare, essential medicines, and vaccination. We examine here how long-standing inequality confounded vaccine availability and excess mortality during the COVID-19 pandemic in LAC. Like much of the world, the pandemic wreaked havoc in LAC. Home to about 8 percent of the world's population, the region accounted for approximately 15 percent of cases and 28 percent of deaths worldwide as of March 2022 (Schwalb et al. 2022). Both poverty and inequality aggravated the humanitarian crises accompanying the pandemic. We use excess mortality and vaccination rate data (Mathieu et al. 2020) to explore their association with poverty and inequality.

In figure 5.4 panels A and B plot the correlation between the vaccination rate per 100 people based on data available until March 2021. We find the association between Gini index and vaccination rate in panel A is weak, but extreme poverty has a statistically strong negative association with vaccination rate in panel B. Further, inequality and extreme poverty positively

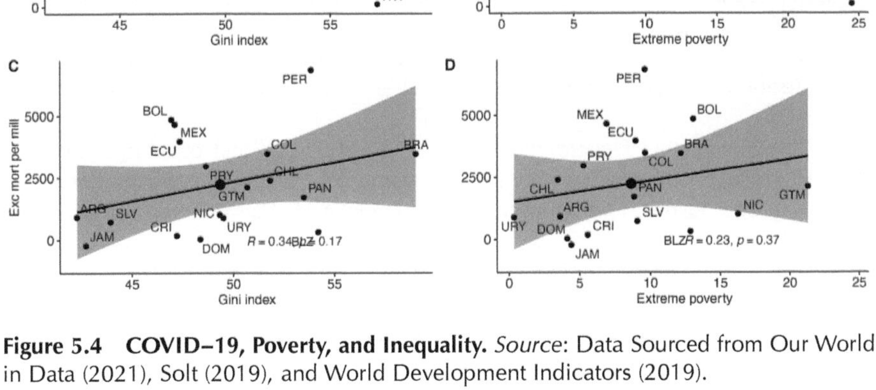

Figure 5.4 COVID-19, Poverty, and Inequality. *Source*: Data Sourced from Our World in Data (2021), Solt (2019), and World Development Indicators (2019).

correlate with excess mortality in panels C and D, but the association is statistically nonsignificant.

5.6 CONCLUSION

Financialization has become a divisive issue. Some present the deepening of financial intermediaries as a force of good that has brought about efficiency, helped many escape poverty, and, more generally, enhanced social welfare. Others dismiss financialization as a false prophet that benefits a few and harms many. Our empirical analyses here present a more complex picture of how gains from financialization are shared across different social groups in the LAC. From the perspective of social inclusion, the different channels of financialization lead to distinctive outcomes. We find that private credit enhances income inequality in the region, worsening relative inclusion. But international private securities benefited the poorest segment of the society. It negatively affects the growth of extreme poverty, thus bolstering absolute inclusion.

How are we to understand the implications of our empirical findings in this and the previous chapter? In the next chapter, we attempt to answer this and related questions by placing these results in the larger discourse of financialization.

NOTES

1. According to Chancel and colleague, global wealth (e.g. interest and dividends) distribution is even starker, with the poorest 50 percent of the world population holding barely two percent of the global wealth.
2. See Demirguc-Kunt, Leora and Dorothe (2017) for a systematic review of the literature. Bruhn and Love (2014), Dabla-Norris et al., (2015); Frisancho and Vera-Cossío (2020); Rojas-Suárez (2016) for LAC.
3. The study of welfare state tends to focus on welfare expenditure which is only an epiphenomenon. The substance of the welfare state is T H Marshall's notion of social rights.
4. The Sustainable Development Goal 8 (decent work and economic growth), Goal 10 (reduced inequality), Goal 11 (sustainable cities and communities), and Goal 16 (peace, justice, and strong institutions) make explicit reference to inclusion (U.N. n.d).
5. The Andese—Bolivia, Columbia, Ecuador, Peru and Venezuela—region had the most disappointing performance terms of inequality in the 1990s (Gasparini et al. 2011). Four of the five countries in the subregion experience an increase in inequality during the period.
6. See Levine (2004) for a comprehensive review of the literature.

7. Henderson, Papageorgiou, & Parmeter (2013) find non-linear relationship between financial development and economic growth. While financial development has a positive effect on growth in middle- and high-income countries, the relationship at best is weak in the case of low-income countries.

8. See Alderson & Nielsen (2002) and also Jha (1996).

9. The Gini coefficient is defined as the ratio of the area of concentration resulting from the deviation of the Lorenze curve between the 45-degree line of perfect equality relative to the area of perfect inequality or the entire region below the line of equality.

10. Further, Atkinson and Marlier (2010) recommend that any indicator of social inclusion should enhance global comparability and be interpretable in the international context.

11. See Gasparini and Guille (2013) and Lusting (2020) for discussion on impact of social policy on poverty and inequality.

12. Bellemare, Masaki, and Pepinsky (2017) find that lagged independent variables can generate bias OLS estimates that are also more likely to produce type I errors in the TSCS setting. We opt for the lagged approach only when there is a paucity of better instruments.

BIBLIOGRAPHY

Acemoglu, Daron, and James A. Robinson. 2002. "The Political Economy of the Kuznets Curve." *Review of Development Economics* 6 (2): 183–203. https://doi.org/10.1111/1467-9361.00149.

———. 2013. "Economics Versus Politics: Pitfalls of Policy Advice." *Journal of Economic Perspectives* 27 (2): 173–92. https://doi.org/10.1257/jep.27.2.173.

Acosta, Pablo, Cesar Calderón, Pablo Fajnzylber, and Humberto Lopez. 2008. "What Is the Impact of International Remittances on Poverty and Inequality in Latin America?" *World Development* 36 (1): 89–114. https://doi.org/10.1016/j.worlddev.2007.02.016.

Aghion, Philippe, and Patrick Bolton. 1997. "A Theory of Trickle-Down Growth and Development." *Review of Economic Studies* 64 (2): 151–72. https://doi.org/10.2307/2971707.

Ahluwalia, Montek S. 2011. "Prospects and Policy Challenges in the Twelfth Plan." *Economic and Political Weekly* 46 (21): 88–105.

Alderson, Arthur S., and François Nielsen. 2002. "Globalization and the Great U-Turn: Income Inequality Trends in 16 OECD Countries." *American Journal of Sociology* 107 (5): 1244–99. https://doi.org/10.1086/341329.

Alesina, Alberto, and Dani Rodrik. 1994. "Distributive Politics and Economic Growth." *The Quarterly Journal of Economics* 109 (2): 465–90. https://doi.org/10.2307/2118470.

Ang, James B., and Warwick J. McKibbin. 2007. "Financial Liberalization, Financial Sector Development and Growth: Evidence from Malaysia." *Journal of*

Development Economics 84 (1): 215–33. https://doi.org/10.1016/j.jdeveco.2006.11.006.

Atkinson, Anthony B. 2018. *Inequality: What Can Be Done?* Cambridge, MA: Harvard University Press.

Atkinson, Anthony B., and Andrea Brandolini. 2001. "Promise and Pitfalls in the Use of 'Secondary' Data-Sets: Income Inequality in OECD Countries as a Case Study." *Journal of Economic Literature* 39 (3): 771–99.

Atkinson, Anthony B, and Eric Marlier. 2010. *Analysing and Measuring Social Inclusion in a Global Context*. ST/ESA/325. New York, NY: United Nations.

Banerjee, Abhijit, and Andrew F. Newman. 1993. "Occupational Choice and the Process of Development." *Journal of Political Economy* 101 (2): 274–98. https://doi.org/10.1086/261876.

Banerjee, Abhijit, Dean Karlan, and Jonathan Zinman. 2015. "Six Randomized Evaluations of Microcredit: Introduction and Further Steps." *American Economic Journal: Applied Economics* 7 (1): 1–21. https://doi.org/10.1257/app.20140287.

Beck, Thorsten, Asli Demirguc-Kunt, and Ross Levine. 2004. "Finance, Inequality, and Poverty: Cross-Country Evidence." Working Paper 10979. National Bureau of Economic Research. https://doi.org/10.3386/w10979.

Bellemare, Marc F., Takaaki Masaki, and Thomas B. Pepinsky. 2017. "Lagged Explanatory Variables and the Estimation of Causal Effect." *The Journal of Politics* 79 (3): 949–63. https://doi.org/10.1086/690946.

Bergstrom, Katy. 2020. "The Role of Inequality for Poverty Reduction." Policy Research Working Paper 9409. Washington, DC: World Bank. https://doi.org/10.1596/1813-9450-9409.

Blanchard, Oliver, and Dani Rodrik, eds. 2021a. *Combating Inequality: Rethinking Government's Role*. Cambridge, MA: MIT Press.

———. 2021b. "Introduction: We Have the Tools to Reverse the Rise in Inequality." In *Compating Inequality: Rethinking Government's Role*, edited by Oliver Blanchard and Dani Rodrik. Cambridge, MA: MIT Press.

Brady, David. 2003. "Rethinking the Sociological Measurement of Poverty." *Social Forces* 81 (3): 715–51. https://doi.org/10.1353/sof.2003.0025.

Bruhn, Miriam, and Inessa Love. 2014. "The Real Impact of Improved Access to Finance: Evidence from Mexico." *The Journal of Finance* 69 (3): 1347–76. https://doi.org/10.1111/jofi.12091.

Cerra, Valerie. 2022. "An Inclusive Growth Framework." In *How to Achieve Inclusive Growth*, edited by Valerie Cerra, Barry Eichengreen, Asmaa El-Ganainy, and Martin Schindler, 1–31. Oxford: Oxford University Press.

Cerra, Valerie, Ruy Lama, and Norman Loayza. 2022. "Links Between Growth, Inequality, and Poverty." In *How to Achieve Inclusive Growth*, edited by Valerie Cerra, Barry Eichengreen, Mayada El-Zoghbi, and Martin Schindler, 32–73. Oxford: Oxford University Press.

Chancel, Lucas, Thomas Piketty, Emmanuel Saez, and Gabriel Zucman, eds. 2022. *World Inequality Report 2022*. Cambridge: Harvard University Press.

Claessens, Stijn, and Enrico Perotti. 2007. "Finance and Inequality: Channels and Evidence." *Journal of Comparative Economics* 35 (4): 748–73. https://doi.org/10.1016/j.jce.2007.07.002.

Claessens, Stijn, and Erik Feijen. 2007. *Financial Sector Development and the Millennium Development Goals*. World Bank Working Papers. Washington, DC: The World Bank. https://doi.org/10.1596/978-0-8213-6865-7.

Clarke, George R. G., Lixin Colin Xu, and Heng-fu Zou. 2006. "Finance and Income Inequality: What Do the Data Tell Us?" *Southern Economic Journal* 72 (3): 578–96. https://doi.org/10.2307/20111834.

Clarke, George, Lixin Colin Xu, and Heng-fu Zou. 2003. "Finance and Income Inequality: Test of Alternative Theories." Policy Research Working Paper 2984. Washington, DC: World Bank. https://doi.org/10.1596/1813-9450-2984.

Commission on Growth and Development. 2008. *The Growth Report: Strategies for Sustained Growth and Inclusive Development*. Washington, DC: World Bank. https://openknowledge.worldbank.org/handle/10986/6507.

Cornia, Giovanni Andrea. 2010. "Income Distribution Under Latin America's New Left Regimes." *Journal of Human Development and Capabilities* 11 (1): 85–114. https://doi.org/10.1080/19452820903481483.

Dabla-Norris, Era, Yixi Deng, Anna Ivanova, Izabela Karpowicz, Filiz Unsal, Eva Van-Leemput, and Joyce Wong. 2015. "Financial Inclusion: Zooming in on Latin America." Working Paper WP/15/206. Washington, DC: International Monetary Fund.

Daron, Acemoglu, and James A Robinson. 2013. *Why Nations Fail: The Origins of Power, Prosperity, and Poverty*. London: Profile Book.

Demirguc-Kunt, Asli, Leora Klapper, and Dorothe Singer. 2017. "Financial Inclusion and Inclusive Growth: A Review of Recent Empirical Evidence." Policy Research Working Paper 8040. Washington, DC: World Bank. https://doi.org/10.1596/1813-9450-8040.

Didier, Tatiana, and Sergio L. Schmukler. 2013. "Front Matter." In *Emerging Issues in Financial Development: Lessons from Latin America*, edited by Tatiana Didier and Sergio L. Schmukler, 1–24. Washington, DC: The World Bank. https://doi.org/10.1596/978-0-8213-9828-9_fm.

Dollar, David, Tatjana Kleineberg, and Aart Kraay. 2016. "Growth Still Is Good for the Poor." *European Economic Review*, Model Uncertainty in Economics 81 (January): 68–85. https://doi.org/10.1016/j.euroecorev.2015.05.008.

Dreze, Jean, and Amartya Sen. 2013. *India: Development and Participation*. Oxford: Oxford University Pres.

ECLAC. 2007. *Social Cohesion: Inclusion and a Sense of Belonging in Latin America and the Caribbean*. Washington, DC: ECLAC - United Nations. https://www.cepal.org/en/publications/31966-social-cohesion-inclusion-and-sense-belonging-latin-america-and-caribbean-summary.

———. 2022a. "Social Panorama of Latin America 2021." LC/PUB.2021/17-P. Santiago: ECLAC - United Nations.

———. 2022b. "Extreme Poverty in the Region Rises to 86 Million in 2021 Due to the Deepening of the Social and Health Crisis Prompted by the Covid-19 Pandemic." ECLAC - United Nations. CEPAL. January 25, 2022. https://www.cepal.org/en/pressreleases/extreme-poverty-region-rises-86-million-2021-due-deepening-social-and-health-crisis.

Esping-Andersen, Gosta. 2002. *Why We Need a New Welfare State*. New York, NY: Oxford University Press.

Feierherd, German, Patricio Larroulet, Wei Long, and Nora Lustig. 2021. "The Pink Tide and Inequality in Latin America." Working Paper 2105. Tulane University, Department of Economics.

Frisancho, Verónica, and Diego Vera-Cossío. 2020. "When Financial Inclusion Proves Noninclusive." In *The Inequality Crisis: Latin America and the Caribbean at the Crossroads*, edited by Matías Busso and Julián Messi, 253–78. Inter-American Development Bank. https://publications.iadb.org/publications/english/document/The-Inequality-Crisis-Latin-America-and-the-Caribbean-at-the-Crossroads.pdf.

Galor, Oded, and Omer Moav. 2004. "From Physical to Human Capital Accumulation: Inequality and the Process of Development." *Review of Economic Studies* 71 (4): 1001–26.

Galor, Oded, and Joseph Zeira. 1993. "Income Distribution and Macroeconomics." *Review of Economic Studies* 60 (1): 35–52. https://doi.org/10.2307/2297811.

Gasparini, Leonardo. 2003. "Inequality and the State in Latin America and the Caribbean." Flagship Report 2003. La Plata, Argentina: World Bank.

Gasparini, Leonardo, and Guillermo Cruces. 2013. "Poverty and Inequality in Latin America: A Story of Two Decades." *Journal of International Affairs* 66 (2): 51–63.

Gasparini, Leonardo, Guillermo Cruces, Leopoldo Tornarolli, and Mariana Marchionni. 2009. "A Turning Point? Recent Developments on Inequality in Latin America and the Caribbean." Working Paper 81. Universidad Nacional de La Plata, Centro de Estudios Distributivos, Laborales y Sociales (CEDLAS). https://www.econstor.eu/handle/10419/127597.

Gasparini, Leonardo, Guillermo Cruces, Leopoldo Tornarolli, and Daniel Mejía. 2011. "Recent Trends in Income Inequality in Latin America." *Economía* 11 (2): 147–201.

Gasparini, Leonardo, and Nora Lustig. 2011. "The Rise and Fall of Income Inequality in Latin America." In *The Oxford Handbook of Latin American Economics*, edited by Jose Antonio Ocampo and Jaime Ros, 691–714. Oxford: Oxford University Press. https://doi.org/10.1093/oxfordhb/9780199571048.013.0027.

Gautam, Rana S. 2015. "Banking Crises and Social Policy: The Case of Latin America and the Caribbean." *Journal of International and Comparative Social Policy* 31 (3): 209–33. https://doi.org/10.1080/21699763.2015.1069206.

Giddens, Anthony. 2000. *The Third Way and Its Critics*. Cambridge: Polity Press.

Gómez León, María. 2021. "The Kuznets Curve in Brazil, 1850–2010." *Revista de Historia Económica / Journal of Iberian and Latin American Economic History* 39 (1): 37–61. https://doi.org/10.1017/S0212610920000166.

Greenwood, Jeremy, and Boyan Jovanovic. 1990. "Financial Development, Growth, and the Distribution of Income." *Journal of Political Economy* 98 (5): 1076–1107.

Hacker, Jacob S. 2019. *The Great Risk Shift: The New Economic Insecurity and the Decline of the American Dream*, 2nd ed. Oxford: Oxford University Press. http://ebookcentral.proquest.com/lib/northgeorgia/detail.action?docID=5647830.

Halac, Marina, and Sergio L. Schmukler. 2004. "Distributional Effects of Crises: The Financial Channel." *Economía* 5 (1): 1–67.

Hausman, Daniel M., and Michael S. McPherson. 2006. *Economic Analysis, Moral Philosophy, and Public Policy,* 2nd ed. Cambridge: Cambridge University Press. https://doi.org/10.1017/CBO9780511754289.

Henderson, Daniel J., Chris Papageorgiou, and Christopher F. Parmeter. 2013. "Who Benefits from Financial Development? New Methods, New Evidence." *European Economic Review* 63 (October): 47–67. https://doi.org/10.1016/j.euroecorev.2013.05.007.

Ianchovichina, Elena, and Susan Lundstrom Gable. 2012. "What Is Inclusive Growth?" In *Commodity Price Volatility and Inclusive Growth in Low-Income Countries*, edited by Rabah Arezki, Catherine A Pattillo, Marc Quintyn, and Min Zhu, 147–60. Washington, DC: International Monetary Fund.

Ianchovichina, Elena, and Susanna Lundstrom. 2009. "Inclusive Growth Analytics: Framework and Application." Policy Research Working Paper WPS4851. Washington, DC: World Bank. https://doi.org/10.1596/1813-9450-4851.

Jayal, Niraja Gopal. 2009. "The Challenge of Human Development: Inclusion or Democratic Citizenship?" *Journal of Human Development and Capabilities* 10 (3): 359–74. https://doi.org/10.1080/19452820903041782.

Jayasuriya, Kanishka. 2006. *Statecraft, Welfare, and the Politics of Inclusion.* New York, NY: Palgrave Macmillan.

Jha, Sailesh K. 1996. "The Kuznets Curve: A Reassessment." *World Development* 24 (4): 773–80. https://doi.org/10.1016/0305-750X(95)00165-9.

Kaufman, Robert R., and Alex Segura-Ubiergo. 2001. "Globalization, Domestic Politics, and Social Spending in Latin America: A Time-Series Cross-Section Analysis, 1973–97." *World Politics* 53 (4): 553–87.

Klapper, Leora, Mayada El-Zoghbi, and Jake Hess. 2016. "Achieving the Sustainable Development Goals: The Role of Financial Inclusion." Washington, DC: CGAP. http://www.meridian.org/wp-content/uploads/2016/12/Achieving-the-Sustainable-Development-Goals-The-Role-of-Financial-Inclusion-April-2016_CGAP.pdf.

Kuznets, Simon. 1955. "Economic Growth and Income Inequality." *American Economic Review* 45 (1): 1–28.

Laruffa, Francesco. 2020. "What Is a Capability-Enhancing Social Policy? Individual Autonomy, Democratic Citizenship and the Insufficiency of the Employment-Focused Paradigm." *Journal of Human Development and Capabilities* 21 (1): 1–16. https://doi.org/10.1080/19452829.2019.1661983.

León, María Gómez. 2021. "The Kuznets Curve in Brazil, 1850–2010." *Revista de Historia Economica - Journal of Iberian and Latin American Economic History* 39 (1): 37–61. https://doi.org/10.1017/S0212610920000166.

Levine, Ross. 2004. "Finance and Growth: Theory and Evidence." Working Paper 10766. Cambridge, MA: National Bureau of Economic Research. https://doi.org/10.3386/w10766.

Levitas, Ruth. 2005. *The Inclusive Society? Social Exclusion and New Labour.* 2nd ed. New York, NY: Palgrave Macmillan.

Lewbel, Arthur. 1997. "Constructing Instruments for Regressions With Measurement Error When No Additional Data Are Available, with An Application to Patents and R&D." *Econometrica* 65 (5): 1201–13. https://doi.org/10.2307/2171884.

Londoño, Juan Luis, and Miguel Székely. 2000. "Persistent Poverty and Excess Inequality: Latin America, 1970–1995." *Journal of Applied Economics* 3 (1): 93–134. https://doi.org/10.1080/15140326.2000.12040547.

López-Calva, Luis Felipe, and Claudia Lusting Lustig, eds. 2010. *Declining Inequality in Latin America: A Decade of Progress?* Washington, DC: Brookings Institution Press. http://www.jstor.org/stable/10.7864/j.ctt6wpdkq.

López-De-Silanes, Florencio, Edgardo Buscaglia, and Norman Loayza. 2002. "The Politics of Legal Reform." *Economía* 2 (2): 91–152.

Lustig, Nora. 2020. "Inequality and Social Policy in Latin America." Working Paper 2011. Tulane Economics Working Paper Series.

Mathieu, Edouard, Hannah Ritchie, Lucas Rodés-Guirao, Cameron Appel, Charlie Giattino, Joe Hasell, Bobbie Macdonald, et al. 2020. "Excess Mortality During the Coronavirus Pandemic (COVID-19)." *Our World in Data*. https://ourworldindata.org/excess-mortality-covid.

Mehrotra, Santosh. 2016. *Realising the Demographic Dividend: Policies to Achieve Inclusive Growth in India*. Cambridge: Cambridge University Press.

Midgley, James, and Kwong-leung Tang. 2001. "Introduction: Social Policy, Economic Growth and Developmental Welfare." *International Journal of Social Welfare* 10 (4): 244–52. https://doi.org/10.1111/1468-2397.00180.

Milanovic, Branko. 2016. *Global Inequality: A New Approach for the Age of Globalization*. Cambridge, MA: Harvard University Press.

Mishra, Ramesh. 2000. *Globalization and the Welfare State*. Northampton, MA: Edward Elgar.

Nussbaum, Martha C. 2000. *Women and Human Development: The Capabilities Approach*. Cambridge: Cambridge University Press.

Palley, Thomas I. 2013. *Financialization: The Economic of Finance Capital Domination*. New York, NY: Palgrave Macmillan.

Park, Cyn-Young, and Rogelio Mercado. 2015. "Financial Inclusion, Poverty, and Income Inequality in Developing Asia." Working Paper 426. Asian Development Bank Economics. http://www.ssrn.com/abstract=2558936.

Pérez Caldentey, Esteban, and Matías Vernengo. 2021. "Financialization, Premature Deindustrialization, and Instability in Latin America*." *Review of Keynesian Economics* 9 (4): 493–511. https://doi.org/10.4337/roke.2021.04.03.

Perotti, Enrico C., and Paolo F. Volpin. 2004. "Lobbying on Entry." *SSRN Electronic Journal*. https://doi.org/10.2139/ssrn.558588.

Petras, James, and Henry Veltmeyer. 2003. "Whither Lula's Brazil? Neoliberalism and 'Third Way' Ideology." *The Journal of Peasant Studies* 31 (1): 1–44. https://doi.org/10.1080/0306615031000169116.

Pettinato, Stefano. 2002. "A Conceptual Primer on the Currents and Trends in Inequality." *Journal of Human Development* 3 (1): 23–56. https://doi.org/10.1080/14649880120105371.

Piketty, Thomas, and Arthur Goldhammer. 2020. *Capital and Ideology*. Cambridge, MA: Harvard University Press.

Pogge, Thomas, ed. 2009. *Freedom from Poverty as a Human Right: Who Owes What to the Very Poor?* Oxford: Oxford University Press.

Power, Timothy J. 2001. "Blairism Brazilian Style? Cardoso and the 'Third Way' in Brazil." *Political Science Quarterly* 116 (4): 611–36. https://doi.org/10.2307/798223.

Rajan, Raghuram. 2006. "Separate and Unequal." *Finance and Development*, March. https://www.imf.org/external/pubs/ft/fandd/2006/03/straight.htm.

Rajan, Raghuram G, and Luigi Zingales. 2003. "The Great Reversals: The Politics of Financial Development in the Twentieth Century." *Journal of Financial Economics* 69 (1): 5–50. https://doi.org/10.1016/S0304-405X(03)00125-9.

Ravallion, Martin. 2005. "Inequality Is Bad for the Poor." Washington, DC: World Bank. https://openknowledge.worldbank.org/handle/10986/9141.

———. 2011. "A Comparative Perspective on Poverty Reduction in Brazil, China, and India." *The World Bank Research Observer* 26 (1): 71–104. https://doi.org/10.1093/wbro/lkp031.

———. 2016. *The Economics of Poverty: History, Measurement, and Policy*. Oxford: Oxford University Press. https://doi.org/10.3386/w27808.

Rawls, John. 1971. *A Theory of Justice*. Cambridge, MA: Belknap Press of Harvard University Press. https://doi.org/10.4159/9780674042605.

Reinhart, Carmen M., and Kenneth S. Rogoff. 2009. *This Time Is Different*. Princeton, NJ: Princeton University Press. https://press.princeton.edu/books/paperback/9780691152646/this-time-is-different.

Riesco, Manuel. 2009a. "Change in the Chilean Social Model." *International Labour Review* 148 (3): 283–300. https://doi.org/10.1111/j.1564-913X.2009.00063.x.

———. 2009b. "Latin America: A New Developmental Welfare State Model in the Making?" *International Journal of Social Welfare* 18 (1): 22–36. https://doi.org/10.1111/j.1468-2397.2009.00643.x.

Robeyns, Ingrid. 2005. "The Capability Approach: A Theoretical Survey." *Journal of Human Development* 6 (1): 93–117. https://doi.org/10.1080/146498805200034266.

Rodgers, Gerry. 1995. "What Is Special About a Social Inclusion Approach?" In *Social Exclusion: Rhetoric, Reality, Responses*, edited by Gerry Rodgers, Gore Charles, and Jose B. Figueiredo, 43–56. Geneva: International Labour Organization.

Rodrik, Dani. 1999. "Where Did All the Growth Go? External Shocks, Social Conflict, and Growth Collapses." *Journal of Economic Growth* 4 (4): 385–412.

———. 2005. *Has Globalization Gone Too Far?* Washington, DC: Institute for International Economics.

Rojas-Suárez, Liliana. 2016. "Financial Inclusion in Latin America: Facts, Obstacles and Central Banks' Policy Issues." Discussion Paper IDB-DP-464. Inter-American Development Bank. https://publications.iadb.org/publications/english/document/Financial-Inclusion-in-Latin-America-Facts-Obstacles-and-Central-Banks-Policy-Issues.pdf.

Roldán, Karem Sánchez de. 2012. "Social Exclusion, Social Cohesion: Defining Narratives for Development in Latin America." *Journal of International Development* 24 (6): 728–44. https://doi.org/10.1002/jid.2864.

Rudra, Nita. 2002. "Globalization and the Decline of the Welfare State in Less-Developed Countries." *International Organization* 56 (2): 411–45.

Savoia, Antonio, Joshy Easaw, and Andrew McKay. 2010. "Inequality, Democracy, and Institutions: A Critical Review of Recent Research." *World Development*, Formal and Informal Institutions and Development, 38 (2): 142–54. https://doi.org/10.1016/j.worlddev.2009.10.009.

Schwalb, Alvaro, Eleonora Armyra, Melissa Méndez-Aranda, and César Ugarte-Gil. 2022. "COVID-19 in Latin America and the Caribbean: Two Years of the Pandemic." *Journal of Internal Medicine*, April, 10.1111/joim.13499. https://doi.org/10.1111/joim.13499.

Sen, Amartya. 2000a. *Development as Freedom*. New York, NY: Anchor Books.

———. 2000b. *Social Capital, Local Capacity Building, and Poverty Reduction*. Social Development Papers 1. Manila: Asian Development Bank.

———. 2000c. "Social Exclusion: Concept, Application, and Scrutiny." Social Development Papers 1. Manila: Asian Development Bank.

———. 2009. *The Idea of Justice*. Cambridge: Harvard University Press. https://doi.org/10.4159/9780674054578.

Seven, Unal, and Yener Coskun. 2016. "Does Financial Development Reduce Income Inequality and Poverty? Evidence from Emerging Countries." *Emerging Markets Review* 26: 34–63. https://doi.org/10.1016/j.ememar.2016.02.002.

Silver, Hilary. 1994. "Social Exclusion and Social Solidarity: Three Paradigms." *International Labour Review* 133 (5): 531.

———. 2015. "The Contexts of Social Inclusion." Working Paper ST/ESA/2015/DWP/144. New York, NY: United Nations. http://www.un.org/en/development/desa/papers/.

Solt, Frederick. 2008. "Economic Inequality and Democratic Political Engagement." *American Journal of Political Science* 52 (1): 48–60. https://doi.org/10.1111/j.1540-5907.2007.00298.x.

Stiglitz, Joseph E. 2012. *The Price of Inequality*. New York, NY: W.W. Norton & Company.

———. 2015. *The Great Divide: Unequal Societies and What We Can Do About Them*. New York, NY: W.W. Norton & Company. https://wwnorton.com/books/9780393352184.

U.N. 2021. "The Sustainable Development Goals Report 2021." New York, NY: United Nations. https://unstats.un.org/sdgs/report/2021/.

———. n.d. "Copenhagen Declaration on Social Development – Introduction." United Nations: Department of Economic and Social Affairs. n.d. https://www.un.org/development/desa/dspd/world-summit-for-social-development-1995/wssd-1995-agreements/cdosd-introduction.html.

———. n.d. "Transforming Our World: The 2030 Agenda for Sustainable Development." United Nations, Department of Economic and Social Affairs. n.d. https://sdgs.un.org/2030agenda.

UNDP. 2022. "New Threats to Human Security in the Anthropocene: Demanding Greater Solidarity." New York, NY: UNDP (United Nations Development Programme). https://hs.hdr.undp.org.

World Bank. 2013. *Inclusion Matters: The Foundation of Shared Prosperity*. Washington, DC: World Bank. https://doi.org/10.1596/978-1-4648-0010-8.

———. n.d. "World Development Indicators." World Bank. https://databank.worldbank.org/source/world-development-indicators.

Zhenmin, Liu. 2021. "View from the Pandemic: Stark Realities, Critical Choices." United Nations, Department of Economic and Social Affairs, Statistics Division. 2021. https://unstats.un.org/sdgs/report/2021/view-from-the-pandemic/.

Chapter 6

Understanding Financialization and Its Consequences

While a great many entries have been made in financialization studies, we were motivated to make an additional entry by an outstanding mystery surrounding financialization, a many-faceted aspect marking the contemporary world. Among the most striking features of financialization is how complex it is and, correspondingly, how poorly understood it remains even as it becomes an apparently immovable fact of life. Even the definition of financialization continues to escape consensus, and its ultimate effects are equally obscure. One significant question that arises, therefore, is why financialization has taken such deep roots in LAC in particular and the developing world in general, given its origins in the markets of highly developed countries. Our primary motivation, though, has been to uncover the downstream effects of financialization on social spending and human welfare indicators, bringing greater clarity to the question as to whether financialization "works" as neoliberal economic theory and its marketized ideology predicts. We believe that answering this question also gives us the answer to the former question. We argued that this requires investigation of how ideas about the good society take root and shape the social world.

As a famous science journalist once posited, the key difference between the natural sciences and the social sciences is that in the natural sciences, "Protons, plasmas and planets are oblivious to what scientists say about them. Social systems, on the other hand, consist of objects that watch television; listen to the radio; read newspapers, journals, books, and blogs; and consequently change their behavior" (Horgan 2013). That is, there is a reflexivity inherent in sciences like economics that complicates the evaluation of any theory and the impact it has on the world. We cannot just focus on the validity of any particular social science theory alone, we must also concern ourselves with what happens when people accept that theory as valid. Horgan also quotes Feyerabend as once saying "[p]rayer may not be very efficient when compared to celestial mechanics, but it surely holds its own vis-à-vis some parts of economics" (Horgan 2013). While people frequently cite this quote when questioning the scientific validity of economics, another possible interpretation is that much like religion, its impact on people's behavior is separate from its scientific validity.

This book and its efforts to evaluate the impact of financialization in Latin America can be understood along similar lines, as the recognition of the complexity of social systems informs our investigation. To sum up our findings so far, we can say that financialization has had consistent and significant impacts on government policy, but its impact on people's lives cannot be easily summarized and defies most existing theories in one way or another. The prescriptive theories in economics as to how to manage government budgets in a financialized world have come to dominate the region, being generally described as a process through which "good economics" arrived in Latin America (Harberger 1996). But if policymakers act as if these ideas are true, the empirical evaluation of their impact on day-to-day lives of millions in the region is far more complex and uneven, calling into question the validity of the theories that support the paradigm. Furthermore, what we make of financialization crucially depends on our choice of how it is conceptualized and operationalized.

6.1 FINANCIALIZATION IN REVIEW

We trace the origins of financialization as a historical process in chapter 2, documenting the radical transformation of LAC economies in the post-World War II period. The originating source of financialization was external, often treated as an ever-watchful observer outside national borders, encapsulated by reference to what the "market" or "Wall Street" wants, and therefore uncontrollable. At the international level, decentralized bond markets pressured governments to adhere to orthodox liberal policies in a way that international banks never could. The diffuse nature of bondholders meant that there were no options for negotiating debts; failure to bring policy and spending in line with orthodox expectations could result in financial disaster if investors deemed a nation unworthy of investment.

The process of financialization is not only an external, foreign influence, however, and the principles of neoliberal economic theory were subsequently embraced at the domestic level, transforming national economies. As external investors pressed from the outside, economic policymakers trained in neoliberal theory deepened their governments' commitment to financialization, resulting in the expansion of domestic credit and thoroughly financializing life in LAC nations. The simple confluence of expectations between national policymakers and international investors fortifies the commitment to orthodox budget-cutting policies.

Financialization proceeded differently in the advanced economies of the capitalist north on one hand, and the less developed economies of Latin American and the Caribbean on the other. While a series of indigenous crises led to financial expansion in the north, financialization in LAC took place in distinctive conditions. Skyrocketing debt and hyperinflation did affect those economies in the 1970s and 1980s, but the logic of financialization assumed a life of its own. Rather than a tool to defang hyperinflation and revitalize economic growth, these economic approaches are deemed by many economists and decision-makers to hold the key to economic development and social transformation.

The Washington Consensus, emerging in the 1980s and 1990s after the inability of state-led economic growth models to cope with the inflationary crises of the 1970s and 1980s, escaped serious scrutiny by major economic advisors and financial institutions for years, reaching the status of conventional wisdom. Without solid evidence of neoliberal success in the varied structural economic conditions of developing countries, its proposals were nonetheless widely adopted. Similarly, financialization became the default mode of capitalist organization for LAC after the crisis-stricken years of the 1980s. From a commitment to heavy financial regulation, the region loosened capital controls, reduced budgets, and privatized state-owned companies. Markets went from being regarded as a tool for development to being considered an independent, and temperamental, entity best left to its own devices.

Despite fears of worldwide homogenization through globalization, neoliberalism, understood as freer trade and economic deregulation, does not produce a mechanistic response to simple economic incentives and does not lead ineluctably to welfare retrenchment. Financial markets, however, have proven to be less malleable. Theoretically, benefits from financialization would derive from capital flows from richer to poorer countries and from access of populations to foreign capital (Kose et al. 2009). Decisions on deregulation and freer capital flows in the United Kingdom and United States necessarily carry profound impacts for LAC, however, and serious concerns have arisen about the implementation of the same mechanisms and effects in the distinctive conditions of Latin America and other emerging economies.

Proponents of financial globalization argue that it allocates finance more efficiently, bringing needed investment from capital-intensive advanced economies where they produce lower returns to less developed economies, where it brings greater returns and plants the seeds for rapid development. Empirical accounts, though, find that the "subordinate financialization" of less developed economies creates potential for heightened economic risks as they participate in financial markets dominated by foreign currencies in which investors are focused on short-term returns, and are subjected to greater volatility and unpredictability (Bonizzi, Kaltenbrunner, and Powell 2020). Rodrik (1998) finds that capital account liberalization has no discernible effect on economic growth. A variety of sources find that financialization has negative effects on economic growth while exposing economies to greater risk of financial crisis, higher unemployment, greater inequality, and a variety of other results that could be expected to create domestic discontent (Assa 2012; Epstein 2005; Levy-Orlik 2013; Tomaskovic-Devey, Lin, and Meyers 2015).

The story we tell in this book is one that is fundamentally about the decoupling of policy and outcomes—it is not that embraced goals and realized outcomes are in concordance or in opposition to each other, but rather that they exist independently and follow different processes. It is in part a story that has been told by many World Polity scholars (Guillén and Capron 2016; Jupille, Jolliff, and Wojcik 2013). But here we try to go beyond noting that disconnect, to highlighting the specific logics that affect policy adoption on one hand and social welfare outcomes on the other.

6.2 MARKET IDEOLOGY, FINANCIALIZATION, AND AGENCY

We maintain that the logics are held together by market ideology which serves as the connective tissue between financialization and budget austerity. In addition to important empirical findings concerning the effects of financialization on social spending and social welfare, we wish to make a contribution to the literature on the significance of ideas in the social world.

The study presents an account of why certain policy decisions take place and persist. The standard economic theory undergirding austerity has it that there is only one efficient organizational framework for an economy. Neoliberal orthodoxy emerging out of the United States and United Kingdom was exported to LAC especially by elite decision-makers educated in the United States, exemplified by the Chicago Boys of Chile. These orthodox ideas have held sway without regard to their actual results. While outcomes have varied widely, sometimes positive and sometimes negative, the commitment to state retrenchment remained robust. We find that an ideational explanation is the most compelling means to account for this outcome.

Departing from many ideational or constructivist theoretical treatments, we refer to this system of ideas as an ideology in order underscore that ideas play an important explanatory role for its holders, but equally important is the normative, programmatic function of ideas. Such an explanation admits space for agentic action, which most agree is an undeniable, even central, aspect of social behavior, but which has proved difficult to account for in social theory.

Structural and psychological explanations appeal to external conditions to account for agents' behavior, leaving no room for the subtleties of idiosyncratic beliefs and dispositions of those agents. This is also true for rationalist and psychological theories, as these assume that all actors with sufficient information will behave similarly in the first case, or that structural conditions imprint themselves in the memories of actors in the second. In contrast, considering the motive role of ideas in contextualizing external conditions, interpreting the world, and supplying roadmaps for action, we bring agents back to the core of our analysis.

In chapter 3, we detailed our ideational explanation for the origins and persistence of financialization, locating its causes in what we call market ideology. We find inadequate the de-socialized explanations that overlook the social constitution of complex systems in accounting for the adoption and persistence of financialization. These theories pose material economic conditions as the ultimate motivator in policy adoption but do not explain the connection between the neoliberal economic model and financialization on the one hand, and budget austerity on the other, since departure from neoliberal orthodoxy does not predict debt default. It is precisely the independence of the process of financialization from its effects that argues in favor of an ideational explanation.

As Bell (2012) argues, ideational approaches have the potential to account for the place of agents but have often missed the opportunity to capitalize on the possibility. By treating the socially constructed world as another structure that only replaces the materially constituted ontology of structuralism with an ideational ontology, still crowding agents out of the picture and reducing them to reaction to forces outside their control. By highlighting ideologies as operative ideas, we believe that we fill a lacuna in ideational literature. Rather than stipulating the existence of ideational structures or attributing their origins to elite imposition, we underscore the fluid and contested lives of ideas, opening the way to understanding their origins and fates.

For this to be true and for ideational theories to avoid simply swapping out one deterministic account for another, there must be an account of how ideas change. We have stressed that there is nothing automatic about the adoption of particular ideologies and policy prescriptions; just as ideas do not simply arise out of external conditions, nor are they simply imposed by elites. Rather, ideologies are action-oriented set of ideas that performs explanatory and normative roles. As interpretations of the social world and guides for acting in it, ideologies connect agents and structures, both constituting important segments of the social world and informing agents' reactions to it.

Market ideology, a distilled form of economic theory favoring the least amount of state regulation, holds markets as the better mechanism for achieving equilibrium and efficiency. Efficiency and equilibrium are conceived as qualities that emerge in the independent functioning of markets, giving rise to the notion of markets as masters. Market ideology arrives at this conclusion by imagining an economy as a machine operating independently of agents, rather than as a social construct inseparable from agents and their interactions with each other.

The advantage of market ideology to policymakers and investors alike is to simplify the complexity of social systems by banishing uncertainty, transforming it into analyzable, manageable risk like gambling. As we saw, neoliberal trade policies and globalization are mediated by a variety of national-level variables such as the power distribution of interest groups and political party ideology. Financialization, though, carries with it a potent force in enforcing orthodox liberal economic policy associated with market ideology. In the 1970s, market ideology served the role of challenging the predominant state-led development programs that crashed on the shoals of stagnation and hyperinflation. Only after a period of economic crisis and ideological upheaval did it attain status as common sense.

As an integral component of late twentieth-century market ideology, financialization can be viewed as the logical extension of the neoliberal reforms of the 1970s and forward. Nonetheless, financialization carries its own logic and is not a necessary extension of the free market reforms of the neoliberal variety. Integration into the global economy through liberalization of trade might be implemented through a variety of mechanisms, and not necessarily in ways that lead to decreases in social welfare spending.

The precise contours of the relationship between neoliberalism, globalization, and financialization on one hand, and budget austerity on the other have motivated an enduring debate and research program. While extensive literature has investigated the determinants of social spending and the role of national-level variables influencing such spending, the effects of financialization on social welfare spending are not well understood. We have attempted to redress this hole in the literature by undertaking an empirical investigation to shed light on the impact of the transition to financialized economies in LAC.

6.3 FINDINGS

Our chief goal in this study has been to bring some clarity to the widely diverging assessments of the real-world consequences that financialization has on ordinary people's lives in LAC. Despite the great deal of attention this phenomenon has garnered, the material results of financialization have proven difficult to nail down.

We find in chapter 4 that financialization has an independent causal effect on certain types of social spending. The type of debt owed by governments exercises a direct form of pressure on the budgeting decisions of national policymakers. While welfare and social security spending are significantly impacted by the strength of labor movements, budget cuts to education and healthcare are directly related to levels of international bond debt. Importantly, there is no direct connection between these budget items and the propensity for governments to default on debt. Wall Street, indeed, wants blood. At what cost to social inclusion are these concessions extracted?

Governmental budgets are only means to ends. In assessing social inclusion, we are ultimately most concerned with how people's lives are lived. We are not aware of a systematic study of the large-scale effects of financialization on social inclusion. This represents an important lacuna, given that contemporary discourse has bruited about the corrosive effects of inequality and social exclusion as these become more evident.

As inroads toward the reduction of poverty worldwide have been significant and perhaps underappreciated, inequality has only more recently gained attention as an undesirable condition for a society. The economic consequences of inequality are themselves serious enough to warrant concern, while also contributing to social erosion and political instability. The widening awareness of the multifaceted nature of poverty, inequality, and their interconnections and impacts on this wide range of social issues has given rise to the study of social inclusiveness, underscoring the multidimensionality and inseparability of these problems.

Given the neoliberal critique of welfare spending and the power of the Washington Consensus, analysis of the effects of neoliberal policies and austerity has become essential in assessing the fate of social inclusiveness in the era of financialization. Not simply an economic measure, this concerns the prevailing understanding of citizenship in the context of freewheeling capitalism.

With this goal in mind, we have modeled the links between financialization and resulting social indicators in an attempt to answer the overarching questions about these important outcomes deriving from financial globalization. In measuring the means in the form of budgeting priorities, though total social spending typically increases, financialization consistently drives governments to reduce health and education outlays. The benefits of financialization, though, are unevenly distributed. While credit increases inequality, social indicators in education and health show no clear direction as nations pursue financial liberalization.

6.4 A FINAL WORD

We set out to bring some clarity to questions surrounding the effects of subordinate financialization in LAC. Here we have recapitulated our principal empirical findings of this process. Another of our chief goals was to determine whether financialization "works."

Financialization in LAC is shaped by preexisting conditions; existing inequality has an impact on the unfolding of financialization. In general, the more affluent are the beneficiaries of the expansion of the financial sector broadly. Credit as an instrument of public policy is intended to spread benefits widely but fails to do so given the marginalization of much of the population of LAC. We believe that the mixed social outcome is due as much to the region's historical inequality as to the nature of private credit and financialization. Household consumer and mortgage credit have outpaced lending to the corporate sector in many countries. While the credit boom has gone hand in hand with a rise in credit to the construction sector, credit has expanded the least in the productive sector of the economy. Access to consumer and home loans depends upon one's creditworthiness. It is also contingent upon access to financial intuitions. LAC is among the laggard regions of the world when it comes to financial inclusion. Unlike private credit, international debt securities benefit the productive sector, which generates growth and employment.

From our empirical results we may conclude that successful and stable financialization is heavily shaped by historical and demographic factors, domestic institutional design, and the character of insertion into the international financial market. As Rodrik (1997, 3) puts it, "it is not openness per se that matters; it is how you handle it," underlining the need for strong institutions and investment in social insurance and education to weather the upheaval that can follow market integration. In the context of LAC and its historically skewed access to resources, financialization has in some cases put the cart before the horse, prioritizing financial openness and deregulation without regard to its appropriateness.

Therefore, we believe that there is no single correct answer to the question of whether financialization "works." The results of our tests reveal that the effects of increased credit availability on a variety of social indicators are neither consistently positive nor negative. Contrary to the most optimistic treatments of expanding finance and standard liberal economics, the case for loosening of capital controls and widening credit as a means to improving economic performance and, consequently, human welfare is weak. Effective implementation of financialization requires a syndrome of favorable structural variables.

On the other hand, the more dire outcomes expected to follow in the wake of financialization are likewise not uniform. This suggests, recalling earlier debates over neoliberalism and globalization, that the socially corrosive potential of financialization can be mitigated and that finance can serve a socially beneficial role. The dichotomous approach to financialization neglects its complexity; financialization manifests through different channels, such as private credit, international and domestic securities, and remittances. These channels do not lead to a unitary social outcome.

Knowing what we do not know, though, tells us a great deal. We can, in fact, draw some positive conclusions based on the muddle of evidence. Importantly, we can conclude that financialization does not function in the manner posited by standard economic theory and does not always bring the salutary effects posited by market ideology. Nor yet does it fit the picture drawn by much critical financialization literature that highlights the baleful influence of finance.

The mechanistic theory of standard economics and market ideology as well as the rigid structuralism of critical views must yield to understanding of financialization as dynamic and unpredictable, and the view that many varying approaches to global integration and financial management are possible.

Among the implications of our findings is that the tight connection between financialization as a process and austerity policies is not one dictated by the objective operation of the market. Since economies and markets are embedded in a social context of many actors and institutions, though, it makes little sense to separate economies and markets from these other social processes. With this recognition it becomes evident that there can be no universally applicable model for economic and financial policy. Like the previous iteration of the debates over globalization and its tendency toward convergence around neoliberal orthodoxy and a race to the bottom, there is no single successful way to integrate into the global market, and there is likewise no single size for financialization. The demands for austerity are ideological, and the means for breaking the link is through ideational change. This becomes important in accounting for how to improve the outcomes of financialization by recognizing the plurality of successful models.

We have placed emphasis on an explicitly ideational framing for examining financialization, concluding that this is necessary for fully appreciating its effects. Does it make a difference, though, to agree that budget austerity following financialization is driven through the ideological realm and that markets are not objects external to social interaction with their own demands, rather than a complex adaptive system integrated with many other such social systems?

We may be tempted to conclude that grasping the influence of ideology allows the transcendence of their influence. We may be certain that we cannot dispense with ideologies altogether and directly experience the material world. Ideas are inescapable, they are the only means we have to navigate the irreducibly complex world we live in. The reduction of social behavior to risk analysis gives false confidence in our power of prediction and management of extraordinarily powerful economic technologies while acknowledging the complexity and uncertainty inherent in the world points our attention to how little we do know.

In recent years the risks associated with unbridled neoliberalism and free market policies have become clear. The global financial crisis of 2008 and the Great Recession led more prominent economists and financial experts to rethink their standard theories. IFIs such as the IMF and World Bank have pushed the brakes on neoliberalism and charted new directions, and the Pink Tide in Latin America suggested the availability of alternatives. Given the recent turbulence in international financial markets and fresh scrutiny on the tenets of neoliberalism, we may be witness to the emergence of new ideas concerning the proper relations between states and markets, or a recrudescence of shopworn ones.

Our recognition of the complex and evolving qualities of social systems, however, leaves space for agents to reshape national choices. The implications of our study are not restricted to LAC but are global, and counsel the need for a balanced, integrated approach to financial liberalization, with particular acknowledgment of the social and embedded nature of these economic processes. Calls for caution with deepening integration into global markets have been issued for decades. But considering recent financial disruptions arising out of the COVID-19 pandemic, cryptocurrencies, and military conflicts, the reminder is never out of place.

BIBLIOGRAPHY

Assa, Jacob. 2012. "Financialization and Its Consequences: The OECD Experience." *Finance Research* 1 (1): 35–39.

Bell, Stephen. 2012. "The Power of Ideas: The Ideational Shaping of the Structural Power of Business: *The Power of Ideas*." *International Studies Quarterly* 56 (4): 661–73. https://doi.org/10.1111/j.1468-2478.2012.00743.x.

Bonizzi, Bruno, Annina Kaltenbrunner, and Jeff Powell. 2020. "Subordinate Financialization in Emerging Capitalist Economies." In *The Routledge International Handbook of Financialization*, edited by Philip Mader, Daniel Mertens, and Natascha van der Zwan, 177–87. Routledge International Handbooks. London New York: Routledge.

Epstein, Gerald A., ed. 2005. *Financialization and the World Economy*. Cheltenham; Northampton, MA: Edward Elgar.

Guillén, Mauro F., and Laurence Capron. 2016. "State Capacity, Minority Shareholder Protections, and Stock Market Development." *Administrative Science Quarterly* 61 (1): 125–60.

Harberger, Arnold C. 1996. "Good Economics Comes to Latin America." In *The Post-1945 Internationalization of Economics*, edited by A. W. Coats, 301–11. Durham, NC: Duke University Press.

Horgan, John. 2013. "Is 'Social Science' an Oxymoron? Will That Ever Change?" Scientific American Blog Network. https://blogs.scientificamerican.com/cross-check/is-social-science-an-oxymoron-will-that-ever-change/.

Jupille, Joseph, Brandy Jolliff, and Stefan Wojcik. 2013. "Regionalism in the World Polity." *Available at SSRN 2242500.*

Kose, M Ayhan, Eswar Prasad, Kenneth Rogoff, and Shang-Jin Wei. 2009. "Financial Globalization: A Reappraisal." *IMF Staff Papers* 56 (1): 8–62. https://doi.org/10.1057/imfsp.2008.36.

Levy-Orlik, Noemi. 2013. "Financialization and Economic Growth in Developing Countries: The Case of the Mexican Economy." *International Journal of Political Economy* 42 (4): 108–27. https://doi.org/10.2753/IJP0891-1916420406.

Rodrik, Dani. 1997. "Globalization, Social Conflict and Economic Growth." In Vol. 24. Conferencia de Raúl Prebisch. Ginebra. Versión revisada (en inglés). http://www. ksg. harvard. edu/rodrik/global. pdf.

———. 1998. "Where Did All The Growth Go? External Shocks, Social Conflict, and Growth Collapses." Cambridge, MA: National Bureau of Economic Research. https://doi.org/10.3386/w6350.

Tomaskovic-Devey, Donald, Ken-Hou Lin, and Nathan Meyers. 2015. "Did Financialization Reduce Economic Growth?" *Socio-Economic Review* 13 (3): 525–48. https://doi.org/10.1093/ser/mwv009.

Index

About the Authors

Rana S. Gautam is Associate Professor of Human Services at the University of North Georgia. He is the author of *Human Rights Practices during Financial Crises* (Palgrave). He serves on the editorial board of *American Journal of Evaluation.*

Diogo L. Pinheiro is Associate Professor of Sociology and Assistant Director of the Center for Undergraduate Research and Creative Activities at the University of North Georgia.

Dwight Wilson is Associate Professor of Political Science and International Affairs at the University of North Georgia.

www.ingramcontent.com/pod-product-compliance
Ingram Content Group UK Ltd.
Pitfield, Milton Keynes, MK11 3LW, UK
UKHW041838031026
15587UKWH00002B/863

9 781793 647955